6/04

Philosophy
& This
Actual World

Philosophy & This Actual World

AN INTRODUCTION TO PRACTICAL PHILOSOPHICAL INQUIRY

MARTIN BENJAMIN

ROWMAN & LITTLEFIELD PUBLISHERS, INC.
Lanham • Boulder • New York • Oxford

ROWMAN & LITTLEFIELD PUBLISHERS, INC.

Published in the United States of America
by Rowman & Littlefield Publishers, Inc.
A Member of the Rowman & Littlefield Publishing Group
4720 Boston Way, Lanham, Maryland 20706
www.rowmanlittlefield.com

PO Box 317
Oxford
OX2 9RU, UK

British Library Cataloguing in Publication Information Available

Library of Congress Cataloging-in-Publication Data

Benjamin, Martin.
 Philosophy and this actual world / Martin Benjamin.
  p. cm.
Includes bibliographical references (p.) and index.
 ISBN 0-7425-1398-X (cloth)—ISBN 0-7425-1399-8 (pbk.)
1. Philosophy. I. Title.
 B72 .B45 2003
 100—dc21

                                        2002008961

Printed in the United States of America

♾™ The paper used in this publication meets the minimum requirements of
American National Standard for Information Sciences—Permanence of Paper for
Printed Library Materials, ANSI/NISO Z39.48-1992.

For my teachers and students

"It is far too little recognized how entirely the intellect is built up of practical interests."

—William James, "The Sentiment of Rationality"

"Language—I want to say—is a refinement, 'in the beginning was the deed'."

—Ludwig Wittgenstein, *Culture and Value*

Contents

Preface

In 1907 William James spoke of the "seriously inquiring amateur in philosophy" who turns to philosophy professors but finds them wanting. The problem is not with the serious amateur, James explained, but the professors. Philosophy should do more than exercise our "powers of intellectual abstraction." It should also "make some positive connexion with this actual world of finite human lives."

If the problem was bad then, it's worse now. A shortcoming of much academic philosophy is its having lost sight of the seriously inquiring amateur—an educated person seeking answers to philosophical questions that, as James puts it, "fit every part of life best and combine with the collectivity of experience's demands, nothing being omitted." What, in the light of contemporary neuroscience, is the relation of mind to brain? How do we reconcile the freedom presupposed by law and ethics with the determinism presupposed by the brain and behavioral sciences? What are the origins and basis of ethics? To what extent can reason resolve or contain moral conflict? Is someone who is totally and permanently unconscious, but breathing without the aid of a machine, alive or dead? Is religious conviction compatible with scientific understanding? Can our lives have meaning if there is no God? And whatever the answers to these and similar questions, how do they all connect with each other?

My aim in this book is to develop, defend, and illustrate an approach to philosophical questions and answers that speaks to James's seriously inquiring amateur and makes some positive connection with this actual world of finite human lives. At the same time, I hope to draw on important advances in recent academic philosophy. In so doing, I combine the spirit, if not the letter, of two thinkers who are in many respects as different as night and day: William James and Ludwig Wittgenstein.

James (1842–1910), an American psychologist and philosopher, wrote on a wide variety of topics for a broad audience. Whatever the subject, James comes across as genial and plainspoken. Reading James, we feel we are listening to a friend who speaks our language and has interesting and important things to say. While James sought and acquired a readership that extended well beyond academic psychologists and philosophers, Wittgenstein (1889–1951), an Austrian who spent much of his life teaching philosophy in England, is little known outside academic philosophy. Where James seems open and friendly—the kind of person you'd like to spend an afternoon with—Wittgenstein seems (and actually was) private and prickly, an exceedingly difficult man. Where James's writing is colloquial and accessible, Wittgenstein's writing is, like the man himself, forbidding. Wittgenstein's first important book, *Tractatus Philosophicus*, was highly compressed and technical. His second great book, *Philosophical Investigations*, was equally difficult, but written in a radically different aphoristic style. It is an unusual reader who will be able to make much sense of Wittgenstein and appreciate his insights and writing without great effort, extensive philosophical background, and formal course work.

Despite these differences, Wittgenstein greatly admired certain of James's writings and read them more than once. Even when he disagreed with him, Wittgenstein felt James's work on psychology and religion had unusual depth and was, for that reason, worth taking seriously. Though each wrote only a single essay with 'ethics' or 'moral' in the title, nearly everything each of them wrote reflected ethical concern. For my purposes the most important similarity is the extent to which each rejected "intellectualist" conceptions of philosophy—conceptions like that of René Descartes (1596–1650), who thought it possible that the asker of philosophical questions could be a *pure* intellect, what I characterize in chapter 1 as an isolated, disembodied spectator. Both James and Wittgenstein emphatically reject this possibility. Askers of philosophical questions, they maintain, are and must be conceived as language-using, social animals. *Embodied social action* is at least as important to philosophical inquiry and understanding, James and Wittgenstein each insist, as *abstract thought or contemplation*.

At one point James put it this way: "The knower is not simply a mirror floating with no foot-hold anywhere, and passively reflecting on an order that he comes upon and simply finds existing. The knower is an *actor*, and coefficient of the truth which he helps to create. Mental interests, hypotheses, postulates, so far as they are bases for *human action—action* which to a great extent transforms the world—help to make the truth" (italics added). Nearly seventy years later Wittgenstein wrote, "Giving grounds, however, justifying the evidence, comes to an end;—but the end is not certain propositions' striking us immediately as true; i.e., it is not a kind of *seeing* on our part; it is our *acting*, which lies at the bottom of the language game." This emphasis on action, agency, and practice is echoed by the contemporary philosopher Hilary Putnam: "The heart of pragmatism, it seems to me—of James' and Dewey's pragmatism, if not of Peirce's—was the insistence on the *supremacy of the agent point of view*. If we find we must take a certain point of view, use a certain 'conceptual system' when we are engaged in *practical activity*, in the widest sense of 'practical activity', then we must not simultaneously advance the claim that it is not really 'the way things are in themselves'" (italics added). James, Wittgenstein, and Putnam are, I think, right about the importance of action, agency, and practice in addressing philosophical questions. In this, they share a *pragmatic temperament*—one that speaks to the whole person, embodied social agent as well as intellect. Philosophical questions are raised by people who have to act as well as think—and satisfactory answers must be responsive to the demands of both.

In addition to Wittgenstein and Putnam, I draw on Richard Rorty and other contemporary philosophers to respond to the questions and concerns of today's seriously inquiring amateur. Taking advantage of the "linguistic turn" in twentieth-century philosophy, they are able to state and defend some of James's important insights more cogently than he could himself.

Though I draw heavily on the insights of academic philosophy, my focus is the questions and concerns of seriously inquiring amateurs. To this end the writing is direct and occasionally conversational—imitating insofar as possible the spirit if not the letter of James's own *Pragmatism*, a set of lectures delivered to educated nonspecialists in the early part of the twentieth century. Technical terms are restricted and, when used, briefly explained. To limit distraction, endnotes are restricted to references. Readers more interested in the thread of the argument than sources of quotations may safely ignore them. Scholarly controversies, further questions, historical background, and additional references are identified in an accompanying bibliographical essay, the structure of which parallels individual chapters and section headings. I presume many readers will not, at least initially, be interested in such matters and including them in the main text would be a hindrance for them. Nothing of scholarly importance is lost by including all such references in an accompanying bibliographical essay that both credits sources and provides guidance for further reflection and research.

For too long academic philosophers have ignored the questions of serious, intelligent, well-educated men and women from all walks of life who do not have the time for concentrated study in philosophy. My aim is to bridge this gap by combining the style and focus of a public philosopher like William James with the insights and discoveries of a philosopher's philosopher like Ludwig Wittgenstein. The result, I hope, is a book that speaks to the general reader while incorporating important developments in recent academic philosophy.

In a review of a book I'd written on moral compromise, Jonathan Moreno said it was unfortunate that I hadn't cited William James. The explanation was that at that point I hadn't actually read much of James. Stimulated by Moreno's comment, however, I began reading more of James. Then I turned to the other two classical pragmatists, Charles S. Peirce and John Dewey. Before long, I realized that most of my teaching, thinking, and writing was a reflection of what I'm calling a pragmatic temperament. The same was true, I thought, of much of the best work in practical and professional ethics. I wanted to share this discovery by recommending a book on the topic to my students and friends, but I discovered there was no short volume that combined the accessibility of James's *Pragmatism* with advances in academic philosophy and current issues in practical ethics, particularly bioethics. So I decided to write such a book myself.

I am grateful to my students for reading and commenting on drafts of individual chapters as they pertained to individual courses. These included graduate seminars on contemporary pragmatism and on Wittgenstein, a senior seminar on contemporary pragmatism, sections of an advanced ethics course, and an introductory course for honors students. I cannot recall or identify each student who made helpful comments. Some graduate students, however, made extensive written comments that resulted in a number of important changes. Mike Squillace's criticisms of the first draft of the first four chapters led to extensive substantive and stylistic revisions. Skott Brill's exceptionally close reading of various chapters did the same. And Scot Yoder, who was writing a dissertation on pragmatism and practical philosophy, taught me as much as I taught him. Like many others, Mike, Skott, and Scot were students who became my teachers.

In 1997–98 I was fortunate to have graduate student M. Lendsey Melton as a research assistant. What helped me most was Lendsey's careful reading and probing questions of various chapters. I learned a great deal from our lengthy conversations over coffee at Espresso Royale. Lendsey was another student who became my teacher.

On various matters I turned to my colleagues for help. Steve Esquith gave me guidance on matters of political philosophy, Fred Gifford on evolutionary biology, Rich Hall on philosophy of mind, Don Koch on classical pragmatism (especially Peirce and Dewey and related bibliographical materials), and Tom Tomlinson on ethics. Friends who read parts of the manuscript and provided useful comments include David Donovan, Carl Hedman, Richard Momeyer, Dolores Rauscher, and Gene Smith. John Arras read the entire manuscript and made a suggestion that led to my emphasis on the pragmatic temperament. As always, Ronna Benjamin read each chapter with her customary good sense and eye for philosophical obscurity.

I received invaluable aid in preparing the manuscript from graduate student Robert Brice and undergraduate Kristen Jarvis Johnson. I am grateful, too, for the useful suggestions from Eve DeVaro and Reid Hester of Rowman & Littlefield. Production editor Julie E. Kirsch and copy editor Luann Reed-Siegel were also very helpful.

Finally, I want to express my gratitude to Gene Cline and his students at Albion College. For three semesters Gene taught an honors seminar that worked through a version of my manuscript. Then, as each seminar came to a close, he invited me to meet with his students. I was impressed with the students' preparation, knowledge, and thoughtfulness and learned a great deal from their hard questions and constructive criticisms.

Some parts of the book are adapted from material published elsewhere. Chapter 7, "Determining Death," includes material from "Pragmatism and the Determination of Death" in *Pragmatic Bioethics*, 2d ed., ed. Glenn McGee (Cambridge, Mass.: MIT Press, 2003). Some paragraphs of chapters 1 and 6 are adapted from *Splitting the Difference: Compromise and Integrity in Ethics and Politics* (Lawrence: University Press of Kansas, 1990) and are reprinted with permission of the University Press of Kansas. Parts of chapters 5 and 6 appeared in a different form in "Between Subway and Spaceship: Practical Ethics at the Outset of the Twenty-first Century," *Hastings Center Report* 31, no. 4 (July-August 2001): 24–31.

Introduction

In a passage worth quoting in full, William James tells of a student who drew a sharp line between the world of philosophy and that of the street.

> The two were supposed, he said, to have so little to do with each other, that you could not possibly occupy your mind with them at the same time. The world of concrete personal experiences to which the street belongs is multitudinous beyond imagination, tangled, muddy, painful and perplexed. The world to which your philosophy-professor introduces you is simple, clean, and noble. The contradictions of real life are absent from it. Its architecture is classic. Principles of reason trace its outlines, logical necessities cement its parts. Purity and dignity are what it most expresses. It is a kind of marble temple shining on a hill.[1]

Variations of this distinction have long been a part of philosophy. From Plato to Descartes to the present day, philosophers often seek refuge from the multiplicity, pain, and confusion of the street in rarefied temples of their own making.

The publication in 1859 of Charles Darwin's *The Origin of Species* challenged this understanding of philosophy. First, the idea of evolution by natural selection made it more difficult to draw a hard and fast line between human beings and (other) animals. This posed problems for more ethereal conceptions of the human mind and of human knowledge. Second, the world could no longer be conceived as fixed or immutable; it was constantly, if slowly, changing due to the blind force of evolution by natural selection. This, too, raised serious difficulties for traditional approaches to knowledge and reality. Finally, the

1

likelihood that our existence is a chance outcome of various contingencies cast doubt on "marble temple" answers to questions of ethics, religion, and life's meaning.

The American philosophers Charles S. Peirce (1839–1914), William James (1842–1910), and John Dewey (1859–1952) were among the first to take this challenge seriously and to develop a conception of philosophy to accommodate it. It came to be called pragmatism (from the Greek word for action) and Peirce, James, and Dewey are generally regarded as the three classic pragmatists. Peirce criticized radical skepticism and the idea that we acquire knowledge of the world as individuals rather than as members of communities. While Peirce focused on language, logic, and science, James extended pragmatism to questions of everyday life, including free will, ethics, and religious belief. An engaging writer and lecturer, James attracted a wide audience. Dewey's pragmatism, which he preferred to call "instrumentalism," combined Peirce's interest in logic and science with James's larger humanistic concerns, especially with respect to education and democracy. Dewey's direct involvement in education and his regular contributions to magazines and newspapers on social issues made him, like James, a "public philosopher."[2]

Peirce, James, and Dewey agreed that the asker of philosophical questions is not a pure subject of consciousness or intellect, but rather one of a number of language-using, higher animals seeking meaningful survival in a complex and occasionally hazardous world. Though united in their opposition to philosophy as "a kind of marble temple shining on a hill," they differed among themselves about the exact nature and scope of pragmatism. In fact Peirce, who coined the term 'pragmatism' in the 1870s, was so offended by James's use of it in 1898 that seven years later he renamed his version "pragmaticism," which, he explained, "is ugly enough to be safe from kidnappers."[3]

Louis Menand's *The Metaphysical Club* is a recent social history of classical pragmatism. The title of the chapter on philosophy— "Pragmatisms"—neatly reflects the differences among Peirce, James, and Dewey.[4] The differences are emphasized, too, by Richard J. Bernstein who writes, "I do not think there is any 'essence' to pragmatism—or even a set of sharply defined commitments or propositions that all so-called pragmatists share."[5] Bernstein warns against what he calls "the danger of nostalgia and sentimentality" among philosophers who regard the works of Peirce, James, and Dewey as definitive of pragmatism. "We may continue to draw inspiration from the classic pragmatists," he adds, "but I cannot think of a more unpragmatic attitude than focusing exclusively on the past rather than on the present and the future. We must also take seriously our commitment to pluralism—even a pluralism in what is appropriated from the pragmatic legacy."[6] In so doing, Bernstein is recommending, in the spirit of James, that pragmatism remain inclusive and receptive to change rather than limited to those who pledge allegiance to the letter of its founding fathers. This, in turn, permits us to acknowledge as pragmatists philosophers like Richard Rorty, who combine the insights and spirit of classical pragmatism with advances in contemporary philosophy of language.

Like Rorty, I believe the linguistic turn—"the switch from talking about consciousness and experience [as did James and Dewey] to talking about language"—is "an instance of genuine philosophical progress."[7] Insights into the relationship between words and the world developed by the twentieth-century Austrian philosopher Ludwig Wittgenstein allow us to reformulate and defend the insights of the classical pragmatists in new and more convincing ways. I like to think Peirce, James, and Dewey would, as pragmatists, welcome this development.

If my approach differs from the letter of the classical pragmatists, however, it shares an important aspect—the *pragmatic temperament*. The pragmatic temperament refuses to accept the sharp line between thought and action assumed by William James's student. The worlds of the philosophy classroom and the street, the student supposed, were so different that "you could not occupy your mind with them at the same time." A pragmatic temperament, however, acknowledges that *genuine* philosophical questions are not a matter of intellect alone. They are raised by the whole person and involve both the street ("multitudinous beyond imagination, tangled, muddy, painful and perplexed") and the classroom. Action without thought, to adapt a phrase from Kant, is *blind*; thought without action is *empty*. If our minds cannot simultaneously occupy the worlds of the street and the classroom when we're doing philosophy, they must at least enact a dialogue between them. Philosophical questions worth asking must be responsive to the demands of both, as must our answers to them.

Chapter 1, "Agent and Spectator," identifies five standard philosophical questions and contrasts the standard intellectualist (Platonic/Cartesian) approach to them with one that is more practical or agent-centered. Chapter 2 then explains and draws on a number of Wittgensteinian insights and arguments to show that the presuppositions of the Cartesian tradition cannot be reconciled with what we now know about the relationships between language, thought, and action. Chapter 3 illustrates this more practical or agent-centered approach as it applies to philosophical questions of knowledge and reality. Chapter 4 does the same for questions of mind and will. In chapter 5 I turn to the origins of ethics and the nature of ethical reasoning and justification. The conception of ethics developed in this chapter is extended in chapter 6, "Democratic Pluralism," to the fact of rationally irreconcilable moral conflict and the possibility of integrity-preserving compromise. Chapter 7 then draws on all the preceding chapters to address a new moral/metaphysical question: determining, in the light of contemporary medical technology, when a person is dead. This new problem provides an illuminating illustration of the approach to philosophical questions that is the subject of the entire book. The book concludes, in chapter 8, with an account of how life can be meaningful in the face of mortality, with or without belief in God and the supernatural.

NOTES

1. William James, *Pragmatism: A New Name for Some Old Ways of Thinking,* in *William James: Writings, 1902–1919,* ed. Bruce Kuklick (New York: Library of America, 1992), 495.

2. George Cotkin, *William James: Public Philosopher* (Baltimore: Johns Hopkins University Press, 1989).

3. Charles S. Peirce, "What Pragmatism Is," in *The Essential Peirce: Selected Philosophical Writings,* vol. 2 (1893–1913), ed. the Peirce Edition Project (Bloomington: Indiana University Press, 1998), 335.

4. Louis Menand, *The Metaphysical Club: A Story of Ideas in America* (New York: Farrar, Straus & Giroux, 2001), 337–75.

5. Richard J. Bernstein, "American Pragmatism: The Conflict of Narratives," in *Rorty and Pragmatism: The Philosopher Responds to His Critics,* ed. Herman J. Saatkamp, Jr. (Nashville: Vanderbilt University Press, 1995), 61.

6. Bernstein, "American Pragmatism," 66.

7. Richard Rorty, "Response to Thelma Lavine," in *Rorty and Pragmatism: The Philosopher Responds to His Critics,* ed. Herman J. Saatkamp, Jr. (Nashville: Vanderbilt University Press, 1995), 53. Richard Rorty, ed., *The Linguistic Turn,* 2d ed. (Chicago: University of Chicago Press, 1992).

Chapter 1

Agent and Spectator

What *you* want is a philosophy that will not only exercise your powers of intellectual abstraction, but that will make some positive connexion with this actual world of finite human lives.

—Williams James, *Pragmatism*

In the early 1970s advances in medical knowledge and technology were creating new ethical problems for doctors and nurses. Physicians were so troubled by debates over "pulling the plug," defining death, and related issues they sometimes turned to philosophers and theologians for help.

My colleague Bruce Miller was among the first academic philosophers invited to explore these questions with medical students and faculty. At first, many physicians were skeptical. How could a discipline as abstract and theoretical as philosophy throw light on the practical concerns of medicine? Miller was aware of these doubts. A hospital case conference, he realized, was no place for a scholarly account of the fine points of Kant's ethical theory. Yet by doing his homework and tailoring his remarks to the concrete reality of medical practice, he made useful suggestions and developed credibility with physicians.

Once, however, during a brown bag case conference at a local hospital, someone with an avocational interest in philosophy made a very obscure comment. When asked what he meant by it and what difference it made to the case under discussion, the person was incredulous: "You're expecting me, *as a philosopher*, to come down to earth?"

"When I heard that," Miller tells me, "I nearly choked on my sandwich." Despite having taken great care in connecting his philosophical

5

remarks to the realities of medical practice, Miller was afraid the speaker's words would rekindle the physicians' skepticism. Yet the speaker was merely echoing a long-standing, popular conception of philosophy.

In *Candide* Voltaire ridicules the philosopher Pangloss (from the Greek, "all tongue") as an ineffectual windbag whose abstract theories have little or nothing to do with real life. At one point, Pangloss and his former pupil Candide are rocked by the tremendous 1775 Lisbon earthquake. Wounded and stretched out under some debris, Candide asks for oil and wine to ease his pain. Pangloss responds with a (dubious) theoretical account of what has happened: "This earthquake is not a new thing. . . . The town of Lima suffered the same shocks in America last year; the same causes, same effects; there is certainly a vein of sulfur underground from Lima to Lisbon." Exasperated, Candide replies, "Nothing is more probable, but for the love of God, a little oil and wine."[1] The idea that philosophy makes little or no contact with everyday reality is reinforced by the way it is often introduced in colleges and universities. Even if certain questions are shown to have practical origins and consequences, their solutions are assumed to be a matter of thought alone.

The roots of this way of thinking about philosophy can be traced at least as far back as Plato. But it is developed most powerfully in the work of René Descartes. In 1641 Descartes presented a seductive argument showing that it is a distinct possibility that the subject of philosophical inquiry—the asker of philosophical questions—might be a pure subject of consciousness, having no body and knowing nothing but the contents of its own mind. Here I use the word 'subject' in the philosophical sense, referring to that which thinks, feels, perceives, and so on, as opposed to the various *objects* of thought, feeling, and perception. When Jill thinks about Jack, Jill (the one doing the thinking) is the subject of thought and Jack (the one thought about) is its object. I use the pronoun 'it' to refer to a *pure* subject of consciousness because it is unclear how, lacking a body, a pure subject consciousness could be either male or female. This understanding of the asker of philosophical questions has been enormously influential. Descartes is often called the "Father of Modern Philosophy" because his questions, and his conception of the *subject* (or asker) of such questions, set the agenda for much of the best work in philosophy in the centuries that followed.

Despite Descartes's influence, however, and the brilliance of many who accepted his assumptions and starting point, his conception of the asker of philosophical questions is no longer defensible. To take it seriously not only relegates philosophy to the margins of contemporary culture, but also diverts it from a number of vital philosophical problems and issues.

If philosophy is, in the words of William James, to "make some positive connection with this actual world of finite human lives," we must replace the Cartesian conception of the subject of inquiry, and all it entails, with a more plausible alternative. The asker of philosophical questions must be conceived not as a pure (possibly isolated and disembodied) intellect or subject of contemplation, but as an embodied, social agent—a flesh-and-blood, language-using, social animal capable of reflective choice and action in an all-too-hazardous world.

Standard philosophical questions often seem so remote from the things that really matter to us—so "academic" in the pejorative sense of the term—because they are formulated in broadly Cartesian terms. In this chapter I identify five standard questions about knowledge, reality, mind, will, and ethics and show that they presuppose that the subject of inquiry is possibly, as Descartes believed, a *disembodied lone spectator*. I then contrast this with a more pragmatic conception—one that takes the subject of philosophical inquiry to be an *embodied social agent* confronted with a variety of more or less *practical* choices about knowledge, reality, mind, will, and ethics in a complex, occasionally hazardous world. Philosophical questions are more meaningful and more answerable if the subject of inquiry is conceived as an embodied social agent. Reformulated in practical or pragmatic terms, both the questions and various answers to them are more closely connected to "this actual world of finite human lives."

NO WAY OUT

Philosophical questions often seem to require fateful choice between two unappealing alternatives. Each has something right about it; but there is some respect in which it is also deeply flawed. Efforts to combine the best of both alternatives seem contradictory. So, we reluctantly try to choose between them.

Knowledge

A standard question in philosophy is whether we can really know anything outside of the contents of our own minds. "How do you know," we may be asked, "that your commonsense beliefs about the world outside your mind accurately represent that world? Granted you have images of your body and books, chairs, tables, and trees. But perhaps your senses deceive you. There were times when you believed that there was water ahead of you on the road, but your belief proved false—it was only a mirage. There were times when you believed you were running from a tiger, naked in a public place, or taking an exam in a subject you knew absolutely nothing about, but—fortunately—you were only dreaming. So how do you *know* that what you see or believe right now is not a mirage or part of a dream?" Perhaps you're only dreaming that you have hands and feet and that there is a book before you and that you are here reading this page.

It's not easy, once we've taken the bait, to free ourselves from this line of questioning. We may, for example, be confident we are not now dreaming. But how do we *prove* it? Whatever reason we give, our interrogator may make the same irritating response: "Well, how do you know that you're not dreaming *that* as well?" Before long, this relentless skeptic has us questioning all our beliefs about the world outside of our thoughts. We are unable to *prove* we are not dreaming and that our images and beliefs are not false. Hence we cannot say that we *know* what our bodies are like or even that we have bodies or that there is a book before us, and so on.

This radical skepticism, developed with great ingenuity by Descartes, presents a daunting challenge—at least in the classroom. We must either (a) show how some of our beliefs about the "external world" can be known *with complete certainty* to be true or (b) admit that we can know nothing but the contents of our own minds. A contemporary, perhaps even more seductive, version of radical skepticism takes the form of a science fiction tale.

Imagine a human being has unwittingly been subjected to a complicated surgical operation by a brilliant, but morally unscrupulous, scientist.[2] The scientist has removed the person's brain and placed it in a vat of nutrients that keep it alive.

By attaching fiber-optic cables to the nerve endings of different parts of the brain and then connecting them to a super-duper computer, the scientist is able to cause the individual whose brain it is to think he or she is leading a normal life. To the individual it seems as if he or she is walking, interacting with other people, entering buildings, admiring beautiful gardens, and so on; but in fact everything he or she experiences is (really) the result of electronic impulses programmed by the scientist to travel from the computer to the nerve endings. Although entirely delusive, the individual's impressions are that everything is normal.

The computer is so powerful and the program so complex that when the individual tries to move its arm the feedback from the computer will cause it to "see" and "feel" its arm move. The scientist can cause the subject to experience any situation or environment the scientist wishes—winning the New York Marathon, climbing Mt. Everest, or being elected president. And so long as the scientist provides a plausible narrative connecting these "experiences," the subject will have no reason to doubt that what it "sees" or "feels" of the world outside its mind is true of it. The scientist can also erase the memory of the brain operation, so that it will seem to the subject whose brain it is that nothing unusual has happened. At this very moment such a subject—a brain-in-a-vat—could believe it is sitting right where you are and reading a book describing the fantastic possibility of a scientist who removes people's brains from their bodies and places them in a vat of nutrients that keep them alive and then attaches them to a super-duper computer that leads them to think they are sitting right where you are and reading a book describing the fantastic possibility of a scientist who . . .

So how do *you* know, despite your current belief to the contrary, you're not a brain-in-a-vat?

"Impossible!" you want to say. "It couldn't be true."

But how do you *know*? How can you be *certain* that *in fact* you are nothing more than three pounds of complex neurological tissue suspended in a small tub of nutrient fluids with everything you believe and experience, including that you have a body and that you are now reading a page of a book on philosophy, being determined by such a scientist with the aid of a super-duper computer?

Well, how do people know this? How can we be certain we are not just brains-in-vats? (Indeed, an orthodox Cartesian would remind us that we may not even be as materially substantial as a brain; since it is possible to doubt that we have brains, but not possible to doubt that we are conscious, we might be nothing more than pure thinking or immaterial things.) Rebutting this skeptical challenge is quite difficult. But, the skeptic insists, you either have to discredit it or else admit you don't really know you're not just a brain-in-a-vat—a humbling and unsettling admission.

So what's it going to be? How are you going to choose? Whichever way you go, it won't be easy. To retain your convictions about the external world, you'll have to come up with a conclusive refutation of radical skepticism. To embrace radical skepticism—and I mean *live* by it, not just score points in philosophical discussion—is to invite a degree of uncertainty that seems likely to undermine commitment and threaten your sanity.

Reality

A similar difficulty applies to the question of whether the world outside our minds exists apart from our ideas of it or whether it is simply a figment of these ideas. *Realists* suppose that the (external) world is prior to and independent of our ideas about it and that our beliefs (or ideas) are true or false insofar as they correspond or fail to correspond with the independent reality of this world. *Idealists* seize on the fact that there is no way for us to conceive of the world except through our ideas or concepts of it to argue that reality is inseparable from mind. Reality, idealists maintain, is *invariably* a part, a product, or a reflection of human thought. The notion of a more or less stable, independent external world is at best an unprovable assumption aimed at explaining the apparent continuity and coherence of some of our ideas. There is no way to identify or characterize the world that does not bear the imprint of our own minds. Reality is, therefore, inseparable from our ideas of it.

The debate between what philosophers call (metaphysical) *realism* and *idealism* confronts us with another uneasy choice between polar opposites. Realism, though congenial to science and common sense, is notoriously difficult to prove. To show that some things are real independent of our ideas of them seems to require that we be able to identify them apart from our ideas of (or words for) them. Yet no one has ever been able to do this—or even been able to say what would count as doing it. Our only access to reality is through the mind and its ideas. Idealism, on the other hand, though in some sense easier to "prove" from the standpoint of a Cartesian subject, is correspondingly more difficult genuinely to believe. It is as difficult *really* to believe in idealism—to live one's life as if it were true—as it is *really* to believe in radical skepticism. Thus we are asked to choose between one alternative (realism), which, while practically indispensable, seems intellectually indefensible, and another (idealism), which, while intellectually defensible, is practically incredible. Is there no way to bridge the apparent gap between thought and action, intellect and practice?

Mind

A third question involves the relation between mind and body. What is the mind? What is the body? And how are they related? Here we are invited, at least initially, to choose between mind–body *dualism* and some form of *physicalism*.

The dualist conceives the mind as a purely mental (or nonmaterial) substance, the body as physical substance, and the relation between them as causal interaction. This is compatible not only with the idea of life after (bodily) death, but also with many commonsense causal explanations. Stubbing your toe (a physical event) causes pain (a mental event); deciding to raise your arm (a mental event) causes your arm to go up (a physical event). The physicalist, on the other hand, identifies the mind with the brain or the central nervous system. This conception of mind—one that regards mental states as nothing but extremely complex physical states—seems more compatible with the presuppositions and findings of contemporary science. Bodily injury may cause pain, but pain may be nothing more than a state of the brain; my decision to raise my arm is actually a complex brain state that then sets off a set of neuromuscular states resulting in my arm's going up.

Mind–body dualism is hard to defend. If, for example, the mind is nonphysical, self-contained, and independent of the body, you could never be sure there were minds other than your own. But (as I show in chapter 3) we are as *certain* that there are minds other than our own as we are of anything. So there must be something wrong about a theory of mind, like dualism, that implies that we can't be sure there are minds other than our own. Second, if mind and body are as radically different as the dualist maintains, how can they possibly interact? How can something entirely nonphysical (that has no length, width, height, or weight, etc.) causally interact with something entirely physical? Causal interaction is, to the scientific mind, always between one physical substance or process and another.

Physicalism, which identifies the mind with the body (or brain), makes easy work of these questions. If others behave like we do or have brains more or less like ours, they have minds like ours. And if mind and body are both physical substances, we can easily explain the commonsense interaction between them. Yet physicalist theories of mind generate problems of their own. How can consciousness possibly be reduced to a state of the brain? There is something about the conscious *experience* of *seeing* red or *tasting* chocolate that cannot be captured by the language of physical science. Someone might know everything there is to know about our bodies and brains and still not know how things look or feel to us. There is more to the mind—for example the conscious *experiences* of seeing red or tasting chocolate—than can possibly be conveyed by even the most comprehensive explanation of what is going on in our brains. And if this is so, the mental (mind or consciousness) cannot be reduced to the physical (the brain).

Though there is much to be said for dualism and for physicalism, each has serious problems. Dualism can account for inner experience, but taking it seriously makes knowledge of other people's minds and interaction between mind and body a complete mystery. Physicalism eliminates these puzzles, but it cannot readily account for what anyone reading this page will affirm—the reality of conscious experience. How can we choose, once and for all, between them?

Will

Aspects of the debates between skepticism and certainty, metaphysical realism and idealism, and mind–body dualism and physicalism combine to generate our fourth traditional problem—the free will question. Suppose, despite your beliefs to the contrary, you *are* actually a brain-in-a-vat. Although it seems that whether or not you move your arm, choose ice cream for dessert, or go to bed early is *up to you*, these and all other "choices" are actually being determined by the scientist and the super-duper computer. You think you're free to do as you please and to will as you please. But this, like your belief that you have a body, is an illusion. In fact, all of your "actions," mental as well as physical, are causally determined by factors wholly outside of (what you falsely believe to be) your knowledge and control.

Even if we are not brains-in-a-vat, *determinists* say, everything we do is still beyond our control. As physical beings, subject to the same cause-and-effect relations as any other physical thing, everything we do is causally determined by prior events that stretch well beyond our understanding (and control). We may believe that whether we choose to watch television or read a book is fully *up to us*, but this belief, determinists say, is false. Given our past history (and/or the state of our brains), whatever we "decide" to do—turn on the TV or open the book—is caused by events over which we ultimately have no control. We cannot, given this chain of events, choose other than we do.

There is at least some truth to this. Our ability to understand and reliably predict the behavior of *others* presupposes causal determination. If we know the causal history of how people have responded to certain circumstances in the past, we can predict with some accuracy how they will respond to similar circumstances in the future. Yet, a more scientific or objective understanding of ourselves suggests that you and I are in this respect no different. Everything *we* do—everything we wish or intend or will—is also the outcome of causal chains ranging well beyond our control. Although you think you're reading this book "of your own free will," it's an illusion. Given your entire causal history, says the determinist, together with the various stimuli and circumstances now working upon you, you cannot at this point in your life do anything but read this book. And if you happen to be one of those people who, after reading the last sentence, just closed the book and turned on the TV to "prove" your freedom, well, given *your* particular causal history, the determinist coolly responds, you couldn't have helped doing that!

Still, determinism is very difficult, if not impossible, *genuinely* to believe, at least about ourselves. Doesn't deliberation, reflection, and choice presuppose that what follows is largely, or at least to some extent, *up to me*? How can I possibly do what I do—live as I live—without believing that many of the things I do are under my control and that I am, accordingly, responsible for them? Consider how deeply these notions of freedom and responsibility are embedded in our everyday lives. Praise and blame, reward and punishment, self-respect and remorse all presuppose the sort of freedom that the determinist tells us is wholly illusory.

The problem is vexing. From one point of view, *everything* we and others do seems to be causally determined. From another point of view, *some of the things* we and others do we regard as freely chosen. Both seem indispensable. But they contradict each other. Which of them is right? Are we even free to ask the question?

Ethics

Suppose there are circumstances in which our wills are free in the sense required for moral responsibility. Some of the things people do in such circumstances are said to be morally right and others wrong; some people, in virtue of the rightness or wrongness of their actions or intentions, are said to be good and others bad. But how do we make such judgments? Are there independent standards of right and wrong, good and bad, to which we appeal? Or are moral judgments nothing more than expressions of personal preferences or the conventions of our culture or society?

At one extreme are those who argue that moral standards must be not only objective (or independent of what people *happen* to value), but absolute (or invariant with respect to time and place). Let us call this position *objective absolutism*. Moral standards, on this view, are prior to and independent of human thought and historically and culturally invariant. The so-called Divine Command Theory provides a clear example.

Suppose God's commands are universal with respect to place and eternal with respect to time. If, then, we define 'morally right' as 'that which is commanded by God' and 'morally wrong' as 'that which is forbidden by God', God's commands provide an objective standard of right and wrong that transcends all differences of time and place. Rightness or wrongness would not be a matter of personal preference or social custom. Nor would it vary from one historical period or culture to another. Right and wrong would be independent of time, chance, and individual or collective human thought. They would be objective and absolute.

The Divine Command Theory, however, has a number of problems. Setting aside questions about God's existence or how we can know what God commands, consider the following objection (based on an argument in Plato's *Euthyphro*). Suppose God commands us to tell the truth. We can then ask whether (a) truth telling is right because God commands it or (b) God commands us to tell the truth because it's right. Each answer spells trouble for the Divine Command Theory. If truth telling is right *for no other reason* than God commands it and 'morally right' *means nothing more* than 'commanded by God', our moral standards are arbitrary. This is because there are no constraints on God's commands. Since 'right' and 'wrong' are defined *in terms of* God's commands, there is no such thing as right or wrong *until* His commands are issued. This means that God's commands are wholly unrestricted by standards of right and wrong. There is no reason, then, for God to command, "Truth telling is right" rather than, "Truth telling is wrong." He could just as well have flipped a coin between them. Thus insofar as our moral standards are based on God's commands and God can command anything He likes (because nothing is moral or immoral on this view *until* God issues His commands), our moral standards are arbitrary. If God's coin had come down differently and He had commanded us to tell lies, truth telling would be wrong.

If, on the other hand, we say that God is good and that being good He only commands us to do what's right, we are led to a different, but equally embarrassing difficulty for the Divine Command Theory. To say, "God is good and a good God would not command us to lie" presupposes criteria of good and bad, right and wrong, that are prior to and independent of God's commands—criteria used not only by God in deciding what to command but also by us in determining what a good God would be like and the sort of things such a God would command. More basic than God's commands, then, are the moral standards that God uses to justify his commands and that we use to shape our idea of a good God. These standards are accessible to us, insofar as we think we know what a good God would be like and what sorts of commands He would issue. We draw on our knowledge of these standards when, for example, we reject the words of mass murderers who claim to be carrying out God's commands. "God is good," we say, "and a good God wouldn't command anyone to murder people like this." Thus, either God's commands are based on certain moral standards or they are not. If they are, then these standards are more basic to morality than God's commands. If they are not, then God's commands are arbitrary and have no moral authority.

Efforts to avoid these and related difficulties with the Divine Command Theory have not been successful. Nor have attempts to provide alternative accounts of how moral standards can be prior to and independent of human experience and reflection. As a result, some have rejected objective absolutism for the other extreme. Moral values, they argue, are nothing but expressions of personal preference or the conventions of a particular society, culture, or subculture. What some individuals or societies regard as right will be regarded as wrong by others. And there is no independent or external standpoint for saying that one is better than the other. Moral judgments are internal to and inseparable from the personal, cultural, and historical circumstances and orientation of those who make them; there is no neutral or objective way to show that one set of values or assessments is better than another.

This general approach—call it *subjective relativism*—is, on reflection, no less problematic than objective absolutism. The main difficulty is that it provides no good grounds for selecting moral standards or for resolving conflicts between them. This is true not only with regard to conflicts between persons, between groups, and between persons and groups, but also with respect to conflicts *within* persons and *within* groups. How, on this view, does an individual resolve an internal moral conflict; and how does a social group resolve such a conflict among its members? If the individual or members of the group can appeal to nothing but the values they already embrace, they have no grounds for rationally resolving the conflict or for revising or improving their values or principles. Neither objective absolutism nor subjective relativism, then, seems to provide an adequate basis for ethics. If these are your only alternatives, it's easy to see why you might become either a moral skeptic—*doubting* whether ethics has any rational justification—or a moral nihilist— flatly *denying* the possibility of such justification.

While exercising what James calls "your powers of intellectual abstraction," these choices between certainty and skepticism, realism and idealism, dualism and physicalism, freedom and determinism, and objective absolutism and subjective relativism, I hope to show, "fail to make some positive connexion with this actual world of finite human lives."

THE CARTESIAN SUBJECT

To find something we cannot possibly doubt, Descartes urges us to suspend belief in anything that could possibly turn out to be false. Because our senses sometimes deceive us, he advises us to suppose that everything we believe on the basis of sense perception may be mistaken. Because we sometimes believe things while dreaming that turn out to be false and because there is at any given time no way to *prove* to ourselves that we are not at that time dreaming, we suppose that any belief that could possibly be the product of a current dream is false. Because we may be deceived by an "Evil Genius" (a seventeenth-century version of the unscrupulous scientist in the tale of the brain-in-a-vat) we may even be mistaken about 2 + 2 = 4. Finally, however, we arrive at a belief that we cannot possibly doubt; namely that we exist as thinking beings or pure subjects of consciousness. This we cannot coherently doubt because every effort to doubt that we exist as thinking beings is, at the same time, an affirmation or proof that we *do* exist as such beings. I cannot doubt my existence as a thinking thing without doubting. But since doubting is a kind of thinking, doubting my existence as a thinking thing is simultaneously to *exhibit and affirm* my existence as a thinking thing!

For Descartes, this absolutely certain belief, that he exists as a thinking thing, provides the bedrock for subsequent reasoning about knowledge and reality. But what must you, as you retrace Descartes's reasoning, be like at this point? For all you know, you're a *lone, disem-*

bodied spectator, or what I call a "Cartesian Subject" of thought or reflection. You're alone because, in doubting whatever can possibly be doubted, you're doubting that other people exist. Other people, for all you *really know*, may be illusions, the product of a dream, or an "Evil Genius." A Cartesian subject is, for much the same reason, supposed to be disembodied. You can be mistaken about the reality of your own body for the same reason you can be mistaken about the existence of other people (and their bodies). Finally, a Cartesian subject is a more or less passive spectator because without a body—and without other physical objects in the "external" world—there is nothing, except reflecting on one's thoughts and beliefs, one can *do*. There is, under these conditions, no important role for embodied action. Indeed, Descartes regarded this as something of a virtue of his method. Knowing, for Descartes, is largely an intellectual or contemplative endeavor and we succumb to error, as he put it, "when the exigencies of action . . . oblige us to make up our minds before having the leisure to examine matters more carefully."[3]

This highly intellectualized conception of the subject of reflection is deeply rooted in Western philosophy. The dominant metaphor, Richard Rorty points out, is that of the mind as a self-subsistent internal mirror, the main task of which is to faithfully represent the world outside of the mind (i.e., external reality) "As It Really Is"—that is, as it is utterly independent of our active, embodied existence in it.[4] The classic seventeenth- and eighteenth-century empiricists (John Locke, Bishop Berkeley, and David Hume), no less than seventeenth- and eighteenth-century classic rationalists (Descartes, Gottfried Leibniz, and Benedict Spinoza) take the Cartesian subject as a starting point of philosophical reflection. The Cartesian subject remains an initial presupposition in the work of Immanuel Kant and continues to play a strong role in contemporary philosophy as revealed by the tale of the brain-in-a-vat.

It is as pure subjects of consciousness that we are invited to contemplate the stark choices posed by standard philosophical questions of knowledge, reality, mind, will, and ethics. They are posed mainly as puzzles for the individual intellect. "Consider the alternatives," say philosophy teachers to their bewildered students. "Certainty or skepticism, realism or idealism, dualism or physicalism, freedom or determinism, objective absolutism or subjective relativism. Think about them carefully, reflect deeply, and decide in each case which is correct."

Seated in a quiet room, dark except for the lamp illuminating the pages of Descartes's first two *Meditations*, painting ourselves into the corner of having to choose between radical skepticism and absolute certainty may not seem problematic. Nor may the other intellectual puzzles seem implausible seated in the philosophy classroom, where, for at least fifty minutes, the activity and requirements of everyday life can be safely bracketed off. But there are serious problems with the idea of a Cartesian subject, its presuppositions, and the philosophical questions to which it gives rise.

First, to employ the sort of methodological doubt recommended by Descartes a subject of consciousness would have to be able to use words *correctly*. It cannot subject its beliefs to systematic doubt without using language to do so. After arriving at the point where the only thing *it* knew for certain was that it existed as a thinking thing, a Cartesian subject would then have to use language to build upon this foundation. A Cartesian subject would have to be confident that its words were meaningful and that what it meant by a word at one time was the same thing it meant at a previous time. This is, however, questionable. The capacity to use words correctly presupposes criteria for correctness. A Cartesian subject cannot, as I will show in chapter 2, be confident it is using words correctly unless there are criteria for correlating what it says with what it and others *do* in various circumstances, criteria of the sort we commonly employ as *embodied* and *engaged* members of linguistic *communities*. Thus a philosophically reflective, language-using Cartesian subject—which is presupposed by our five standard problems—is not possible.

On the contrary, we who raise genuine questions about knowledge, reality, mind, will, and ethics are not, first and foremost, isolated, disembodied Cartesian observers *of* the world, but rather embodied social agents *in* it. When we reflect, we do so not from some point outside the world, but rather at a particular time and place—and with one or more practical purposes—within it. Given our biological origins and nature and our consequent vulnerability—our need for nurture, food, shelter, clothing, protection from disease and aggression, and so on—we must, in order to survive, formulate and *act upon* certain conceptions of ourselves and the world. Action and agency are, in this respect, at least as basic as observation and contemplation. Indeed, abstract thought very likely owes its origin, development, direction, and value to the demands of practice.

The Darwinian overtones of this picture are no coincidence. Darwin's account of biological evolution plays an important role in the shift from a Cartesian (or contemplative) to a more pragmatic (or practical) conception of the subject of philosophical inquiry. The emergence of philosophical pragmatism as an explicit alternative to the Cartesian tradition comes in the wake of the publication of *The Origin of Species* (1859). The founders of philosophical pragmatism—Charles S. Peirce, William James, and John Dewey—were among the first to grasp the far-reaching philosophical implications of the Darwinian Revolution.

Like Plato, Descartes and those influenced by him generally assume that reality is for the most part fixed and immutable, as is genuine knowledge of that reality. They assume, too, that there could be no order in matter unless it was first conceived by mind and that human beings, as creations of God, enjoy a unique and exalted status. These assumptions are plausibly challenged by Darwin. A principal thesis of *The Origin of Species* is that the world, including the various species of plants and animals, is not fixed or immutable. Moreover, natural selection—the principal mechanism for evolutionary change—undermines both the idea of final ends or purposes of human existence and the idea of radical differences between human beings and nonhuman animals. Human beings are, for Darwin, vulnerable biological organisms whose existence is attributable to blind contingency rather than Divine purpose. There is, in the Darwinian understanding of the world, no fixed end or purpose for human beings; nor is there any particular design in the universe. Human beings are another species of animal that has slowly evolved over a long period of time through biological variation, heritability, and natural selection. The distinction between humans and other animals is thus a matter of degree rather than kind.

Like other animals, human beings are vulnerable biological organisms in a changing, occasionally threatening, competitive environment in which survival depends, in part, on the capacity to adapt to changing conditions. A feature of human life that has proved especially useful in enabling humans to contend intelligently with complexity and change is language. Language use—including the various specialized vocabularies and subvocabularies developed and employed in special circumstances, such as in the different sciences—is a tool for anticipating and contending with the hazards and complexities of life. It extends, in a wide variety of ways and circumstances, our capacity to survive. It is through language that human beings are able to anticipate a wide variety of complex, dangerous circumstances and then to coordinate survival-enhancing responses to them. And it is as language-using biological organisms that we raise philosophical questions.

THE PRAGMATIC SUBJECT

This more naturalistic conception of the subject of reflection underlies a more practical or pragmatic approach to philosophical inquiry. Pragmatic considerations are inseparable from certain social *practices*—and practices are themselves constituted by patterns of (embodied) human action. It is because we *must* act—because we are primarily interdependent biological agents rather than possibly self-sufficient ethereal spectators—that we have developed certain practices. In so doing we avail ourselves of language—understood not simply as a set of words, but rather as a complex variety of linguistic *practices* that, as humans have evolved, have greatly enhanced the sophistication and effectiveness of human action. An important use of language, so understood, is effective action, not simply description or reflection for its own sake. And the main function of action, for vulnerable biological organisms like ourselves, is *meaningful* survival (see chapter 8) in an occasionally hazardous environment that reinforces or selects for, among other things, informed, far-sighted choice. Language—by enabling us to escape the immediate present through (a) locutions of past and future; (b) reference to distant and hypothetical places, circumstances, and events; (c) conditional ("if-then") constructions; (d) imagining alternative ways of doing and construing things; and so on—is what makes such choice possible. To use language effectively, however, we must use it correctly. And correct language use, as I show in chapter 2, presupposes membership in a community of embodied, language-using agents. Intelligible expression of doubt, then, presupposes a social as well as an embodied subject of inquiry.

Conceiving the subject of inquiry as pragmatic (an embodied social agent) rather than Cartesian (a possibly lone, disembodied spectator) results in different philosophical questions about knowledge, reality, mind, freedom, and ethics. Gone are the polarities of the Cartesian tradition—the "all or none" choices between skepticism and certainty, realism and idealism, dualism and physicalism, freedom and determinism, and objective absolutism and subjective relativism. In their place are various families of questions that, while in some respects more complicated, are more answerable than those of the Cartesian tradition. Though not resolvable in one fell swoop, they can, in many *contexts*, be resolved *for all practical purposes*—which are, for those of us with a pragmatic temperament, the purposes that matter most. Both the pragmatic formulation of these questions and their possible resolutions will be examined in subsequent chapters.

AGENT AND SPECTATOR

One reason "so few human beings truly care for philosophy," William James observed, is its "monstrous abridgment of things, which, like all abridgments is got by the absolute loss and casting out of real matter."[5] The "real matter" to which James refers includes the wide variety of rich and concrete realities that comprise our daily lives. Abstract ethical theories, for example, cannot capture the various complexities of everyday moral decision making. "The entire man [or woman], who feels all needs by turns," James points out, "will take nothing as an equivalent for life but the fulness [sic] of living itself."[6]

James does not, however, want to *substitute* action and agency for contemplation and intellect. Among the false choices pragmatists want to reject are those between theory and practice, agent and spectator. The subject of philosophical inquiry is not an agent *rather than* a spectator, but both an agent *and* a spectator. Without agency, philosophical inquiry would be unnecessary; without the capacity to approximate the viewpoint of a spectator it would be impossible. Philosophy is both necessary and possible because we are *both* agents and spectators.

Philosophical questions of knowledge, reality, mind, will, and ethics can be traced to our capacity to view the world from two very general, interrelated perspectives. The first is a personal, subjective, or internal viewpoint—the standpoint of a participant. The second views the world from a more impersonal, objective, or external standpoint. This is the perspective of a detached spectator. Thomas Nagel calls this more impersonal perspective "the view from nowhere" and Hilary Putnam characterizes it as a "God's-eye point of view."[7] It is, in its purest form, the view of no human being in particular.

The distinction between the two standpoints is, as Nagel points out, "really a matter of degree and it covers a wide spectrum." Infants and animals are, for the most part, confined to the subjective perspective. During the normal course of linguistic, psychological, and intellectual development, however, a person gradually develops the capacity to approximate an increasingly objective or impersonal viewpoint. We learn to abstract from our personal position so as to assume a more disinterested or external perspective—viewing ourselves and our relation to the animate and inanimate world from "the outside." The development of self-consciousness, putting ourselves in other people's shoes, and seeing ourselves as others see us are aspects of this perspective—as is coming to see ourselves as no more important or valuable from the standpoint of impersonal justice than anyone else. Moreover, Nagel adds, "a standpoint that is objective by comparison with the personal view of one individual may be subjective by comparison with a theoretical standpoint still farther out. The standpoint of [impartial] morality is more objective than that of private life, but less objective than the standpoint of physics."[8] From a certain point of view my life is no more valuable than any other person's, but as persons we are all more valuable than, say, rocks or trees. From the standpoint of physics, however, there is no difference between persons, on the one hand, and rocks and trees, on the other; each is just a particular configuration of matter.

We can now express our five philosophical questions in terms of the two general standpoints: (1) Is what we believe from an internal (or personal) standpoint true from a more external (or impersonal) standpoint? (2) Is reality confined to the contents of our internal standpoints or is it what would be seen from a "God's-eye point of view"? (3) Is the mind what we experience from the inside (for example, pain) or is it what we can only understand from the outside (various functions of the brain)? (4) Are decisions that seem from the inside to be "up to us" really, when understood from a more external perspective, actually determined by factors over which we have no control? and (5) Is ethics based on the preferences and dispositions we (or our cultures or subcultures) happen to have or are there independent and unchanging standards to which these preferences and dispositions ought to conform?

As traditionally formulated, these questions ask us to choose, once and for all, between variants of the internal and external perspectives. If, however, we identify with James's "entire" person—"who feels all needs by turns"—we will resist doing so. Each perspective is necessary for whole or integrated persons—reflective, embodied social agents like ourselves—and insofar as a certain conception of philosophy asks us to choose between them, we are likely to reject it in favor of one more hospitable to "the fulness of living itself."

In ordinary life we regard an individual who becomes *locked* into one of these perspectives at the expense of the other as seriously incapacitated. People who cannot approximate a more detached or impersonal viewpoint are likely to overpersonalize their inevitable losses and frustrations and find it nearly impossible to contend with the darker sides of life. Consider how in consoling the bereaved we sometimes remind them that we are all mortal and that if death had not come now to the person for whom they mourn, it would have come eventually. We point out, too, that time is a great healer and that they will not always feel as empty and sad as they now feel. In so doing we encourage those suffering a great loss to balance (but not replace) their painful personal perspective with a more impersonal perspective—to temper despairing or suicidal thoughts with a more detached or disinterested view of the situation. Attempts at this sort of balancing are common enough in certain situations to be embodied in some of our clichés, as, for example, when we remind the bereaved that "we all have to die sometime" or console a rejected and despondent lover or suitor by pointing out, "There are other fish in the sea."[9]

Persons can also become locked into the objective or impersonal perspective, and here the balancing must go the other way. Those who find themselves full-time spectators—incapable of forming close personal attachments and relationships as well as uncommitted to any particular projects—are usually as desperately unhappy and in need of our sympathy and support as the bereaved. In some cases, their emptiness may be more critical, leaving them seriously depressed or suicidal. They need to embrace a less detached worldview and way of life, one that will allow them to participate in the joy and risks of human relationships and to commit themselves to specific projects, giving shape and meaning to their lives.

The metaphor or image suggested by these examples is that of tacking. In sailing into a wind we cannot set a direct course. Instead we proceed indirectly, heading first toward one side of our eventual destination, then toward the other side, then back to the first side, and so on. We sail back and forth along these opposing, counterbalancing tacks until we get where we are going. In life, too, we often find ourselves "heading into the wind," and we must judiciously tack between the personal and impersonal perspectives. Although there are situations in which we largely commit ourselves to one tack rather than another—for example, in falling in love or in studying physics—most of us cannot do so permanently nor should we so desire. Successful navigation in life, as on the sea, requires knowing when and how to tack between viewpoints. Those who remain utterly blind to a more objective or detached picture of their betrothed or lovers are ill-advised to make long-standing personal commitments to them; psychotherapists who cannot resist analyzing every action, motive, and choice of those around them are not yet ready for friendship or love.

But exactly who or what is doing the tacking? From what standpoint, to expand the metaphor, do we determine our destination and tack between viewpoints? If we think of the various standpoints arranged on a spectrum with the most internal or subjective at one end (for example, that of animals or young children) and the most external or objective at the other (for example, that of physics), we might place the standpoint of *reflective agency* (that of our sailor) at about the middle. It is from this standpoint that we informedly and reflectively formulate various personal goals and identify and implement the means most likely to realize them. The sailor's goal may be a particular harbor and the means a particular pattern of tacking. You or I might decide to become a parent and subsequently tack back and forth between books and studies on child development and spontaneous, loving play with our infant. The books and studies may influence our play and our playful experience may temper our assessment of what we have read.

The capacity to view the world from the two kinds of standpoints and to tack between them contributes significantly to our capacities for self-reflection and self-direction—and therefore to survival and well-being. Each general perspective provides a standpoint for critically examining and tempering the other, providing the possibility for intelligently adapting to new circumstances and assuming some degree of control and responsibility for our lives. This capacity also allows us to understand and enjoy the works of Sophocles, Aristophanes, Shakespeare, Ingmar Bergman, and Woody Allen. Comedy, no less than tragedy, depends on the capacity to view the world (and ourselves) from different, often incongruous, perspectives. Human life—as represented by great literature, explored by interpretative social scientists, and experienced by each of us—involves an indispensable, creative tension between them.

No wonder, then, we find the traditional dichotomies between certainty and skepticism, realism and idealism, mind and body, freedom and determinism, and objective absolutism and subjective relativism so uninviting. To opt for one pole or the other is to deny a complex capacity that both enhances our ability to survive and partly defines individual and social identity. Exclusive identification with the personal perspective exaggerates the significance of our biological (or animal) origins; exclusive identification with the more *im*personal perspective overstates the significance of our intellectual understanding and transcendent (or God-like) aspirations. To conceive of human beings as whole or integrated persons—embodied social agents whose continued existence, identity, and flourishing depend on judiciously tacking between personal and impersonal perspectives—is therefore to reject the standard philosophical dichotomies. Yet, as I will show in subsequent chapters, philosophical questions of knowledge, reality, mind, will, and ethics do not disappear if we adopt a more pragmatic conception of the person. They must still be addressed—not once and for all and in the abstract, but day in, day out in a never-ending variety of concrete situations.

In the chapters that follow I fill out this sketch of the pragmatic subject—a being who is both agent *and* spectator—and trace its significance for philosophical reflection. I identify and defend a pragmatic account of language, meaning, and truth, and show how it contributes to mutually reinforcing responses to *practical* philosophical questions about knowledge, reality, mind, will, and ethics. I turn then to social and political philosophy and to a new, far-reaching philosophical question raised by advances in medical knowledge and technology. Finally, I develop a pragmatic conception of transcendence to show how our lives can have meaning and value in the face of mortality.

THE IRREPRESSIBLE SKEPTIC

But what of our friend, the radical skeptic? Readers wedded to the Cartesian tradition are unlikely to be persuaded by what I've said so far. "You're just begging the question," I can imagine one of them saying.

> You can't avoid the deep philosophical problems of knowledge, reality, mind, will, and ethics that easily. *Postulating* the inquiring self as a pragmatic agent rather than a Cartesian subject, as Bertrand Russell remarked in another context, has the same "advantages of theft over honest toil."[10] After all, how do you *know* Darwin's theory is true or that there even was such a person as Darwin? Come to think of it, how do you *know* you're not a brain-in-a-vat or a Cartesian subject? How can you be *certain* you're not just dreaming that you're an embodied agent? Anyone seeking *the truth* would rightly be unconvinced by your reasoning, which presupposes what you are trying to prove.

It's an open question whether this sort of doctrinaire skepticism can be answered on its own terms. Determined and resourceful skeptics always seem to be able to redeploy their argument, no matter what our response. There's always another story they can tell—a *deeper* layer of illusion, a *more encompassing* dream, *another* scientist playing tricks with our "vatted" brain, and so on.

I have two responses to the persistent radical skeptic. The first draws on contemporary philosophy of language to show that the capacity to use words correctly presupposes that we are pragmatic rather than Cartesian subjects of inquiry. We cannot seriously believe and express radical skepticism and, at the same time, be confident that our words have a clear and definite meaning. I develop the argument for this in the next chapter.

Though I find the argument persuasive, I realize that a hard-core skeptic may not be convinced. So there is, in these pages, a second, more indirect response aimed at marginalizing (rather than directly refuting) radical skepticism. To the very end of *Candide*, Dr. Pangloss maintains that this, as it is, is the "best of all possible worlds." Despite all the pain, misery, and death he and the others have witnessed and experienced, he refuses to relinquish his doctrine. Though Candide comes to reject Pangloss's teachings, as the book ends he no longer wastes his time trying to prove to his former teacher's satisfaction that he is wrong. The concluding sentence expresses Candide's simple and eloquent response to yet another tiresome refrain of Pangloss's "best of all possible worlds" philosophy: "'That is well said', replied Candide, 'but we must cultivate our garden.'"[11] At which point, I like to think, Candide turns from Pangloss and resumes weeding.

To cultivate a garden is not to accept everything that happens as for the best. Weeds, disease, and drought are part of nature, but to a gardener these are things to be reduced or eliminated. What Candide *does* in cultivating his garden (where cultivating a garden is a metaphor for doing our best to improve the conditions of our earthly lives) is in some respects a more powerful and eloquent "refutation" of Pangloss's doctrine than anything he could at this point *say*. Deeds, not words, are the most fitting response. Pangloss's abstract generalizations are simply beside the point; they don't matter, do any work, or make any "connexion to this actual world of finite human lives." For Candide it's no longer worth trying to refute Pangloss on his own terms; he has better things to *do*.

After a point, it seems to me, our response to radical skeptics ought to resemble Candide's response to Pangloss. Even if we cannot refute them to *their* satisfaction, the fact that their doctrine makes "no positive connexion with this actual world of finite human lives" may be sufficient to relegate it to the margins of contemporary philosophy (though *not* to the margins of the *history* of philosophy, where it remains of the greatest importance). As embodied social agents we have a number of more interesting and important philosophical questions to address than those posed by the radical skeptic. Like Candide, then, let's not worry too much about matters that make no difference to the way we (must) lead our lives. There are more fertile fields that need cultivating. And we'll never get to them unless we can turn our backs on radical skepticism.

NOTES

1. Voltaire, *Candide*, in *Candide, Zadig and Selected Stories*, trans. Donald M. Frame (New York: New American Library, 1961), 26.

2. Hilary Putnam, "Brains in a Vat," in *Reason, Truth, and History* (Cambridge: Cambridge University Press, 1981), 1–21.

3. René Descartes, *Meditations*, in *Philosophical Works of Descartes*, trans. Elizabeth S. Haldane and G. R. T. Ross (Cambridge: Cambridge University Press, 1969), 198–99.

4. Richard Rorty, *Philosophy and the Mirror of Nature* (Princeton, N.J.: Princeton University Press, 1979.

5. William James, "The Sentiment of Rationality," in *William James: Writings 1878–1899*, ed. Gerald E. Myers (New York: Library of America, 1992), 508.

6. James, "Sentiment of Rationality," 508.

7. Thomas Nagel, *The View from Nowhere* (New York: Oxford University Press, 1986); Hilary Putnam, *Reason, Truth, and History* (Cambridge: Cambridge University Press, 1981), 49.

8. Nagel, *View from Nowhere*, 5.

9. This paragraph and the four that follow are adapted from Martin Benjamin, *Splitting the Difference: Compromise and Integrity in Ethics and Politics* (Lawrence: University Press of Kansas, 1990), 97–99.

10. Bertrand Russell, *Introduction to Mathematical Philosophy*, 2d ed. (London: George Allen & Unwin, 1920), 71.

11. Voltaire, *Candide*, 101.

Chapter 2

Language, Meaning, and Truth

[T]he knower is not simply a mirror floating with no foot-hold anywhere, and passively reflecting an order that he comes upon and finds simply existing. The knower is an actor, and coefficient of the truth which he helps to create. Mental interests, hypotheses, postulates, so far as they are bases for human action—action which to a great extent transforms the world—help to make the truth.

—William James, "Remarks on Spencer's Definition of Mind as Correspondence"

We raise philosophical questions about knowledge, reality, mind, will, and ethics in *words*—words we think have a more or less definite *meaning*. We then try to determine which of a variety of possible answers is *true*. In this chapter I show that the most plausible understanding of language, meaning, and truth presupposes that the asker of philosophical questions is a pragmatic rather than a Cartesian subject—an embodied social agent rather than (possibly) a lone disembodied spectator.

LANGUAGE

What would language have to be like if you were actually a Cartesian subject? First, it would have to be self-taught. Second, it would have to be *private* in the sense that even if there were other people, they couldn't possibly understand this language because its words would be defined in terms of your own (inner) thoughts and experiences that are, by their nature, inaccessible to others. Third, there would have to be some way for you to know your words were meaningful rather than just gibberish. Could there be such a language? Is a Cartesian subject—a pure (disembodied) subject of consciousness—really capable of learning and using language? A powerful line of argument developed by Ludwig Wittgenstein answers "no" to both questions.

Suppose you were to follow the path of methodological doubt recommended by Descartes. Seeking absolute certainty, you assume that any type of belief that might be false *is* false. Because your senses can deceive you, you assume anything based on sense perception is false; because dreams can deceive you and you cannot be sure you're not dreaming, you assume anything that could be part of a dream is false; and because you can't know for certain that a very powerful "evil genius" isn't playing tricks with your mind, you even suppose mathematical "truths" like 2 + 2 = 4 are false. Having doubted the existence of everything physical, including your own body and those of others, you then try to doubt your own existence. This, however, proves impossible: "I cannot doubt my existence *as a thinking thing*," you say, "because whenever I try to doubt this I must (insofar as doubting is a kind of thinking) *exist* as a thinking thing." This (or something like it) provides the basis for Descartes's claim that while you can doubt you have a body (and that there are physical objects or other persons), you cannot possibly doubt you exist as a thinking thing or pure subject of consciousness. Of this—and only this—can you be absolutely certain as you seek, as a foundation for knowledge, a belief that cannot possibly be doubted. With this as a premise you will then (following Descartes) try to deduce an equally certain set of beliefs about yourself, the world outside your mind, and the relation between them.

But how would you (as, by hypothesis, a lone disembodied subject of consciousness) have acquired the language in which you say, "I cannot doubt my existence as a thinking thing because whenever I try to do so I must (insofar as doubting is thinking) *exist* as a thinking thing"? As a radically skeptical inquirer, how can you be certain your words have a fixed meaning? Of course, you *think* your words are meaningful. You think, for example, you know what the word 'doubt' means and that you're using it the same way from one time to the next. But can you, as a possibly lone disembodied inquirer, be *certain* of this?

As a radical skeptic, you must have taught yourself language. You cannot have learned it from other people because you're assuming that there aren't any. You can't accept it as a given, because it may have been given to you by an "evil genius" who tricks you into believing you're talking sense while your words are just gobbledygook. But how can you have taught yourself language from the bottom up? How as a Cartesian subject—a lone disembodied spectator—could you have learned what the word 'doubt' means?

One possibility is that you experience a feeling of doubt, make up the word 'doubt', and then attach it to the specific experience. The word would be defined in terms of what it refers to—namely the (inner) experience of doubting. In this way, perhaps, you develop a vocabulary with which to express and reason about your thoughts and experiences *even if* there is nothing in the world apart from yourself and your mental states.

Such a language would, in a very strong sense, be *private*. It's not simply that you keep your thoughts from others, as, for example, by devising a secret code for an intimate diary. Rather you couldn't share your thoughts with others even if you wanted to. You could, if you wished, teach another person the secret code in which you keep a diary, but as a Cartesian subject you couldn't possibly teach someone else what you mean by 'doubt'. This is because the word would be defined solely in terms of your (inner) experience of doubting—and this is accessible to no one but yourself. Since you've defined the word in terms of what it refers to and no one but you has access to what it refers to, no one but you can possibly know what it means.

There are, however, formidable difficulties with the very idea of such a language. First, it's not clear there is a distinctive and uniquely identifiable inner experience of doubting. Try it. Express doubt about something and see if you can identify a distinctive inner feeling or experience. I'm fairly confident you can't. But if, after trying, you think you can, compare the feeling of doubt with what you experience when you're puzzled or feel hesitant about something. Do you still think you can identify a *distinctive* experience of doubting—one that is markedly different from what you experience when you're puzzled or hesitant? I'd be surprised if you can.

Even if you could identify a distinctive inner experience of doubting, how could you use it, and it alone, to define the word 'doubt'? You would, presumably, inwardly "point" to the particular experience, think the word 'doubt', and then resolve to use this word to refer to this type of experience in the future. Here another question arises: how would you know you're linking up the word 'doubt' with a certain *type* of experience rather than a specific *instance* or *aspect* of the experience?

As embodied social agents you and I do sometimes define words by pointing to what they refer to. Suppose, for example, you tell me the color of a friend's new carpet is mauve. "What's mauve?" I ask. In response you could look for a mauve object, direct my attention to its color, and say, "That's mauve." This is called *ostensive* definition—defining a word by pointing to what it refers to. Ostensive definitions contrast with verbal or dictionary definitions, which define a word in terms of other words. There would, in this case, be no problem with your ostensively defining 'mauve' for me. But it is one thing for an (embodied) language user like you to ostensively define a word like 'mauve' for another language user like me, and quite another for a lone disembodied subject of consciousness to define *all* the referring words in its vocabulary ostensively. This, when you think about it, is impossible.

As pragmatic subjects, you and I share certain behavioral and contextual criteria for determining the meaning and correct use of our words. We also share an extensive vocabulary. This is what allows us to communicate about colors despite the fact that neither of us has access to the other's (inner) experience of color. When you ostensively define 'mauve' for me, you rely on various words and gestures to direct my attention to a mauve object and indicate that 'mauve' refers to its color. There are public (linguistic/behavioral/contextual) criteria for (1) identifying mauve objects, (2) focusing on their color, and (3) correlating a particular word with a particular color. These criteria enable you first to teach the word to me and then to determine whether your teaching has been successful; whether, for example, I can then go on to identify mauve objects and distinguish them from those that are pink or purple.

To illustrate, suppose you have a limited color vocabulary ('blue', 'light blue', 'dark blue', and so on) and you've asked an artist friend to help you expand it. Whenever you're together she points to certain objects and ostensively defines their colors. Before long you've picked up 'mauve', 'indigo', 'umber', 'puce', 'sepia', and so on. One afternoon she sees a woman in a long heliotrope coat. "See the woman at the bus stop?" she says. "That's heliotrope." Given the context, you know exactly what she means. You locate the woman, look at the coat, focus on the color, and associate this color with the word 'heliotrope'. Assuming you can use the word correctly in the future, you've now learned what 'heliotrope' means.

If, however, you'd never expressed an interest in expanding your color vocabulary and the same thing had happened—your friend says,

"See the woman at the bus stop? That's heliotrope."—you'd be baffled. What's she talking about? Even if she were to point, how would you know whether she were pointing to the woman herself (an acquaintance, perhaps, with the unusual name "Heliotrope") or to the coat or to its fabric or its texture or its cut or its color or to a particular part of the coat? Only if your friend were to say something like, "See the woman at the bus stop? *The color of* her coat is heliotrope," would you know what she's talking about (even if you were to wonder *why* she's talking about it!). A person's simply lining up her forefinger with an object and uttering a word is *by itself* insufficient for successful ostensive definition. We cannot, without further information, know what she is pointing to (or, indeed, whether she is pointing at all). Try it yourself. Silently point to this page. Then to its shape. Next to its texture. Now to its color. Would someone who was watching know exactly what you were pointing to in each case? Could you indicate exactly what you're pointing to without using words like 'page', 'shape', 'texture', or 'color'?

The moral of the story is that successful ostensive definition requires a good deal of stage-setting, including some prior mastery of language. Ostensive definition cannot, by itself, be *the* basis for language learning. The implications for the idea of a Cartesian subject should be clear. A Cartesian subject could not teach itself language through ostensive definition alone. Even if it could identify a distinctive (inner) experience of doubting, it would lack the linguistic, behavioral, and contextual resources for linking the word 'doubt' to a *type* of experience as opposed, say, to a specific *instance* of it or to its *duration,* its *intensity,* or something else. The situation of a Cartesian subject would be similar to yours if you didn't know the meaning of 'heliotrope' and out of the blue a friend suddenly looks or points in a certain direction and says, "Heliotrope." Without further (linguistic) explanation you would have no idea what your friend meant. For much the same reason, a Cartesian subject couldn't rely on ostensive definition to teach itself language from the ground up. Ostensive definition depends on some prior ability to use and understand language.

Moreover, even if we were to grant that a Cartesian subject could (as in fact it could not) identify a distinctive experience of doubting and could (as in fact it could not) connect the word 'doubt' to it, it still wouldn't have taught itself what 'doubt' means. To know the meaning of 'doubt' it would have to be able to connect the same word with the same type of experience in the future. This, in turn, would require *cor-*

rectly remembering the experience and the connection between it and the word 'doubt'. But the distinction between correct and incorrect memories is one that a Cartesian subject cannot draw. As embodied social agents you and I have the capacity to test our memory beliefs for correctness by comparing them with various types of physical evidence and what other people say and do. Yet these sorts of criteria are unavailable to a Cartesian subject. A subject of consciousness that denies the existence of physical objects and other people has no way to distinguish correct from incorrect memory beliefs. Whatever is going to *seem* right with respect to its memory beliefs is going to be right. "And that," as Wittgenstein points out, "only means that here we can't talk about 'right'."[1]

If a Cartesian skeptic cannot distinguish true memories from false, it must, in the spirit of methodological doubt, assume all its memory beliefs are false. But if it cannot rely on memory, it cannot know it is using words correctly or consistently. And if it cannot do this it cannot know it is talking sense rather than nonsense. Descartes, then, seems to have pulled his punches with respect to methodological doubt. He says he is going to doubt whatever can be doubted, but he fails to question whether, as a pure subject of consciousness, he can be certain that his words have any meaning or the same meaning from one time to the next. "The argument 'I may be dreaming,'" Wittgenstein writes, "is senseless for this reason: If I am dreaming, this remark ['I may be dreaming'] is being dreamed as well—and indeed it is also being dreamed that these words have any meaning."[2]

Thus a Cartesian subject will not even be able to say, "I cannot doubt my existence as a thinking thing because whenever I try to do this I must exist as a thinking thing," let alone use this as a foundation from which to infer other beliefs about the world. If he were consistent, Descartes would, at the end of the chain of methodological doubt, be literally speechless. All he could say, Wittgenstein once remarked in conversation, would be "Ah!"[3]

If this is all a Cartesian subject could say, it would certainly not be capable of philosophical reflection. Philosophical reflection requires language. You can't raise questions about knowledge, reality, mind, will, and ethics without being confident your words mean something and that you're using them consistently. But a Cartesian subject would have no grounds for such confidence. The problem is not that it can't answer such questions; it's that it *can't even raise them.* We should not, therefore, take seriously philosophical questions that presuppose the possibility of our being Cartesian subjects.

A more adequate understanding of language reveals that an individual cannot formulate philosophical questions unless he or she is (or has been) a member of a community of embodied agents. Language is not, in the first place, something we superimpose over a preexisting network of complex thought. The picture of language as an overlay—related to thought as a sports announcer's play-by-play account of a soccer game is related to what's happening on the field—is mistaken. Though the game is entirely independent of the sports announcer's account, there is no sharp distinction between the capacity to engage in complex thought—such as systematically doubting the truth of one's beliefs—and formulating this thought in language. Language and complex thought are intimately related. We cannot doubt without language. Animals cannot doubt, nor can young infants. Only linguistic beings can doubt, and only embodied social agents can be linguistic beings.

Even a Robinson Crusoe alone on an island must at one time have been closely connected to other embodied language users if he is to have any but the simplest thoughts in his solitude. As the unfortunate example of abandoned or socially isolated children reveals, normal human beings do not develop their genetic capacities for language apart from interactions with members of a linguistic community. Such children are dubbed "feral" or wolflike not only because of the myth that they have been raised by wolves, but also because their thought and behavior are more like those of nonhuman animals than linguistic human beings. A Robinson Crusoe will have learned and cultivated his thoughts as a member of a linguistic community. If, alone on an island, he is denied the corrective interactions with other language users, he still has his body and the surrounding environment to serve as a check on memory. Unlike a Cartesian subject, he has means for determining whether he is using words the same way from one time to the next.

Words are bound up with certain patterns of behavior that provide criteria for their application. It is not, however, that the patterns of behavior precede the words or that words refer to nothing but patterns of behavior, but rather that language and behavior—thought, words, and deeds—are interconnected. Learning a language is thus in many respects like learning a game. Knowing a game requires knowing the rules governing what one may and may not do in various situations. We assess a person's knowledge of and proficiency in a game by observing their conduct against the background of a number of constitutive and strategic rules. Such comparisons also provide the basis for further instruction. The same is true of language. Mastering an entire language or a specific linguistic activity (like teaching various color words or bargaining with a car dealer) requires knowing what to say *and do* in a variety of situations—"how to play the game."

Wittgenstein devised the term 'language game' to emphasize the connection between saying, doing, and rule-following. A language game, he says, consists of "language *and the actions* into which it is woven" (italics added).[4] The metaphor is especially apt. Language is "woven" into (we might better say "interwoven with") the nonlinguistic actions of language users rather than superimposed on them. The actions not only give language much of its point—language has evolved largely because of its capacity to extend the range and sophistication of individual and collective, survival-enhancing human action—but also provide pegs for learning words and distinguishing correct from incorrect ways of using them. What we *do* is fundamental. Properly understood, thinking and saying are not only inseparable from doing, but they are also kinds of doing. "Words," as Wittgenstein puts it, "are also deeds."[5]

This should be no surprise to anyone whose conception of language can account for a child's acquisition of its first language. Left to themselves and their own devices, individual humans will not develop their capacity for language. It is largely through selective training and reinforcement by members of their linguistic community that a child's playful babbling and undifferentiated expressions of distress, desire, satisfaction, and joy gradually evolve into the intelligible use and understanding of words. A child's initial acquisition of language is a matter of training—learning to *use* words by means of examples, practice, and reinforcement rather than learning to *comprehend* words by means of definition. Were there no way to correlate certain vocalizations with certain contexts, objects, and patterns of action, there would be no way for children to grasp the meanings of certain adult utterances or for adults to determine whether children had mastered the various words or sentences. The same connection between verbal expression, physical objects, social context, and patterns of behavior holds true for language use among adults. Even rudimentary communication with those having an entirely different language from our own requires making some connection between the sounds they make and various objects, contexts, and patterns of behavior. This, in brief, is what it means to say that language use presupposes a community of embodied agents. And it is why subjects of philosophical inquiry, if they are to formulate questions about knowledge, reality, mind, will, and ethics, cannot possibly be Cartesian subjects.

Children and childhood are, for the most part, neither seen nor heard in the work of the Cartesian tradition—nor are women, whose traditional roles have included bearing and raising children and nursing the sick and dying. To be reminded of childhood and the needs of the young, the sick, and the dying is to be reminded of the human life cycle and the normal stages of birth, growth, learning, development, decline, and death. It is to be reminded, too, of social and biological dependence and interdependence. In a discussion of the foundation of ethics, Annette Baier points out that "philosophers who remember what it was like to be a dependent child, or know what it is like to be a parent, or to have a dependent parent, an old or handicapped relative, friend, or neighbor," will take a different approach than those for whom the paradigm of ethical relations is that between free and equal adult strangers.[6]

Philosophers who remember such things will also, I suggest, take a different approach to the subject of philosophical inquiry than those for whom the paradigm of such a subject is possibly a Cartesian subject— a lone, disembodied spectator. Recent work in cognitive science and early child development shows that the playful, embodied interactions between parents and children and the world result in a child's readily solving a number of traditional philosophical problems: whether there is a world independent of its own mind; whether such a world contains minds other than its own; and how to decipher the sounds that come out of the mouths of its parents and others. These are simply not genuine (or practical) problems for normal children of a certain age. For example, a typical three-year-old being given a hard time at the dinner table, as Gopnik, Meltzoff, and Kuhl point out, "experiences his brothers teasing him, not skin-bags moving. He sees tables and spoons . . . not undifferentiated colors and shapes. And he immediately understands the significance of the rude joke and the apology that are actually no more than the most fleeting vibrations."[7] The child learns that there are minds other than its own, that there is a world independent of its mind, and that some sounds (or signs) have meanings partly through its genetic endowment and partly through embodied interaction with people and things.

MEANING

A Cartesian subject could not define the word 'doubt' for itself unless there were something common to all (and only) experiences of doubting. This common feature (or set of features) would be necessary for such a subject's distinguishing doubt from other mental experiences and classifying two separate experiences as experiences of doubting. To identify what is uniquely common to all instances of doubting is to identify what is essential to it—what philosophers have traditionally called its *essence*. To know the meaning of 'doubt' is, on this view, to know its essence: what is common to all and only experiences of doubting.

Since a Cartesian subject could not use language at all, it could not define the word 'doubt' in this or any other way. Still, the idea that the meaning of a word like 'doubt' is a function of what is common to all and only instances of doubting is at least as old as the dialogues of Plato, where Socrates repeatedly asks for the essence of piety, knowledge, justice, love, and so on, not just instances of them. In the *Euthyphro*, for example, Socrates presses Euthyphro for a definition of piety:

> *Socr.* . . . What I asked you, my friend, was What is piety? And you have not explained it to my satisfaction. You only tell me that what you are doing now, namely, prosecuting your father for murder, is a pious act.
> *Euth.* Well, that is true, Socrates.
> *Socr.* Very likely. But many other actions are pious, are they not, Euthyphro?
> *Euth.* Certainly.
> *Socr.* Remember, then, I did not ask you to tell me one or two of all the many pious actions that there are; I want to know what is characteristic of piety which makes all pious actions pious. You said, I think, that there is one characteristic which makes all pious actions pious, and another characteristic which makes all impious actions impious. Do you not remember?
> *Euth.* I do.
> *Socr.* Well, then, explain to me what is this characteristic, that I may have it to turn to, and to use as a standard whereby to judge your actions and those of other men, and be able to say whatever action resembles it is pious, and whatever does not, is not pious.[8]

The idea is intuitively appealing. To understand piety is to grasp its *essence*, what all and only pious actions have in common. Once we know the essence of piety, we have a clear standard for methodically distinguishing pious from impious actions.

A simple example of the sort of definition Socrates seeks is: "A bachelor is an unmarried adult male." The combination of being (1) unmarried, (2) adult, and (3) male is something all and only bachelors have in common. Each of the three conditions is individually necessary for someone's being a bachelor. An unmarried boy or woman isn't a bachelor, nor is a married man. Yet none of the conditions is (by itself) sufficient for someone's being a bachelor. All bachelors are unmarried, but so are many nonbachelors (unmarried women); all bachelors are adult, but so are many nonbachelors (married men and all women); and all bachelors are males, but so are many nonbachelors (married men and boys). Taken together, however, the three conditions are, when satisfied, sufficient for someone's being a bachelor—anyone characterized by all three is a bachelor. While nonbachelors might satisfy one or two of the conditions, *all and only* bachelors will satisfy all three of them. Conditions (1), (2), and (3) are thus said to be (individually) *necessary* and (jointly) *sufficient* for someone's being a bachelor.

Though the example is simple and nonphilosophical, its form is a model for philosophers who try to specify necessary and sufficient conditions for more philosophically significant words like 'knowledge', 'reality', and 'justice'. We have a checklist of features for distinguishing bachelors from nonbachelors. So the aim is to devise similar checklists for distinguishing knowledge from (mere) belief, the real from the unreal, and justice from injustice.

Essentialism, as this approach to meaning is sometimes called, has played a prominent role in the history of Western philosophy. For some, a commitment to essentialism defines what it means to be a philosopher. Philosophers are distinguished from others, on this view, by their unremitting efforts to get to the bottom of things—to identify the (often hidden) *essences* of knowledge, reality, justice, and so on by determining what is uniquely common to all instances of knowledge, reality, and justice, respectively. As a contemporary Socrates might put it, "Don't give me examples of knowledge; I want to know what distinguishes all knowledge from (mere) belief. What are the necessary and sufficient conditions for something's counting as knowledge?" To refrain from seeking essences is regarded by those committed to the process as shallow or unphilosophical.

Yet, after nearly 2,500 years, essentialism has borne little fruit. We are no closer to understanding the essences of such philosophically interesting notions as knowledge, reality, and justice than was Socrates. Yet most of the time most of us seem to do pretty well with words like 'knowledge', 'reality', and 'justice'. How can this be? One plausible answer, parts of which are clearly anticipated by, if not indebted to, the earlier work of William James, has been developed by Wittgenstein.

Meaning and Use

I have already mentioned Wittgenstein's idea of a *language game*—"language and the actions into which it is woven." Words are used by embodied social agents in a wide variety of social and physical contexts for a wide variety of purposes. Insofar as these uses are governed by rules related to both context and purpose, they are similar to moves in a game. Both language use and game playing require compliance with (mutable) rules constitutive of certain practices in certain contexts. A word's meaning, on this view, is generally a function of its roles in the various language games into which it is woven. "For a *large* class of cases—though not for all—in which we employ the word 'meaning'," Wittgenstein writes, "it can be defined thus: the meaning of a word is its use in the language."[9]

Because we use words not just for one purpose—for example to state or describe matters of fact—but for a wide variety of purposes, the meanings of our words are often complex, varying, in significant respects, from language game to language game. It is useful, in this connection, to compare words with tools. Wittgenstein puts it this way:

> Think of the tools in a tool-box: there is a hammer, pliers, a saw, a screwdriver, a rule, a glue-pot, glue, nails, and screws.—The functions of words are as diverse as the functions of these objects. (And in both cases there are similarities.)
>
> Of course, what confuses us is the uniform appearance of words when we hear them spoken or meet them in script and print. For their *application* is not presented to us so clearly. Especially when we are doing philosophy![10]

Consider, in addition, the multiplicity of language games—those now extinct and those yet to be devised, as well as those presently in use—and the *activities* of which they are a part. Wittgenstein lists the following examples of language games:

> Giving orders, and obeying them—
> Describing the appearance of an object, or giving its measurements—
> Constructing an object from a description (a drawing)—
> Reporting an event—
> Speculating about an event—
> Forming and testing a hypothesis—
> Presenting the results of an experiment in tables and diagrams—
> Making up a story; and reading it—

Play-acting—
Singing catches—
Guessing riddles—
Making a joke; telling it—
Solving problems in practical arithmetic—
Translating from one language into another—
Asking, thanking, cursing, greeting, praying.[11]

There are striking differences, Wittgenstein emphasizes, between the actual *multiplicity* of kinds of words and sentences and the *singularity* of what philosophers have said about the structure of language. The discrepancy is attributable, in large part, to philosophers having abstracted words from the wide variety of *activities* (or language games) in which they *do their work.*

Nowhere is this more apparent than in essentialist accounts of meaning. Philosophers who presuppose or attempt to provide such accounts, Wittgenstein points out, have rarely examined the ways in which language is actually (and successfully) used in everyday life. Such an examination would reveal that words like 'knowledge', 'reality', and 'justice' are correctly and effectively used day in, day out in a wide variety of contexts by a wide variety of persons who would be tongue-tied if asked to provide essentialist definitions of them. Consider the word 'language'. What is its essence? What do all and only things called 'language' have in common? What are the necessary and sufficient conditions for something's being a language? It is, on reflection, very hard to say. The meaning of 'language' cannot be specified in terms of a single function because language has a wide variety of functions. We use language not only to communicate with others, but also to soliloquize, to express pain, to make notes, to keep private diaries, to sing songs, and so on. But how can we know how to use the word 'language' if we cannot specify what all and only those things called language have in common? "Instead of producing something common to all that we call language," Wittgenstein responds, "I am saying that these [linguistic] phenomena have no one thing in common which makes us use the same word for all,—but that they are *related* to one another in many different ways. And it is because of this relationship, or these relationships, that we call them all 'language'."[12] The relationship(s) in question Wittgenstein likens to the kind of phenotypic resemblances we find among biologically related members of a family.

Family Resemblances

Suppose a friend invites you to meet her family. First you encounter her older brother. Apart from his eyes, he bears little resemblance to his sister. She is tall, slight, and blonde, while he is short, heavy, and dark-haired. It crosses your mind that one or both of them may have been adopted. Then their father emerges from the kitchen. He is of medium height, his hair is light like his daughter's, and he is built like his son, yet his face is markedly different from theirs. Finally, your friend's mother and younger brother appear. The mother is tall and thin like your friend and dark like her older brother. Your friend and her older brother have their mother's eyes, but not her younger brother. He has his father's eyes, his mother's hair, his sister's smile, and his brother's chin.

If you'd seen only two biologically related members of this family without the others, it probably wouldn't occur to you that they were blood-related. Yet viewed together over a period of hours, the five have the unmistakable look of a biologically related family because of a set of overlapping resemblances with respect to build, features, facial expressions, and so on. Although there may be no distinguishing phenotypic feature common to all, taken together they share a certain "family resemblance." And, Wittgenstein suggests, the same sort of relationship obtains among different uses of the same word. Like members of a family, these uses are related by "a complicated network of similarities overlapping and criss-crossing: sometimes overall similarities, sometimes similarities of detail."[13]

Take, for example, the word 'game'. If we put our essentialist preconceptions aside and actually *look* at its various uses—in talking about board games, card games, ball games, Olympic games, computer games, and so on—we will see that there is nothing distinctive and common to all and only uses of 'game'. Wittgenstein puts it this way:

Look for example at board games, with their multifarious relationships. Now pass to card-games; here you find many correspondences with the first group, but many common features drop out and others appear. When we pass next to ball-games, much that is common is retained, but much is lost.—Are they all "amusing"? Compare chess with noughts and crosses [tic-tac-toe]. Or is there always winning and losing, or competition between players? Think of patience [solitaire]. In ball games there is winning and losing; but when a child throws his

ball at the wall and catches it again, this feature has disappeared. Look
at the parts played by skill and luck; and at the difference between skill
in chess and skill in tennis. Think now of games like ring-a-ring-a-
roses; here is the element of amusement, but how many other characteristic features have disappeared! And we can go through the many,
many other groups of games in the same way; can see how similarities
crop up and disappear.[14]

Thus we identify and call things "games," not because they share a
certain essence or have a number of distinguishing features in common, but because they form a family and are related by *family resemblance*. The same is true of such more philosophically interesting notions like language, knowledge, reality, justice, and so on.

Wittgenstein employs a second metaphor in explaining how the
various uses of the word 'number' are related. The relationship among
cardinal numbers, rational numbers, real numbers, negative numbers,
and so on, he suggests, may be compared to the relationship among
the individual fibers constituting a single thread: "[W]e extend our
concept of number as in spinning a thread we twist fibre on fibre. And
the strength of the thread does not reside in the fact that some one fibre runs through its whole length, but in the overlapping of many
fibers."[15] So, too, with overlapping similarities among the various uses
of words like 'game', 'number', 'language', and so on.

The moral of the story, then, is that we do not have to identify an
essence or specify necessary and sufficient conditions for words like
'game', 'number', 'knowledge', 'reality', or 'justice' to be meaningful
and for us to be able to use them (which are, for the most part, the
same thing). The intuition that we can understand such words only if
we can identify their essences or specify conditions necessary and sufficient for their application turns out, on examination, to be based on
a mistaken preconception about language—one that fails to take account of how language is actually used by embodied social agents like
ourselves.

Context

Another important determinant of meaning is context. If the meaning
of a word, phrase, or sentence is mainly a function of its use in the language, and its use cannot be determined apart from close examination
of the language game into which it is woven, meaning is highly contextual. We cannot determine the meaning of a word by writing it on

the blackboard and focusing our attention on it, trying to divine its essence (as, for example, a Cartesian subject would have to divine the essence of doubting). We generally understand what words like 'truth', 'knowledge', 'real', and so on mean when we use them in everyday situations to *do* one thing or another. "The confusions which occupy us," Wittgenstein has said, "arise when language is like an engine idling, not when it is doing work."[16]

Though Wittgenstein never identified himself as a pragmatist, a connection with pragmatism is, as many have noted, unmistakable. "The *words* you utter or what you think when you utter them," he wrote in a notebook, "are not what matters, so much as the difference they make at various points in your life. . . . *Practice* gives words their sense."[17] William James (writing in 1907) anticipates Wittgenstein (writing in 1950) when he asks:

'things,' what are they? Is a constellation properly a thing? or an army? or is an *ens rationis* such as space or justice a thing? Is a knife whose handle and blade are changed the 'same'? . . . The moment you pass beyond the practical use of these categories (a use usually suggested sufficiently by the circumstances of the special case) to a merely curious or speculative way of thinking, you find it impossible to say within just what limits of fact any one of them shall apply.[18]

James was not as familiar with automobiles as Wittgenstein, but there is little doubt that he would agree that problems with the meaning of the word 'thing' arise only when the engine is "idling, not when it is doing work."

To understand the meaning of the vast majority of words, phrases, and sentences is to understand how they are *used* for particular purposes in particular settings. Meaning cannot, therefore, generally be abstracted from the social practices or rule-governed patterns of behavior into which the use of words is woven; to learn the meaning of a word we must, as a rule, catch on to the way(s) it is used. The most plausible general account we have of linguistic meaning, then, presupposes that words and sentences are used by social, embodied beings (rather than Cartesian subjects) in performing a wide variety of *actions* in a wide variety of *contexts*. We cannot understand the meaning of words, phrases, or sentences without understanding the language games—the rule-governed, purposive patterns of action—into which they are woven. And we cannot understand a rule-governed pattern of action unless there are external (in part bodily) criteria for determining when the rules—linguistic and nonlinguistic—have been followed and when not. As with language in general, then, our understanding of the meanings of particular words and sentences presupposes that those who utter or write them are pragmatic (active, embodied, social) rather than Cartesian (lone, disembodied, passive) subjects.

TRUTH

Philosophers have long sought a comprehensive theory of truth—one that identifies its essence and specifies necessary and sufficient conditions for distinguishing true beliefs and sentences from false. An aim of such a theory is to make distinguishing truth from falsity as methodical as distinguishing bachelors from nonbachelors.

Truth as Correspondence

At one level, of course, we all know what 'truth' means. Truth is agreement with reality. But what do we mean by 'agreement' here? And what do we mean by 'reality'? Defining truth as agreement with reality is okay at a certain level of generality, but it will not give us a useful *method* for distinguishing true beliefs and sentences from false unless we can make the definition more precise. One possibility—one with a long philosophical pedigree—is that true beliefs and sentences somehow *picture, represent,* or *correspond* to certain *facts* about the world in the same way, say, that an accurate photograph of the Taj Mahal pictures, represents, or corresponds to the most famous building in India. True beliefs or sentences are, on this view, those that accurately *copy* or *mirror* the facts.

This is sometimes called the *correspondence theory of truth* and it is intuitively very appealing. First, its broad outline promises a comprehensive method for distinguishing truth from falsehood. Just as we can more or less methodically assess the accuracy of an ordinary photograph by comparing it with what it represents, we can test the truth of any belief, sentence, or utterance by comparing *it* with what it represents. Second, we can easily think of examples. I pick up a coin, bring my hands behind my back, and then present you with two closed fists. Is the coin in my right hand, I ask, or my left? Here you might actually *picture* two possibilities: one with the coin in my right hand, the other with it in my left. One of the two pictures is true (or represents or corresponds to the location of the coin) and the other false. You make a decision and express it in words: "It's in your right hand." You learn whether your guess is true or false by comparing what you *say* (your "word picture") with what you *see* when I open my hands. Something similar, we might say, occurs in science when we formulate a hypothesis, devise and conduct an experiment to test it, and then compare the hypothesis with the outcome of the experiment. The hypothesis predicts a certain outcome, one we can often visualize. If, when we conduct the experiment, the results correspond to the one "pictured" by the hypothesis, the hypothesis is true; if they don't (to oversimplify a bit), it's not.

As a comprehensive theory, however, this conception of truth is riddled with difficulties. First, the analogy between a photograph and a belief or sentence is at best strained. We can show which elements of a photograph of the Taj Mahal correspond to which elements of the actual building. This sort of representation is much more obscure in the case of beliefs or sentences, especially insofar as the same belief can be formulated in radically different ways in different languages and different sentences within the same language can be used to express the same belief. Defenders of the correspondence theory presume that the relation between a true belief or sentence and what it represents is something like the relation between an onomatopoetic word (one that incorporates or copies the sound to which it refers, as, for example, 'click', 'boom', or 'hiss') and what it represents. But most words are not onomatopoetic and, apart from some words written in languages like hieroglyphics, Chinese, or Japanese, there is no visual analogue of onomatopoeia. Moreover, many true beliefs and sentences are not even metaphorically pictorial. Think, for example, of "Life is nearly always preferable to death," "E equals mc^2," and "The class of natural numbers is infinite."[19]

Second, a large part of the theory's appeal is that it promises to compare a belief or sentence with something independent of beliefs or sentences. The ultimate test of the accuracy of a photograph is, as a rule, a *direct comparison* with its object, not with another photograph. If you suspect a photograph of an aging political leader has been "doctored" to make him or her look younger, your doubts will not be allayed by other photographs unless you can be assured that their accuracy has been determined by *direct* comparison with the leader himself or herself. To defend the accuracy of one questionable photograph by comparing it to others that are no less questionable is to argue in a circle. Similarly, according to the correspondence theory, the ultimate test of the truth of a belief or sentence would have to be a direct comparison with the "facts," not with other beliefs or sentences (unless, of course, we can be assured that these beliefs or sentences have reliably been determined to be true by direct comparison with the facts).

But here the analogy breaks down. There is no way to classify and identify the things we call facts *apart from the use of language*. The elements of the world do not come self-labeled, nor do the various things we call "facts." If the world is God's creation, no one has discovered the original blueprint, the document that would definitively identify its building blocks and identify basic facts apart from human language and interests. Nor have scientists been able to identify what Richard Rorty calls "Nature's Own Language"—a language that would identify the "facts" in a way that is prior to and independent of the way various (parts of) human languages identify and classify what we call facts.[20] All efforts to "climb out of our own skins"—to apprehend the "facts," directly and nonlinguistically, and then use them to compare what we *say* about the world with the world *as it is in itself*—have, as I will show in chapter 3, ended in failure. There is no way to make *cognitive* contact with the world (or reality or the facts) apart from the way we talk about it; and, as indicated above, no way to separate how we *talk about* the world from how we *act in* it. The sort of direct comparisons between (language-dependent) beliefs and sentences and nonlinguistic reality presupposed by the correspondence theory of truth is, at least given our present understanding and capacities, impossible. We cannot *show* some beliefs or sentences to be true without relying, in one way or another, on other beliefs or sentences (which is not, as I show in chapter 3, to say that the latter can be anything we want).

Is there a better comprehensive theory of truth? One that identifies its essence and specifies necessary and sufficient conditions for distinguishing all true beliefs and sentences from false ones? There is no shortage of contenders. Trading on the deficiencies of the correspondence theory, the coherence theory identifies truth with harmony or consistency among certain beliefs and sentences. The (traditional) pragmatic theory identifies truth with the usefulness or utility of certain beliefs and sentences. Yet all comprehensive theories—correspondence, coherentist, and (traditional) pragmatist—whatever their individual difficulties, share the same shortcoming. Assuming truth has an essence more specific than "agreement with reality," they identify an important feature of a *large number* of true beliefs and sentences and mistakenly claim it applies to *all* such beliefs and sentences. But the complexity of our various uses of 'true' (and its cognates and antonyms) resists essentialist definition.

The Truth about Truth

There is, as the conceptions of language and meaning outlined in the previous two sections suggest, no philosophically interesting essence to truth, no methodical (and quasi-mechanical) way to distinguish all true beliefs and sentences from those that are false. The words 'true' and 'false' (and their cognates) are family resemblance terms as shown by the following list of true sentences compiled by Rorty (from which I've already borrowed):

> Bacon did not write [the plays of] Shakespeare.
> It rained [or didn't rain] yesterday.
> E equals mc².
> Love is better than hate.
> *The Allegory of Painting* was Vermeer's best work.
> 2 plus 2 is 4.
> There are nondenumerable infinities.[21]

Assuming these sentences to be true, it is impossible to specify a single characteristic that all and only these and other true sentences have in common. Though they agree with reality, "agreement with reality" is too general to serve as such a characteristic. There is no single method, no set of necessary and sufficient conditions, that we can use to determine whether any given belief or sentence agrees with reality or not. The sentences on Rorty's list are related, perhaps, as members of a family or as overlapping fibers in a thread, but not because they share a *specific*, distinguishing characteristic—one that could actually be *used* to distinguish all of them from false sentences.

To reject the possibility of a "master theory" of truth—one that provides a method for systematically distinguishing any and all true beliefs from those that are false—does not, however, mean we cannot distinguish truth from falsity. There are tests for the truth (or falsity) of each of the sentences on Rorty's list, but they cannot be specified apart from the particular language games in which the sentences are used. Within the language game of determining authorship, for example, there are criteria for determining whether Bacon wrote any of the plays of Shakespeare; within the language game of weather reporting, there are criteria for determining whether it rained yesterday; within the language game of physics, there are criteria for determining whether E equals mc²; and so on. Yet the language games of determining authorship, reporting the weather, establishing laws of physics, adding numbers, evaluating art, and doing set theory differ in various respects. There is no super-duper method, prior to and independent of these linguistic activities, that will allow one to magisterially pronounce on the truth of various claims made within them. It is the different language games themselves—their more or less complex and interrelated rules, practices, conventions, purposes, standards of judgment, and so on—that provide the ground rules or criteria we use in determining truth or falsity within them.

But what about language games themselves? Can they be true or false? How do we decide, in cases of conflict, to adopt one language game or another? Whether, for example, to adopt a Ptolemaic (or geocentric) or a Copernican (or heliocentric) way of talking and thinking about the universe? A Newtonian (or classical mechanical) or Einsteinian (or relativistic) way of talking and thinking about physics? A biblical (or creationist) or Darwinian (or evolution by natural selection) way of talking and thinking about human origins? Here, as will be explained further in chapter 3, we appeal more directly to our overall aims, the comparative usefulness of different ways of talking, thinking, and acting, and the extent to which certain ways of talking, thinking, and acting usefully cohere with other ways of talking, thinking, and acting. On such grounds educated people now largely agree that the Copernican conception of the universe is true and the Ptolemaic false. Among physicists, the Newtonian conception of the physical world has been replaced by the Einsteinian one. And, since it has such far-reaching implications for our self-understanding, the truth of the Darwinian account of our origins, though affirmed by nearly all biologists, remains a matter of public controversy.

Following Rorty, I will use the word 'vocabulary' to identify certain kinds of language games.[22] As language games, *vocabularies* consist of complex, interwoven patterns of words and actions. They are distinguished, however, by their identifiability and scope. Academic disciplines such as physics, chemistry, biology, philosophy, history, psychology, sociology, and anthropology are examples of vocabularies, as are medicine, nursing, architecture, law, and so on. To study and master a certain discipline, like molecular biology, is to study and master a complex language game—a certain vocabulary (words) *and* the actions into which they are interwoven. A molecular biologist is someone who is fluent in "molecular biologese." He or she can speak and interact with other molecular biologists, read and understand journal articles, formulate and conduct experiments, distinguish most true from false molecular biological beliefs and theories, and recognize (if not make) new discoveries and assess their significance. Similar things are true of those who have mastered the vocabularies (or language games) of physics, philosophy, psychology, medicine, law, and so on.

Other types of vocabulary are even more general. In chapter 4 we will examine the *vocabulary of causal determinism*—a very general way of talking and thinking about human behavior that implies that human beings are never really responsible for what they do. This very general vocabulary is often presupposed by (and incorporated in) more specific vocabularies, like some types of psychology and psychiatry. We will also examine the *vocabulary of personal responsibility*—a general way of talking and thinking about human behavior that implies that human beings *are* morally and legally responsible for some of the things they do. This very general vocabulary is presupposed by (and incorporated in) more specific vocabularies, like law and ethics.

Whether determinism is true or false will be discussed later. The main point, for present purposes, is that (1) questions of truth and falsity cannot be separated from our language games (or vocabularies); (2) our language games (or vocabularies) cannot be separated from our actions; (3) our actions cannot be separated from our various aims and interests; and (4) these aims and interests are those of embodied social agents.

SUMMARY AND CONCLUSION

After painting himself into the corner of radical skepticism, Descartes tries to reason his way out. Once he proves he exists as a thinking thing, he finds among his ideas that of a supremely perfect being, God. The idea of God, Descartes reasons, is so great that he couldn't possibly have come up with it himself. It could only have been placed in his mind by what it represents, a supremely perfect being, God. Thus, in addition to his own existence as a thinking being, he is now absolutely certain of the existence of God. Descartes then notices that some of his ideas about the world outside his mind are "clear and distinct" while others are "obscure and confused." He is strongly inclined to believe that his clear and distinct ideas are true. But could he be dreaming or deceived by an "Evil Genius" about this? Not anymore. Since God exists—and deception being an imperfection, God, a supremely perfect being, would not be a deceiver—Descartes concludes that his clear and distinct ideas about the world must be true. Since among these ideas are those of his own body, other persons, and physical objects, he concludes that these things exist and that his ideas of them are true.

Like most people, you probably find the reasoning leading into radical skepticism more persuasive than Descartes's way of reasoning himself out. For over three hundred years philosophers have sought alternatives, hoping to show how, starting with the contents of its own mind, a possibly solitary, disembodied subject of reflection could determine which of its ideas about the external world were true and which false. To this day, however, no proposal for escaping the Cartesian corner has met with success. Once you paint yourself in, it looks like there's no way out.

To take the problem of the Cartesian corner seriously is to take the possibility that you might be a Cartesian subject seriously. But this, as I have argued in this chapter, is incompatible with our most plausible understanding of language, meaning, and truth and the relationships among them.

What would language, meaning, and truth have to be like if you were to take seriously the possibility of being a Cartesian subject? *Language* would be something you could teach yourself by ostensive definition and you would have to be able to tell solely by appeal to your own mind that you were using words correctly and consistently. The *meaning* of words would have to be determined by your thought alone—apart from the way words are woven into various contexts and patterns of individual and social behavior. And the *truth* of your beliefs about the world outside of your own mind would have to be determined by directly comparing what you say and believe about the world with the way the world is in itself.

Yet these and related conceptions of language, meaning, and truth are indefensible. Language use is not something in addition to (or superimposed on) most distinctively human activities, including complex thought; rather it is constitutive of them. Meaning is not a function of private ostensive definition or linguistic essences; rather it is a function of the way words are used for certain purposes in certain language games. And truth is not determined by *directly* comparing what we say about the world with what the world is like in itself; rather it is a property of either (a) individual beliefs or sentences that together with certain events or states of the world satisfy the rules internal to a particular (useful or justifiable) language game or vocabulary or (b) entire language games that, given their purposes and their comparative advantages over competing language games, are more useful or justifiable than any practical alternative.

Implicit in these interlocking conceptions of language, meaning, and truth is a conception of the subject of thought and reflection as a social, embodied agent rather than (possibly) a lone disembodied spectator. "The knower," as William James states in the quotation at the beginning of this chapter, "is not simply a mirror floating with no foot-hold anywhere, and passively reflecting an order that he comes upon and finds simply existing. The knower is an actor, and coefficient of the truth which he helps to create. Mental interests, hypotheses, postulates, so far as they are bases for human action—action which to a great extent transforms the world—help to *make* the truth."[23] The sense in which the knower is a "coefficient of the truth which he helps to create" is the sense in which truth is largely a function of sentences, sentences a function of language games, and language games a function of human aims and interests, which are themselves a function of embodied social agency. This is not, however, to say that knowledge of the world is whatever we make it or that there is no reality independent of our words and ideas. But to show this we must turn, in the next chapter, to a more comprehensive inquiry into knowledge and reality.

The main point of this chapter is that a Cartesian subject couldn't possibly paint itself into the corner of radical skepticism because it wouldn't have the words—the linguistic paint and brush—needed to do so. If we take the Cartesian corner seriously, it is only because we are being inconsistent in our skepticism. We assume a capacity for linguistic reason while pretending to deny an important precondition for it: the ability to distinguish correct from incorrect uses of words, which, in turn, presupposes membership in an embodied linguistic community. We shouldn't worry, then, about the Cartesian corner's lacking an exit. Since there's no way to get in, there's no real problem about getting out.

NOTES

1. Ludwig Wittgenstein, *Philosophical Investigations*, 3d ed., trans. G. E. M. Anscombe (New York: Macmillan, 1953), §258.

2. Ludwig Wittgenstein, *On Certainty*, ed. by G. E. M. Anscombe and G. H. von Wright, trans. Denis Paul and G. E. M. Anscombe (New York: Harper & Row, 1969), §383.

3. O. K. Bouwsma, *Wittgenstein: Conversations 1949–1951*, ed. J. L. Craft and Ronald E. Hustwit (Indianapolis: Hackett, 1986), 13–14.

4. Wittgenstein, *Philosophical Investigations*, §7.

5. Wittgenstein, *Philosophical Investigations*, §546.

6. Annette Baier, "Trust and Anti-Trust," in *Moral Prejudices* (Cambridge, Mass.: Harvard University Press, 1994), 115.

7. Alison Gopnik, Andrew N. Meltzoff, and Patricia K. Kuhl, *The Scientist in the Crib: Minds, Brains, and How Children Learn* (New York: Morrow, 1999), 6.

8. Plato, *Euthyphro* in *The Euthyphro, Apology, and Crito of Plato*, trans. F. J. Church, rev. and introduced by Robert D. Cumming (Indianapolis: Bobbs-Merrill, 1956), 6–7.

9. Wittgenstein, *Philosophical Investigations*, §43.

10. Wittgenstein, *Philosophical Investigations*, §11.

11. Wittgenstein, *Philosophical Investigations*, §23.

12. Wittgenstein, *Philosophical Investigations*, §65.

13. Wittgenstein, *Philosophical Investigations*, §66.

14. Wittgenstein, *Philosophical Investigations*, §66.

15. Wittgenstein, *Philosophical Investigations*, §67.

16. Wittgenstein, *Philosophical Investigations*, §133.

17. Ludwig Wittgenstein, *Culture and Value*, ed. G. H. Von Wright, trans. Peter Winch (Chicago: University of Chicago Press, 1980), 85e.

18. William James, *Pragmatism: A New Name for Some Old Ways of Thinking*, in *William James: Writings 1902–1919*, ed. Bruce Kuklick (New York: Library of America, 1992), 566.

19. Richard Rorty, *Consequences of Pragmatism* (Minneapolis: University of Minnesota Press, 1982), xiii.

20. Rorty, *Consequences of Pragmatism*, 195.

21. Rorty, *Consequences of Pragmatism*, xiii.

22. Richard Rorty, *Contingency, Irony, and Solidarity* (Cambridge: Cambridge University Press, 1989), 7.

23. William James, "Remarks on Spencer's Definition of Mind as Correspondence," in *William James: Writings 1878–1899*, ed. Gerald E. Myers (New York: Library of America, 1992), 908.

Chapter 3

Knowledge and Reality

Let us not pretend to doubt in philosophy what we do not doubt in our hearts.

—Charles S. Peirce, "Some Consequences of Four Incapacities"

Giving grounds, however, justifying the evidence, comes to an end;—but the end is not certain propositions' striking us immediately as true; i.e., it is not a kind of *seeing* on our part; it is our *acting*, which lies at the bottom of the language game.

—Ludwig Wittgenstein, *On Certainty*

Profusion, not economy, may after all be reality's key-note.

—William James, *Pragmatism*

According to the Cartesian tradition, the fundamental question about knowledge requires choice between two, and only two, alternatives. Either we *prove* that some beliefs about the world outside our own minds are true or we acknowledge that we can know nothing but the contents of our own minds. The fundamental question about reality takes the same form. Either we *prove* there are real (physical) objects apart from our ideas of them or we concede that as far as we can tell, there is no genuine difference between reality and our ideas of it. In each case, the required proof is to consist of a set of statements or propositions, which, when *apprehended by the intellect*, provide definitive support for the conclusion.

53

Insofar as each question assumes that the subject of philosophical inquiry may turn out to be a lone, disembodied spectator, it is, however, misconceived. A lone, disembodied spectator could not, as I argued in chapter 2, even formulate such questions, let alone answer them. Once we conceive the subject of philosophical inquiry as an embodied social agent, I show in this chapter, these questions and the problems they create disappear. Certainty—*objective* certainty—about aspects of a world we are equally certain exists independently of our minds is implicit in the capacity to use language.

Though my conclusions will be those of common sense, I cannot rely on common sense to support them. Common sense is not, as the history of science reveals, self-certifying. Common sense tells us that the earth is flat and stationary with respect to the sun. But the earth is not flat, nor is it stationary with respect to the sun. We must often go beyond common sense to see why some of our commonsense convictions about rocks, tables, chairs, and other persons are correct, especially in the light of centuries of philosophical arguments to the contrary. "Philosophy," as Wittgenstein once put it, "unties knots in our thinking; hence its results must be simple, but philosophizing has to be as complicated as the knots it unties."[1] Philosophical problems about whether we can be certain about anything outside our own minds and whether there is a difference between reality and our ideas of it are, as I will now show, the result of complex "knots" in our thinking. Once the knots are untied, the problems don't arise. Except for when we're under the spell of the Cartesian tradition in philosophy, we are absolutely (and *rightly*) certain of the independent existence of rocks, tables, and other persons.

There are, however, a number of genuine philosophical questions about knowledge and reality. They take a different and more answerable shape, however, when formulated by embodied social agents like ourselves. I identify some of these questions at the end of this chapter.

KNOWLEDGE

Real Doubt vs. Philosophical Doubt

Pragmatist philosopher Charles S. Peirce was among the first to challenge the basic assumptions of Cartesianism. One of his strongest criticisms turned on distinguishing *genuine* doubt from its Cartesian counterpart. "We cannot," Peirce wrote in 1868, "begin [philosophiz-ing] with complete doubt."

> We must begin with all the prejudices which we actually have when we enter upon the study of philosophy. . . . Hence this initial [Cartesian] skepticism will be a mere self-deception, and not real doubt. . . . A per-son may, it is true, in the course of his studies, find reason to doubt what he began by believing; but in that case he doubts because he has a posi-tive reason for it, and not on account of the Cartesian maxim. Let us not pretend to doubt in philosophy what we do not doubt in our hearts.[2]

That doubt is a matter of the body as well as the mind is an important insight. An examination of *real* doubt (as opposed to the sort of parlor-game "doubt" still dear to the hearts of some academic philosophers) reveals that to doubt something one must be an embodied social agent—one who *knows* some things and is *certain* of others.

Suppose someone were to doubt whether you'd correctly multi-plied $2,600 times four while doing your income taxes. You respond that you'd used a calculator. "Well," the person might say, "perhaps you'd entered a wrong number or punched a wrong key."

That's possible, you think. Mistakes happen and you're no less fal-lible with a calculator than anyone else. So you retrieve the calculator, carefully enter $2,600, hit the multiplication key, enter four, and hit the equals key. The result, once again, is $10,400. Now the person doubts whether the calculator is working properly. "You can't always trust technology," he says grimly. "These gadgets are sometimes out of whack."

Acknowledging this, you repeat the calculation with pencil and pa-per and get the same result. "I don't know," the person says. "Maybe you made a mistake. You've made mistakes in arithmetic before, haven't you? Maybe you've done it again."

So, with the patience of a saint, you repeat the calculation—this time expressing what you're doing verbally. "Four times zero is zero," you say. "Four times zero is zero. Four times six is twenty-four. . . ."

"Wait a minute," the person interrupts. "How do you know four times six is twenty-four?" It occurs to you that you could count out four groups of six coins, merge them, and then count them again, ar-riving at twenty-four. But then he'd probably question your eyesight, your memory, or your ability to count! Finally, it dawns on you. This guy isn't serious. Maybe he's pulling your leg; maybe he enjoys jerk-ing you around; maybe he's mentally disturbed. But whatever it is, he's not really doubting your calculation. If he were doing *his* taxes and had to multiply 2,600 by four, you can be sure (assuming he's not mentally disturbed) he'd come up with and enter the same result as you did.

Doubting is a language game—a complex interplay of words, rules, norms, and actions—with a family of distinguishing features. Among them, as Peirce emphasized, is the need to give positive reasons for doubt. You cannot doubt something for no reason at all. Nor can you doubt for any "reason" whatsoever. The reason must be plausible; there must be some sort of connection between the reason and that which is doubted. The problem with the person doubting your calculation that 4 x 2,600 = 10,400 is that as soon you discount one reason he reflexively fishes for another. When you discredit this, he does the same thing again until, when you're finally driven to dig in your heels, his "reasons" have become increasingly far-fetched.

A second distinguishing characteristic of doubt is that it must, at least in principle, be resolvable. This is one of the ground rules of the societal practice of doubting. Even if we cannot, at a particular time or circumstance, resolve a particular doubt, we must have some idea of what sort of situation or occurrence *would* resolve it. Someone who expresses a doubt and adopts a policy of refusing, in principle, to accept any proposed resolution is not expressing what Peirce calls "real doubt." That's another problem with the person in the multiplication example. Whatever you do, it's apparent he's going to come up with something, no matter how fantastic, as a ground for questioning your result. Perhaps he's playing a different language game than doubting—the game of pulling your leg or a game unique to academic philosophy—or perhaps he's mentally disturbed. But there's no longer any reason to take his "doubts" seriously. As propping a door with a baseball bat is not playing baseball, this person's use of the word 'doubt' is not part of the language game of doubting. Whatever "game" this person is playing, he's not really *doubting* your calculation.

A third important feature of doubt is that we can't doubt everything at once. Insofar as we need reasons for doubt, doubting some things requires *knowing* others; and knowing anything at all, as I will soon show, requires a certain kind of *certainty*.

Knowledge and Belief

What is knowledge? What is belief? And how are the two related? There is no quick answer to this set of questions. A full response requires a careful examination of the wide variety of contexts and ways in which we actually *use* the words 'knowledge' and 'belief' (and their cognates). There is neither time nor space to undertake such a comprehensive examination here. We can make a start, however, by considering three ordinary conversations adapted from Wittgenstein.[3]

Case 1:
You're walking with Randy, who has bad eyesight. At one point Randy asks, "Do you believe what we see over there is a tree?"
"I *know* it's a tree," you reply. "I can see it clearly; and I'm familiar with it."

Case 2:
Terry asks, "Is Jeri home?"
You respond, "I believe she is."
Terry then asks, "Was she home yesterday?"
"Yes," you say, "yesterday she was. I know she was; I spoke to her."

Case 3:
Kelly asks, "Do you know or only believe that this part of the house was built on after the rest?"
"I *know* it was," you respond. "I asked the owner about it."

In the first case you cite your clear vision and prior familiarity as support for saying you *know*, not merely believe, that what you and Randy "see over there" is a tree. Because of Randy's poor sight and lesser familiarity with the area, initially he only believes it's a tree. Upon hearing your response, Randy can also claim to *know* it's a tree. The second case contrasts your believing Jeri's being at home today with your knowledge that she was home yesterday. What's the difference? It's that you spoke to Jeri (at her home or about her being at home) yesterday, but you have *no comparable reason* to believe she's home today. In the third case, you are denying that you only believe this part of the house was an addition. Since you asked the owner and she said it was built on later, you have *grounds* for knowledge. Note, too, that in all three cases the claim to know is a response to a *genuine* question. Whether something is a matter of knowledge or merely belief is often quite significant. Compare, in this connection, a prosecution witness who plausibly claims to know the defendant was at the scene of the crime with a defense witness who merely believes the defendant was elsewhere.

As the cases suggest, knowledge generally requires more in the way of grounds or support than mere belief. "If someone believes something," Wittgenstein points out, "we needn't always be able to answer the question 'why he believes it'; but if he knows something, then the question 'how does he know?' must be capable of being answered."[4] Suppose, for example, Lisa says she believes God exists while Bart says he *knows* it. Lisa doesn't have to justify her belief in God's existence in order to retain it. Belief in God can be personal and subjective and without grounding or support. If someone asks for her reasons, she can refuse to provide them or even admit she hasn't any without having to surrender her belief. Lisa's belief in God may be based on little more than feeling, intuition, or faith. Bart's claim to knowledge, however, bears a burden of justification—in this case a particularly heavy one. Claims to knowledge are impersonal or objective in a way that mere belief is not. Questions like "How do you know?" and "On what basis?" demand an answer. If Bart can't provide plausible answers to such questions with respect to God's existence, he'll have to relinquish his claim to *knowledge*. He can retain a belief in the existence of God, but this is more modest, and will carry less weight in, say, political debates about the relationship between church and state than a plausible knowledge claim.

Despite this difference, however, knowledge and belief are similar insofar as neither ordinarily requires certainty. That (mere) belief can be mistaken is perhaps obvious. But knowledge claims are *fallible* as well. In all three of the previous cases, we can imagine (rather unlikely) variations in which the claim to knowledge would be mistaken: the tree with which you are familiar could have been cut down and replaced with a fake; the person you took for Jeri yesterday could have been a skilled imposter; and the owner of the house (who may not be the original owner) may have been mistaken or trying to mislead you about one part of the house having been built later than the rest. Even when justified, then, claims to knowledge are fallible. It is always possible, with varying degrees of likelihood, that the things we justifiably claim to know are false. Someone who identifies knowledge with certainty, Wittgenstein remarks, "always forgets the expression 'I thought I knew'."[5]

Claims to knowledge are generally supported by other, presumably more secure but nonetheless fallible, knowledge claims. There is, however, no indubitable foundation to empirical knowledge of the sort sought by Descartes; no absolutely certain *premises* about the world from which we can validly *infer* other sentences or beliefs whose truth is no less certain. Our system of empirical knowledge is a more or less coherent network of mutually supportive, revisable parts rather than a rigorously deductive system based on indubitable premises.

The Ship of Knowledge

In an illuminating metaphor, social scientist Otto Neurath compares humans as knowers to "sailors who must rebuild their ship on the open sea, never able to dismantle it in dry-dock and to reconstruct it there out of the best materials."[6] We acquire our capacity for critical reflection against the backdrop of a complex network of beliefs and claims to knowledge. Some elements of the network were acquired from our families, others from church, neighborhood, school, books, television, and so on; still others have their origins in personal experience. This network of knowledge and belief is our ship, the vessel on which we navigate the occasionally hazardous, ever-changing, only partially charted sea of life. The "ship of knowledge" is not, however, as seaworthy as we would like it to be. Some parts, we discover, are worn out, others no longer seem to serve any purpose, and, perhaps most important, we have encountered unprecedented conditions for which the ship is ill-equipped. It needs repair and rebuilding, but we can't do it all at once and from the bottom up. We are, after all, on the open sea. We need to use and stand on some parts of the ship while restoring and reconstructing others.

The comparison of rebuilding a seaborne ship from the bottom up with Descartes's project of rejecting anything that could be doubted should be obvious. Totally dismantling a ship on the open sea in order to rebuild it would soon find us uttering (shortly before drowning), "Glug, glug." Doubting everything that can possibly be doubted in order to rebuild our system of knowledge from the bottom up would, as Wittgenstein remarked, enable us to utter nothing but "Ah" (chapter 2, p. 33). As the mariner must use and stand on some parts of the ship while examining, repairing, and improving others, we must rely on some (fallible) parts of our network of knowledge and belief while doubting, testing, and revising other parts. As each part of the boat is subject to repair or replacement, no aspect of our empirical knowledge is, in principle, immune to correction or improvement. But neither a *seaborne* ship nor a *working* system of knowledge can be rebuilt all at once and from the bottom up.

In questioning some things, then, and in doubting others, there must be some things we do not *at that time* question or doubt. Perhaps later, in other circumstances, we will have reason to question or doubt what we now take for granted as we conduct our investigations (in which case there will be still other things that we cannot *at that time* question or doubt). Some parts of our network of knowledge and belief must remain fixed or constant, at least provisionally, if we are to doubt or question others. Doubt therefore presupposes knowledge or belief. This is, in part, what Peirce is getting at when he characterizes *radical* skepticism as "a mere self-deception, and not real doubt." As we cannot repair some parts of a seaborne ship without relying on others, we cannot coherently doubt some things without knowing or believing others.

Before the Copernican Revolution, for example, it was "common knowledge" among astronomers that the earth occupied a stationary position at the center of the universe. This proposition—the earth is the center of the cosmos—had for centuries been one of the fixed points of the prevailing Ptolemaic system of astronomy; and it provided a basic assumption of inquiry in astronomy. As observation of the planets became more accurate, however, it became increasingly difficult to plot their movements under the Ptolemaic (or geocentric) system. Dissatisfied with this system, Copernicus turned to the works of certain Greek philosophers who, he discovered, had suggested as far back as the third century that the sun, rather than the earth, was the center of planetary orbits. In formulating his doubts about the earth's being at the center of the universe, Copernicus took as fixed points a number of other beliefs, calculations, and claims to knowledge. Though initially counterintuitive, the proposition that the sun was stationary and the earth and other planets revolved around it seemed to him to have a number of advantages over the proposition that the earth was stationary and the sun and other planets revolved around it. And, as we know, despite considerable scientific, theological, and popular opposition, the Copernican (or heliocentric) conception eventually (and fruitfully) prevailed over the Ptolemaic (or geocentric) conception.

Generalizing over examples of this kind, Wittgenstein writes: "It might be imagined that some propositions, of the form of empirical propositions, were hardened and functioned as channels for such empirical propositions as were not hardened but fluid; and that this relation altered with time, in that fluid propositions hardened, and hard ones became fluid."[7] Prior to Copernicus, the proposition that the earth is the center of the universe was "hardened" and functioned as a channel for more "fluid" propositions expressing predictions of solar and planetary motion. After the Copernican Revolution, however, the relation altered: propositions about the location of the sun, which were formerly fluid, now became fixed; and propositions about the motion of the earth, which were formerly fixed, became fluid. As Wittgenstein also puts it, "the same proposition may get treated at one time as something to test by experience, at another as a rule of testing."[8]

Pragmatic Certainty

There may, however, be something unsettling about this conception of knowledge. If (fallible) knowledge claims can be justified only in terms of other (fallible) knowledge claims, knowledge may seem to be so relative as to possibly lose contact with the world. If there is nothing about the world about which we can be certain—no place at which our understanding makes direct and more or less sustained contact with the world apart from any particular set of fallible knowledge claims—our *entire network* of knowledge, no matter how coherent internally, may be wholly out of touch with reality. Is the relativism of the foregoing conception of knowledge so extreme as to collapse the distinction between reality and what we say about it?

The answer, I think, is no. There are a number of things about the world outside our minds of which we are objectively certain. The source of certainty is not, however, as Descartes and many philosophers presume, certain indubitable statements or propositions accessible to the intellect. As Peirce suggests with his reference to the heart and as Wittgenstein argues in his last writings, the locus of certainty is the *actions* of embodied social agents, *not the intellect* of a (possibly) lone, disembodied spectator. Certainty turns out to be practical or pragmatic rather than propositional or intellectual, a matter of embodied social action rather than self-evident axioms or propositions apprehended by a lone disembodied intellect.

Here are just a few things of which you and I are pragmatically certain: we have bodies; our hands don't disappear when we're not paying attention to them; our feet are still there when we get up from where we are sitting; the earth exists and has existed for a long time before we were born; and there are minds other than our own.[9] Though we are certain of these and similar things, it is unlikely we have ever uttered many of them before. Some of these certainties, my guess is, have never explicitly crossed your mind. Yet these and similar certainties are, as Wittgenstein puts it, "the [*nonpropositional*] hinges" on which our entire system of propositional knowledge and belief turn, "the rock bottom of our convictions," and "the inherited background against which [you and] I distinguish between true and false."[10]

These *non*propositional hinges (certainties) must be carefully distinguished from the propositional hinges (fallible knowledge claims, such as those about planetary motion) identified earlier. Various knowledge claims or beliefs serve as propositional hinges for inquiry as, for example, when we assume that the earth and the other eight planets revolve around the sun when we conduct astronomical inquiry. As illustrated by the Copernican Revolution, however, such provisionally fixed points may come to be regarded as false. Insofar as they are certain, then, they are *relatively* certain. Pragmatic certainties, like our having bodies and other persons having minds more or less like our own, on the other hand, cannot be mistaken. They cannot be questioned by ordinary inquiry because they are the hinges on which *all* inquiry turns, the scaffolding that frames our entire system of knowledge and belief and stands fast as we use, test, and revise it.[11]

Our pragmatic (or nonpropositional) certainty that we have bodies or that our feet will not disappear when we get up from a chair is, strictly speaking, neither knowledge nor (mere) belief. Knowledge, as indicated above, is fallible and requires justification. "How do you know?" and "On what basis?" are reasonable responses to claims to knowledge. "I know because of this" or "On the basis of that" we might say, where 'this' and 'that' refer to propositions that are presumably more secure than the claim they are called on to support. If, however, someone questions our certainty that we have bodies or that our feet will not disappear when we get up from a chair, there is nothing we can *say* that could possibly convince him or her (supposing, as is unlikely, his or her doubt is real rather than merely "philosophical"). My certainty, for example, that I have a body is *revealed* in my unhesitatingly seeking doorways when entering or leaving a room rather than walking into walls, by my ducking if I unexpectedly see something coming at my head, by my immediately touching and looking at my arm if I suddenly feel a pain in it. Nothing we can utter is more basic or certain than our conviction that we have bodies or that the floor will not all of a sudden disappear. The only meaningful articulation and defense of such certainties are the ways in which we act. "Why do I not satisfy myself that I have two feet when I want to get up from a chair?" Wittgenstein asks. "There is no why. I simply don't. This is how I act."[12]

The certainties I identified are not *mere* beliefs because while belief may be personal or subjective, our certainty that the earth has existed for a long time before we were born or that there are minds other than our own is as objective as anything can be. It's not just that these things are certain only from our particular viewpoint, but that they are certain from the viewpoint of anyone like you or me. Individuals who seriously doubt that the floor will support them if they get up out of a chair *and thus refuse to get up* or who seriously doubt whether their hands continue to exist if they stop paying attention to them *and thus keep them before their eyes* do not simply hold idiosyncratic beliefs; they're seriously mentally disturbed, what we sometimes (and revealingly) call "unhinged"! That the floor will not fall away and that our hands do not disappear when we are not paying attention to them are objectively certain. Equally unhinged are individuals (if there are any) who (seriously) doubt there are minds other than their own *and conduct themselves accordingly*. You and I do not (merely) believe there are minds other than our own; we're certain of it. *It goes without saying.*

This expression—"It goes without saying"—is a key to understanding what I'm calling pragmatic certainty. Empirical knowledge is basically propositional. To say that someone knows something is to say that there is a certain proposition (or sentence or statement) that he or she knows to be true. Philosophers often express this schematically as: '*S* knows that *p*', where *S* stands for a subject or individual and *p* stands for a particular proposition (sentence or statement). Propositional knowledge is, then, largely a function of language and intellect. We determine people's propositional knowledge by what they *say*, in conversation, on paper, or online. It is the sort of thing for which we give (oral or pencil-and-paper) exams. If we doubt whether Bart knows something he claims to know, we ask him *how* he knows it. In response he may offer a number of other knowledge claims (propositions) that we may in turn, if we have reason for doubt, subject to scrutiny. That we have bodies, however, and that the floor will not fall away when we get up from a chair are, despite superficial similarities, not first and foremost propositional. They neither need nor are susceptible of what we ordinarily think of as proof—a set of propositions providing conclusive support for one or more other propositions. We have to work hard to imagine (far-fetched) situations in which a sentence like 'I have a body' or 'The floor will not fall away when I get up from my chair' would, as explicit utterances, do any real work for us. Such certainties "go without saying." We hardly ever think them, let alone say them. And there are generally no plausible reasons to doubt them. They are revealed in and partly constituted by what, as embodied social agents, we *do*, not by what we *say*. Questions of truth or falsity generally don't arise. ("If the true is what is grounded," Wittgenstein writes, "then the ground is not *true*, nor yet false."[13]) *Of course* we have bodies, there are minds other than our own, and the floor will not fall out from under us as we get up from our chairs. *It goes without saying.*

These and other pragmatic certainties anchor our fallible system of knowledge and belief to the world, providing boundaries beyond which skeptical questioning cannot usefully proceed. If, for example, Bart asks when the Magna Carta was signed, you would, if you know, say 1215. If he then asks how you know it was signed in 1215, you might say you learned it in school. If he then asks whether the teacher might have been wrong or your memory may have failed, you might look it up in one or more encyclopedias or history books. If, having taken a philosophy course, Bart then asks how you know that both you and the earth were not created five minutes ago with all of the evidence (including encyclopedias and the things written in them) and people's memories falsely pointing to a longer history—there is probably nothing you can *say* that will satisfy him. That the earth is very old *goes without saying.* Much of what we know and *do* reflects it—the study of history, geology, paleontology, biology, and religion as well as our practices of honoring the dead, celebrating holidays, commemorating certain events, and so on—and there is no plausible reason for doubt. If Bart is *genuinely* concerned about whether the earth is more than five minutes old (as reflected, for example, in his staying awake at night thinking about it, being unable to eat or concentrate on other things, refusing to study history or paleontology, and so on), he has come *unhinged.*

Wittgenstein's Pragmatic Temperament

Though he did not consider himself a pragmatist, Wittgenstein, as he was dying from cancer, wrote a remarkable series of notes that first identified what I am calling "pragmatic certainty." Published in 1969, eighteen years after his death, the notes, as the editors indicate, are all "first-draft material, which he did not live to excerpt and polish."[14] Wittgenstein's polished writings are intentionally indirect, highly compressed, and notoriously demanding. Problems of understanding are compounded in his exploratory, highly original, unfinished notes published under the title *On Certainty*. Among a wealth of insightful, often brilliant, epigrammatic insights are a number of questions and possible inconsistencies that he was, under the circumstances, unable to address. Refusing to oversimplify, however, and aware of the radically new direction he was taking, Wittgenstein writes at one point, "I believe it might interest a philosopher, one who can think himself, to read my notes. For even if I have hit the mark only rarely, he would recognize what targets I had been ceaselessly aiming at."[15] One such philosopher is Avrum Stroll, whose study of *Moore and Wittgenstein on Certainty* contains an illuminating exegesis of both Wittgenstein's targets and his approach to them.

The most important of these targets, according to Stroll, is the view that certainty is propositional, the product of reasoning, reflection, or intellection.[16] Wittgenstein's conception of certainty is, by contrast, nonpropositional, consisting, as Stroll puts it, of three different, but interrelated, strands: (1) *instinct* ("certainty is something primitive, instinctual, or animal"); (2) *training* ("that it derives from rote training in communal practices"); and (3) *action* ("that it is acting").[17] There is, it seems to me, a marked correspondence between the three strands identified by Stroll and the pragmatic conception of the subject of reflection as an embodied ("instinctual" or "animal") social ("communal practices") agent ("acting"). The source of certainty, if I can put Stroll's reading of Wittgenstein into my terms, is to be found in the actions of embodied social agents, not in the thoughts of a possibly lone, disembodied spectator. The following (numbered) selections from Wittgenstein's notes on certainty, that I have grouped under the headings of *Embodiment, Social Practice,* and *Action,* respectively, suggest that he was working his way toward this conclusion.[18]

Embodiment

359. But that means I want to conceive it [certainty] as something that lies beyond being justified or unjustified; as it were, as something animal.

475. I want to regard man here as an animal; as a primitive being to which one grants instinct but not ratiocination.

Social Practice

144. The child learns to believe a host of things. I.e., it learns to act according to these beliefs. Bit by bit there forms a system of what is believed, and in that system some things stand unshakably fast and some things are more or less liable to shift.

What stands fast does so, not because it is intrinsically obvious or convincing; it is rather held fast by what lies around it.

153. I do not explicitly learn the propositions that stand fast for me. I can *discover* them subsequently like the axis around which a body rotates. This axis is not fixed in the sense that anything holds it fast, but the movement around it determines its immobility.

160. The child learns by believing the adult. Doubt comes *after* belief.

161. I learned an enormous amount and accepted it on human authority, and then I found some things confirmed or disconfirmed by my own experience.

Action

110. . . . But the end is not an ungrounded presupposition: it is an ungrounded way of acting.

204. Giving grounds, however, justifying the evidence, comes to an end;—but the end is not certain propositions' striking us immediately as true, i.e., it is not a kind of *seeing* on our part; it is our *acting*, which lies at the bottom of the language game.

205. If the true is what is grounded, then the ground is not *true*, nor yet false.

342. That is to say, it belongs to the logic of our scientific investigations that certain things are not *in deed* doubted.

343. But it isn't that the situation is like this: We *can't* investigate everything, and for that reason we are forced to rest content with assumption. If I want the door to turn, the hinges must stay put.

344. My *life* consists in my being content to accept many things.

402. . . . [Quoting Goethe] "In the beginning was the deed."

Weaving the three strands together, we obtain a pragmatic, as opposed to propositional, account of certainty and its relations to doubt, knowledge, and belief.

First, a revealing truism: human beings are human animals. As vulnerable biological beings, animals have evolved through random variation and natural selection. Animals that instinctively sought certain kinds of food and shelter and fled such dangers as fire were likely to live long enough to produce descendants with the same sort of biological instincts. Animals lacking such instincts were less likely to survive and reproduce. Forest-dwelling mammals are, for example, instinctively certain they should flee fire. This certainty is not, however, a matter of knowledge or justification. These animals haven't learned to avoid fire from experience (they've never been burned) nor have they learned it from parents, books, or teachers. "Animal certainty," as we might call it, is a matter of biological instinct, not rational justification. The outcome of natural selection, these and similar survival-enhancing animal certainties are shaped by—and thus conform to—the broad contours of the world outside the animal's own skin. If such animal certainties did not, in general, track the "external" world, the animals exhibiting them would be unlikely to survive and reproduce.

Human infants, studies have shown, share in certain animal certainties. Take, for example, the instinct to avoid the edges of a cliff. Rodents, birds, turtles, cats, sheep, goats, dogs, and primates instinctively avoid high places where they are at an increased risk for falling or dropping off to the ground. A laboratory study involving a purely "visual cliff" (a controlled environment eliminating all but visual input of the drop-off) reveals that these animals will instinctively avoid the cliff edge and choose the safe, shallow edge on the basis of visual information alone. "This," as the authors indicate, "surely has value for survival." Moreover, "cliff avoidance develops very early and, in some species, without any opportunity for learning." Human infants, they add, "avoid a cliff as early as they can crawl."[19] Insofar, then, as it makes sense to say that infants are certain that getting too near a cliff edge is bad for them, it is a matter, not of knowledge or justification, but of animal certainty. The outcome of biology and natural selection, the infant's instinct tracks the contours of the natural world, the world outside its developing mind. If it did not, the child's certainty would not, as in this instance it does, contribute to survival.

There is, however, an important difference between human and nonhuman animals—the capacity for language. With the passage of time, the human infant develops, through a complex interplay of genetic endowment, social instruction, and embodied action, the ability to learn and communicate through the use of words. Bit by bit the child acquires a system of propositional knowledge and belief that extends its horizons beyond the stimuli of the more or less immediate present. In mastering various language games, the child learns about the underlying structure of some things (people have bones, blood, hearts, and brains) and about things in different times and places (the birth of Christ, what's happening elsewhere, and how long until one's next birthday). Much, if not all, of this network of knowledge and belief the child initially accepts on faith. It is inculcated by family, community, and society.

Children cannot, at this point, question or challenge what they are taught because they have neither the cognitive nor linguistic facility to do so. (At this stage of development, by the way, cognitive and linguistic development are two sides of a single coin.) "The child," as Wittgenstein puts it, "learns by believing the adult." It accepts a network of knowledge and belief "on human authority."[20]

Before long, however (sooner perhaps than some parents would like), children develop a capacity to question some of what they have learned. In some situations they notice inconsistencies among certain bits or types of knowledge and belief; in others personal experience conflicts with something they've learned from their parents and society. In each case, the child's capacity to question or doubt some element of its network of knowledge and belief turns on its accepting others. Like a mariner rebuilding a ship on the open sea, the child relies on some parts of the "ship" of knowledge and belief while questioning and repairing other parts. To doubt or question some things the child must know or believe things that are not *at that time* doubted or questioned. These are not, however, certain; for there may, in other contexts, be good reasons to subject them to doubt. Recall here the Copernican Revolution and Wittgenstein's metaphor of the way hardened channels and fluid propositions may over time change so that the "fluid propositions hardened, and hard ones became fluid."

Some aspects of our understanding, however, "stand fast," constituting what Wittgenstein variously calls "our frame of reference," "world-picture," "inherited background," "the element in which arguments have their life," "the substratum of all my enquiring and asserting," or "the *scaffolding* of our thoughts."[21] These are the objective certainties—for example, our having bodies, the earth's being very old, there being minds other than our own—that *go without saying*, the hinges on which our entire system of knowledge and belief turns. Our certainty that we have bodies is a kind of higher animal certainty—*higher* because it accompanies the development of language; *animal* because it is nonpropositional, revealed by what we do rather than by what we say. That we have bodies, that our hands don't disappear when we're not looking at them, that the floor will not fall away from our feet when we get up from a chair, and so on are not explicitly taught. They are, however, implicit in the things we are taught and they are absorbed and revealed, day in, day out, in the way we *live* our lives. No one who, for example, comforts the sick or goes to the aid of the injured seriously doubts there are minds other than his or her own. These are things that, as Wittgenstein puts it, are *in deed* not doubted and that constitute the nonpropositional scaffolding, background, or framework of linguistic knowledge and inquiry. Like animal certainties, such *human* animal certainties conform to the broad contours of the world outside of our own minds, thereby contributing to the likelihood we will survive and reproduce.

Still, you might ask, isn't it conceivable that one day the floor *will* fall away from my feet when I get up from a chair (because, for example, someone has, unbeknownst to me, put a trapdoor there) or there are no minds other than my own (because while I slept a force of ultrapowerful, ultra-intelligent extraterrestrials replaced all human beings on earth with super-duper, mindless robots whose behavior can simulate that of persons like you and me)? The answer is yes, it's (remotely) possible we'll one day turn out to be *wrong* about some of these basic certainties, but we won't have been mistaken. We could be wrong because many things are remotely possible, including that the world will all of a sudden go completely haywire. We wouldn't have been mistaken because there are presently no good reasons for doubt or for acting as if things were otherwise. There is nothing to mis-take.

But "[w]hat if," as Wittgenstein asks, "something *really unheard-of* happened?—If I, say, saw houses gradually turning into steam without any obvious cause, if the cattle in the fields stood on their heads and spoke comprehensible words; if trees gradually changed into men and men into trees."[22] If these things were to occur, we would be thrown for a loop, perhaps become "unhinged" (though not irrationally unhinged, because some of the most important certainties on which knowledge and belief are hinged would have disintegrated). Our first thought might be that we're going crazy, or that someone had slipped LSD into our orange juice. We wouldn't know what to think or say. Suppose, however, we first determine that we're not going crazy, aren't on LSD, and so on. Then we discover the world has in fact undergone radical change—what we called "houses" now *do* turn into steam, what we called "cattle" now *do* stand on their heads and converse, and what we called "trees" gradually *do* change into what we called "human beings" and vice versa. If these things were to occur, our previous (human) animal certainties to the contrary would now be *wrong*. They would not, however, have been mistaken. At the time they stood fast for us we had made no errors in reasoning or cognition, nor were there reasons for doubt. Nor do such possibilities have any direct bearing on what we should *do* now. You have no more reason after reading of these possibilities to *avoid* houses, to *converse* with cattle, or to *treat* trees as human beings or vice versa than you did before. If you were *in deed* to do some of these things, your mind would have come off its hinges; you'd have lost your sanity.

REALITY

Having unknotted the thinking leading to the question of whether we can be certain about anything outside our own minds, we can now make relatively short work of the related question of whether physical objects exist apart from our ideas of them. According to the Cartesian tradition, the fundamental question about reality is whether there are real (physical) objects apart from our ideas of them. If, however, we take the subject of inquiry as an embodied social agent and understand knowledge, belief, doubt, and certainty as outlined above, the question can't even arise. Of course there's a physical world the existence of which is independent of and prior to our existence. Nearly everything we *do* and much that we say reflect our pragmatic certainty that our bodies, books, tables, chairs, and the earth exist apart from our ideas of them. *It goes without saying.* "Let us not," as Peirce puts it, "pretend to doubt in philosophy what we do not doubt in our hearts."

Anyone who knows something about the history of science and medicine also knows that the complexities of the world continually expose the limits of our ideas about it. Something like the AIDS virus was able in the earliest stages of the epidemic to make *physical* (and, in this case, lethal) contact with us before we were able to make *cognitive* contact with it. And there is no reason to believe that the AIDS virus will be the last of the tricks the world plays on our aspirations to complete and eternal knowledge. Has the world ever confuted your warranted convictions? Dashed your reasonable expectations? Thwarted your well-laid plans? Then you know from experience there's a big difference between the world and your ideas of it. To anyone but a certain kind of academic philosopher, it goes without saying.

We can't, however, *prove* the independent existence of physical objects if by 'prove' you mean write down a set of true premises from which we can validly derive the conclusion that "there are real (physical) objects apart from our ideas of them." But there's no need for such a proof. Only if you think of yourself as a Cartesian subject would you, *if you could think and reason at all,* feel the need for a pencil and paper (or propositional) proof of the independent existence of rocks, tables, and other persons. But the reason for italicizing "if you could think and reason at all" in the previous sentence is to remind you that, as I have argued in this and the previous chapter, you could *not*, as a pure subject of consciousness, think and reason at all. If you can think and reason at all, you are an embodied social agent rather than a possibly lone, disembodied spectator and you are pragmatically certain of the independent existence of rocks, tables, and other persons. What should be puzzling here is not the lack of a proof, but the *request* for one—a request symptomatic of various "knots in our thinking."

KNOWLEDGE AND REALITY: PRAGMATIC QUESTIONS

There are, however, genuine philosophical questions about knowledge and reality, even for pragmatists. I spoke earlier of the "ship" of knowledge. Yet this is somewhat misleading. There are actually a number of different ships of knowledge and, at the risk of running the metaphor into the ground (or should it be the sea?), they do not always travel in the same direction. Let me explain.

Knowledge

As general definitions go, defining 'knowledge' in terms of 'justified true belief' is as good as any. Claims to knowledge are generally supported by other, presumably more secure but nonetheless fallible, knowledge claims. This means that knowledge is inescapably linguistic. To justify or support a belief is to give reasons for it. And reason-giving is a linguistic undertaking. Whether a particular justification is adequate is usually determined by the rules of the language game in which it occurs. Language games, as you will recall (chapter 2, pp. 35, 39–40), are various patterns of words and the actions into which they are woven. Examples include giving and obeying orders, expressing doubts, and entire practices (like the disciplines of biology and history) composed of subpractices (for example, molecular biology and intellectual history) composed, in turn, of other subpractices (for example, evaluating an experiment and dating a document). To determine whether a knowledge claim in molecular biology or intellectual history is justified, we must turn to the context and the rules governing these language games (or vocabularies or disciplines) and the linguistic and nonlinguistic practices into which they are woven. The same is true of most any knowledge claim. Justification is context and language game relative.

The various language games and academic disciplines (and sub-disciplines) are what I mean by the various "ships of knowledge." There is no such thing as knowledge *as such*. There is no Department of Knowledge at a college or a university, nor is there a single comprehensive and consistent language game called "knowledge." Rather there are kinds (and subkinds) of knowledge, with their own (occasionally overlapping) subject matter, presuppositions, modes of reasoning, ground rules, and so on. We have developed and maintained these various disciplines and language games because of a combination of the world's complexity, our limited cognitive and perceptual capacities, and the pragmatic requirement that knowledge enhance our capacity to understand and effectively *contend* with the world. A single, overarching category or language game called "knowledge" would (for our minds, at least) be so vague or general as to be practically *useless*. Each of our current cognitive language games or academic disciplines (and subdisciplines) has, on the other hand, proved its worth by fulfilling particular, more or less practical, purposes that, I presume, cannot currently be satisfied by any alternative language game or discipline (or subdiscipline). Indeed, as science has progressed it has, in many respects, become more fragmented—more highly diverse and specialized—than unified. What was once simply biology has now split into population biology, microbiology, evolutionary biology, cell biology, neurobiology, biochemistry, and so on. The respective vocabularies—or language games—are now so complex that they take years to master and individuals "fluent" in one area of biology (that is, able to understand and conduct original research) may have little more than "reading knowledge" of the others (that is, the ability to understand and appreciate significant results). The same is true at the frontiers of other natural and social sciences and in the humanities as well. Progress in the various cognitive disciplines—the development of more useful vocabularies for understanding and contending with the world—has, given the size and complexity of the world together with the limits of our minds, seemed to require a proliferation of specialized disciplines and subdisciplines rather than unification.

Since, however, language games consist of actions as well as words, different knowledge claims occasionally require that we undertake different courses of action. And here's where the trouble starts. What do we do when two or more knowledge claims, embedded in two or more useful language games, require opposing courses of action? How do we adjudicate between conflicting language games when they are not each part of some more comprehensive language game identifying more or less specific rules for making such decisions? Writ small, this is the problem of, for example, deciding between a psychotherapeutic and a biochemical diagnosis (and corresponding course of treatment) for clinical depression. Writ large, it is the problem, identified by Thomas Kuhn, of deciding between two scientific "paradigms," such as the Copernican and the Ptolemaic conceptions of planetary motion.[23] Writ even larger, it is the problem of deciding between a wholly deterministic conception of human beings and one that makes room for some degree of freedom or choice.

The fact that there are these various "ships" of knowledge and that they occasionally travel in opposing directions creates questions and problems that transcend the capacities of any particular ship to resolve. These are distinctly philosophical questions. Pragmatically conceived, philosophy adjudicates or mediates conflicts between various language games, ways of talking, thinking, and acting, when they conflict. In many cases, as James and Dewey emphasize, such conflicts will be between new and old ways of thinking and acting. In other cases they will be between two or more current ways.

How exactly do we resolve conflicts among knowledge claims embedded in different language games or disciplines? What methods can we employ? Though I cannot answer these questions here, I will make a stab at it in the remainder of the book, especially chapters 4, 5, and 7. Let us now have a quick look at related questions about reality.

Reality

"I have settled down to the task of writing these lectures," Sir Arthur Eddington says in introducing his book on *The Nature of the Physical World*, "and have drawn up my chairs to my two tables. Two tables! Yes; there are duplicates of every object about me—two tables, two chairs, two pens."[24] One of the tables is the familiar, solid, colored table of common sense—the sort of thing we can touch and photograph. The other Eddington calls his "scientific table": "It is a more recent acquaintance and I do not feel so familiar with it. . . . My scientific table is mostly emptiness. Sparsely scattered in that emptiness are numerous electric charges rushing about with great speed; but their combined bulk amounts to less than a billionth of the bulk of the table itself."[25] Appalled by the suggestion that there are two tables, philosophers have traditionally insisted that one must be "real" and the other not. Is it the solid, static, brown table of common sense? Or is it the

table consisting of mostly empty space, occupied by the rapidly moving, colorless particles of microphysics? The pragmatist's answer is a
gently teasing "Yes."

Whether the table is that of common sense or microphysics depends
upon the context of inquiry. We employ a wide variety of different language games or vocabularies in making our way in the world and
there is, as indicated above, nothing to be gained and much to be lost
by choosing *once and for all* between them.

There are, however, those who maintain it is the physical sciences,
particularly physics, that uniquely put us in touch with reality. Yet as
physicist Richard Gregory points out, the vocabulary of physics is
more like a tool than an accurate photograph:

> We normally think of science as the discovery of the facts about the nat-
> ural world and the laws that govern its behavior, that is, we view science
> as the uncovering of an already-made world. In this book we will follow
> another course. We will trace the history of physics as the evolution of a
> language—as the invention of new vocabularies and new ways of talk-
> ing about the world. Concentrating on the language physicists use to
> talk about the world will establish a perspective vitally important for
> understanding the development of physics in the twentieth century. But
> even more important, tracing the development of physics will provide a
> powerful way of looking at the much broader question of how language
> looks at the world.
>
> Although it may be surprising at first, we will find that physics is re-
> ally not about making accurate pictures of the world. If you go to an art
> gallery and ask yourself which of the paintings are realistic and which
> are abstract, and why, you will discover that realism in painting is
> largely a convention. A physicist is no more engaged in painting a "real-
> istic" picture of the world than a "realistic" painter is. For a physicist, a
> realistic picture is far too complex to be useful as a tool, and physics is
> about fashioning tools.[26]

The history of modern physics, as Gregory understands and explains
it, is the history of a complex (network of) language game(s) that has
been developed as one strand of the "endless human project of learning to deal with the world."[27] Questions formulated in the vocabulary
of physics are addressed within this vocabulary and in some cases,
where satisfactory answers are not forthcoming, lead to the imagina-
tive invention and development of a radically new vocabulary or
branch of physics.

But, Gregory rightly adds, not all questions—including questions
about reality—are formulated in the vocabulary of physics:

For thousands of years questions have been raised about the nature of reality. Is reality material or is it spiritual? Is reality one or is it many? Is everything determined or is there room for freedom? The answers have not proved persuasive, since the questions are still being debated. Physics shows us a different way to look at these questions—a way that asks what vocabulary, what theory, we should use to talk about the world. The word *should* makes sense in terms of the ends we hope to achieve. The question need not be whether reality is material or spiritual; it can be, what follows from talking about reality one way or the other? What do we gain, and what price do we pay, for adopting one vocabulary and giving up another?[28]

As indicated above, human beings have devised a wide variety of vocabularies—or language games—for contending with their experience and the world, and each of these vocabularies, insofar as it is retained, seems to do some important work that cannot be done nearly so well by any of the others. Choosing, in particular situations, between competing vocabularies turns therefore on comparative overall *usefulness* rather than on accuracy of representation.

There are few if any contexts in which we must make practically significant choices between Eddington's "two tables." The two vocabularies differ, but are not, in most practical contexts, genuine rivals. In other areas, however, peaceful coexistence among differing vocabularies is more difficult to achieve. Both the mind–body and the free will problems seem to require fundamental choice between mutually incompatible vocabularies. I now turn to these problems, both for their intrinsic interest and to develop a pragmatic approach to practically significant questions of knowledge and reality.

NOTES

1. Ludwig Wittgenstein, *Zettel*, ed. G. E. M. Anscombe, trans. G. H. von Wright and G. E. M. Anscombe (Berkeley: University of California Press, 1967), §452.

2. Charles S. Peirce, "Some Consequences of Four Incapacities," in *The Essential Peirce*, vol. 1 (1867–1893), ed. Nathan Houser and Christian Kloesel (Bloomington: Indiana University Press, 1992), 28–29.

3. Ludwig Wittgenstein, *On Certainty*, ed. G. E. M. Anscombe and G. H. von Wright, trans. Denis Paul and G. E. M. Anscombe (New York: Harper & Row, 1969), §483.

4. Wittgenstein, *On Certainty*, §550.

5. Wittgenstein, *On Certainty*, §12.

6. Otto Neurath, "Protocol Sentences," in *Logical Positivism*, ed. A. J. Ayer, trans. George Schick (Chicago: Free Press, 1959), 201.

7. Wittgenstein, *On Certainty*, §96.

8. Wittgenstein, *On Certainty*, §98.

9. Wittgenstein, *On Certainty*, §244, §153, §273; Ludwig Wittgenstein, *Philosophical Investigations*, 3d ed., trans. G. E. M. Anscombe (New York: Macmillan, 1953), §303, p. 224e.

10. Wittgenstein, *On Certainty*, §341, §248, §94.

11. Wittgenstein, *On Certainty*, §341, §211, §151.

12. Wittgenstein, *On Certainty*, §148.

13. Wittgenstein, *On Certainty*, §205

14. Wittgenstein, *On Certainty*, vi.

15. Wittgenstein, *On Certainty*, §387.

16. Avrum Stroll, *Moore and Wittgenstein on Certainty* (New York: Oxford University Press, 1994), 154.

17. Stroll, *Moore and Wittgenstein*, 157–58.

18. The passages that follow are numbered sections from Wittgenstein's *On Certainty*.

19. Eleanor J. Gibson, "The Development of Perception as an Adaptive Process," *American Scientist* 58, no. 1 (January–February 1970): 98–107.

20. Wittgenstein, *On Certainty*, §160.

21. Wittgenstein, *On Certainty*, §151, §83, §162, §94, §105, §162, §211.

22. Wittgenstein, *On Certainty*, §513.

23. Thomas S. Kuhn, *The Structure of Scientific Revolutions*, 2d ed. (Chicago: University of Chicago Press, 1970).

24. Sir Arthur Eddington, *The Nature of the Physical World* (Ann Arbor: University of Michigan Press, 1958), xi.

25. Eddington, *Nature of Physical World*, xii.

26. Richard Gregory, *Inventing Reality: Physics as Language* (New York: Wiley, 1988), 3.

27. Gregory, *Inventing Reality*, 3.

28. Gregory, *Inventing Reality*, 197–98.

Chapter 4

Mind and Will

Pretend as we may, the whole man within us is at work when we form our philosophical opinions. Intellect, will, taste, and passion co-operate just as they do in practical affairs. . . . The absurd abstraction of an intellect verbally formulating all its evidence and carefully estimating the probability thereof by a vulgar fraction by the size of whose denominator and numerator alone it is swayed, is ideally as inept as it is impossible.

—William James, "The Sentiment of Rationality"

We have a deeply entrenched, highly useful set of language games involving the mind. Much of what we are and do is expressed and explained in terms of what we feel, believe, desire, intend, hope, fear, and so on. Advances in neuroscience, however, reveal that at least some of our mental states are intimately related to the brain. Clinical depression, for example, seems to be connected to the activity of certain neurotransmitters. Alter this activity (in ways not yet fully understood) and you often lift or mitigate the depression. Is it possible that clinical depression is nothing but a complex state of the brain? Will we one day be able to talk about certain brain states rather than depression, as we could now, if we wished, talk of "H_2O" instead of "water"? If we can do this for depression, can we do it for all mental states, so talk of the mind could, at least in principle, be fully replaced by talk of the brain (or central nervous system)? Why would we want to make such a change? What would it mean for our understanding of reality and of ourselves? These are some contemporary questions about the relationship between mind and body.

A related question is whether freedom and responsibility are compatible with a scientific understanding of human behavior. Some of the things we do, we commonly assume, we do of our own free will. These are actions for which we can be praised or blamed, rewarded or punished—and for which we can take credit or feel remorse. If, however, the mind is nothing but the brain, and the workings of the brain can be fully described and explained in terms of biology and physics, the vocabularies of freedom, choice, and responsibility may be outmoded. Everything we think and do may be caused by states of the brain, which are themselves the effects of causes over which we ultimately have no control. Is it possible, then, that the vocabularies of freedom, choice, and responsibility could eventually be replaced by vocabularies in the natural sciences? Can explanations of human behavior in terms of a person's brain states replace explanations in terms of a person's reasons for acting? How can we decide whether to pursue or make such a replacement? Can we even talk of "decision" here? What are the implications for our understanding of reality? What are the implications for morality and law? If we retain both our psychological and biophysical vocabularies, what do we do when, in certain cases, they seem to require different (and opposing) courses of action? These are some contemporary questions about free will.

In this chapter, I make a start at answering these questions. I begin with the mind and then turn to the will. Drawing on the ideas of a pragmatic subject (chapter 1), language games (chapter 2), and pragmatic certainty (chapter 3), I steer a narrow course between the Scylla of Cartesian dualism (which holds that the word 'mind' refers to an entity or substance separate from the brain) and the Charybdis of reductive or eliminative physicalism (which holds that everything we say about the mind is ultimately reducible to or replaceable by talk of the brain). We may, for the most part, combine what's right about dualism and what's right about physicalism while avoiding their difficulties by conceiving the subject of thought and action as an embodied social agent, acknowledging the various uses of language, and distinguishing pragmatic certainty from scientific knowledge. The result we might call *pragmatic physicalism*.

MIND

Dualism

Cartesian dualism—mind as purely mental substance, body as purely physical substance, and causal interaction between them—has few contemporary defenders. First, there has been no progress in solving long-standing philosophical problems with dualism. If, for example, dualism were true, we couldn't know there were minds other than our own; yet we are certain—*pragmatically* certain—that there are (chapter 3, pp. 61–69). Moreover, no one has ever been able to explain how a purely nonphysical substance like a Cartesian mind could causally interact with a purely physical substance like a human brain or body. Second, the idea of nonphysical substance is incompatible with contemporary science. If science cannot answer all our questions, it places formidable constraints on what can. A Cartesian conception of mind and the mental is therefore unlikely to be correct. Third, research into the relation between mind and brain is proving extraordinarily fruitful, both for theoretical understanding and practical intervention (especially, for example, with respect to various mental disorders). Thus the prevailing view of the mind–body relation among philosophers and brain and behavioral scientists is some form of physicalism.

Reductive Physicalism: The Identity Theory

One way to retain the reality of the mind while avoiding the problems of Cartesian dualism is to show, appearances to the contrary, that mental states are in fact identical with physical states. Science tells us, for example, that water just *is* H_2O and lightning just *is* an electronic discharge. There aren't two separate things, water and H_2O or lightning and electronic discharges, respectively, but one thing referred to in two different ways. And one of the ways, H_2O or electronic discharge, is somehow more basic or revealing of ultimate reality than the other. In some instances we talk of the less basic category or description (water or lightning) being "reduced" to the more basic (H_2O or electronic discharge).

Now suppose clinical depression just *is*, in the same way, a certain state of the brain. The two are identical. There aren't two things, clinical depression and the brain state, but just one. Everything true of depression would be true of the brain state, and vice versa. If depression makes you feel terrible, so does being in the particular brain state. If the brain state can be altered or eliminated by various serotonin re-uptake inhibitors (like Prozac), so too can depression. Since the term 'brain state' is more basic or revealing about what's ultimately going on than the term 'depression', we say that depression has been reduced to (a certain kind of) brain state.

If this could be generalized to all mental phenomena, the two main difficulties with Cartesian dualism would disappear. If mental states are identical with certain brain states and we can know others have such brain states, we can know they have mental states as well. Thus we could know whether there are minds other than ours. If others have brain states like ours, they have minds like ours. Second, if mental states are identical with or reducible to brain states and brain states are physical states that interact with other parts of the body, there is no special problem of understanding the causal relationships between mind and body. They can be reduced to interactions between one part of the body, the brain, and others.

This, in brief, is the mind–brain identity theory. Though making short work of the difficulties with Cartesian dualism, it has problems of its own. One, acknowledged even by physicalists, is that the same kind of mental state, say, toothache, may be identical with a wide variety of brain states. Given what we are learning about the complexity and plasticity of the brain, particularly that one part may take over for damage to another, there are unlikely to be one-one matchups between each *kind* of mental state or condition and each *kind* of physical state or condition that would allow us to "reduce" or replace the vocabulary of psychology with that of neurophysiology. My toothache may be "identical" with my C-fibers firing and yours with the firing of your D-fibers. At one stage of my life my toothache may be "identical" with my C-fibers firing and at a later stage (after a serious head injury, say, or in the later stages of some neurological disease) it may be "identical" with the firing of my E- or F-fibers. It's also quite possible that human beings will eventually encounter extraterrestrials or construct conscious "robots" whose aches and pains are "identical" not with states of brains like ours, but rather with states of a silicon-based, lime-Jell-O-like substance in the case of the extraterrestrials, and states of the silicon chips (or whatever we're using as hardware in the future) in the case of the "robots." So the best identity theorists may be able to do is to show that each individual mental state is identical with some *particular* physical state or other, not that mental states of certain *kinds* are identical with physical states of certain kinds. This would be no small accomplishment, insofar as it would conclusively refute Cartesian dualism. It would not, however, go as far as physicalists hoping to *reduce* psychology to neurophysiology (as water is reduced to H_2O) would like. Even if each instance of toothache is in some sense identical with some particular physical state or other, the language or vocabulary of psychology will not *in general* be reducible to (and in principle replaceable by) that of neurophysiology. To do this we should have to show that each instance of a mental state of *a certain type* is identical with a brain state *of a certain type*. And this is unlikely to be true. We will still, therefore, need the concept of a toothache to indicate what you and I have in common when, for example, my C-fibers are firing and your D-fibers are firing. And we will need the concept of pain to indicate what you and an extraterrestrial or *Star Wars*'s C-3PO have in common when each of you moans and groans after falling off a bike.

Eliminative Materialism

Some physicalists respond to this and related problems with the identity theory by proposing that we simply eliminate talk of the mental. Recent discoveries in neurophysiology, they argue, suggest that our psychological vocabulary is a vestige of an outmoded, prescientific understanding of human behavior. There was a time when certain illnesses were explained in terms of a witch's spell or demons in the patient's blood. The development of scientific medicine, however, led to the replacement of such explanations with explanations in terms of the germ theory of disease. It's not that a witch's spell or demons in the blood are identical with, say, a certain infection, but that in fact there are no such things as witches or demons in the blood. Since what people attributed to demons in the blood was actually produced by various kinds of (physical) microorganisms, we simply eliminated the idea of demons as causes of disease and replaced it with germs. The same is likely true, eliminative physicalists argue, of commonsense psychological explanations of behavior. Describing and explaining behavior in terms of beliefs, desires, intentions, hopes, wishes, and fears is probably, from the standpoint of contemporary neuroscience, no better than, and ultimately deserves the same fate as, explaining illness in terms of demons in the blood. The language of beliefs, desires, intentions, and so on is part of "folk" psychology—a prescientific way of describing and explaining human behavior that has now outlived its usefulness. As we learn more about the "real" or neurophysiological bases of behavior, we will eliminate folk psychology (and its mentalistic or "folk psychological" conception of the mind) and replace it with a more scientific, neurophysiological conception of psychology.

Paul M. Churchland, a leading eliminativist, puts it this way:

> As the eliminative materialists see it, the one-to-one match-ups [required by the identity theory between certain kinds of mental and physical states] will not be found, and our common-sense psychological framework will not enjoy an intertheoretic reduction, *because our common-sense*

psychological framework is a false and radically misleading conception of the causes of human behavior and the nature of cognitive activity. On this view, folk psychology is not just an incomplete representation of our inner natures; it is an outright misrepresentation of our internal states and activities. Consequently, we cannot expect a truly adequate neuro-scientific account of our inner lives to provide theoretical categories that match up nicely with the categories of our common-sense framework. Accordingly, we must expect that the older framework will simply be eliminated, rather than be reduced, by a matured neuroscience.[1]

Since what we now call "mind" would be assimilated by the biological and physical sciences, philosophical questions about the relation between mind and body would totally disappear.

Eliminativists assume that what they disparagingly call "folk psychology"—what you and your friends knew about the mind before you ever picked up a psychology book—is a prescientific *theory* for describing and explaining behavior. Like any theory, they argue, it is fallible. It's always possible that we will come up with a better theory—one that is more comprehensive, accurate, fruitful, etc.—to replace it. This is what happened in astronomy when the Ptolemaic (geocentric) theory of planetary motion gave way to the Copernican (heliocentric) one. And, they predict, it is about to happen with the mind as a "matured neuroscience" provides better explanations and predictions of human behavior than does folk psychology. In some cases, explanations of depression in terms of laziness or a poor mental attitude have already been replaced by explanations in terms of neurotransmitters and serotonin levels. Before long all of folk psychology will be eliminated by the vocabulary of neuroscience.

The main difficulty with eliminativism is its narrow understanding of our ordinary psychological framework. To eliminativists it is basically a theory for describing and explaining (other people's) behavior. Granted, *one* of the uses of commonsense psychology is to explain behavior. But our everyday psychological vocabulary has other important uses as well. We use it, for example, to imagine, wonder, speculate, make up stories, write poetry, sing songs, ask questions, and so on. Commonsense psychology is also inseparable from some of the certainties—the hinges or fixed points—on which all our scientific knowledge, research, and theorizing turn.

Each of us is, for example, *certain* that we and others like us are subjects of experience or phenomenal consciousness. ("I am as certain that I am sentient as I am certain of *anything*," writes cognitive scientist Steven Pinker, "and I bet you feel the same."[2]) Our certainty is revealed more by what we *do* than what we *say*. (Indeed, it is hard to imagine contexts in which a sentence like "I am sentient" would actually have a use or do any work. What would we be saying? And to whom?) We keep away from fire, raise the thermostat on the furnace, lower the volume on the stereo, comfort a frightened child, commiserate with the bereaved, condemn torture, and so on. As *pragmatic* certainties, these anticipations of and responses to subjective experience are not part of a fallible theory or system of knowledge. Our certainty that we and others can experience pain is not propositional—not the outcome of a conclusive chain of reasoning. Like the pragmatic certainties discussed in the previous chapter, that we and others can experience pain *goes without saying*. We cannot really doubt whether we and practically all other human beings are capable of certain mental states because these and related states are among the *hinges* on which language—and hence doubt and inquiry—turn. They are the scaffolding that frames our entire system of knowledge and belief, including our various scientific theories. (We might, in a particular situation, doubt whether someone is actually in pain. Perhaps she's only pretending. But the idea of feigning pain would make no sense if there were no such thing as real pain and our capacity to experience and detect it.) Among the pragmatic certainties that *stand fast* for us, then, both in everyday living and in conducting scientific research, are some that involve the concepts and categories of "folk" psychology.

Suppose, for example, you're doing research in neuroscience. This requires, among other things, that you be able to critically sift through various theories, hypotheses, and experiments. In so doing you will, as a matter of course, *doubt* some theories, *assert* some hypotheses, and *judge* some experimental results to be invalid. Conducting such research assumes, too, that you are a member of a research community—a "community of inquiry" as Peirce put it—that establishes criteria for resolving doubt, testing hypotheses, and determining validity. As a member of this community you are *concerned* about what other people will *think* about your doubts, assertions, and judgments. But doubt, assertion, and judgment, as Avrum Stroll points out, are just the sort of "folk" psychological notions that eliminativists hope to eliminate.

The eliminativist proposes that the disappearance of our everyday mental vocabulary would entail the revision or elimination of our common sense framework. But what the hypothesis would also entail, if correct, is that much of our inherited background, namely the totality of such [commonsense] practices, would then be revised or disappear since, as we have seen, it is these practices that are essential components of the common sense framework. And that in turn would entail that such specific practices as doubting, asserting, and judging will also be revised or disappear.[3]

In other words, eliminativists propose to eliminate the very framework upon which the *practice* of science, including neuroscience, depends.

The commonsense framework that includes doubting, asserting, judging, feeling, and so on is among the hinges of scientific practice. It is not a *theory*—a set of revisable claims or conjectures to be subjected to testing—but part of what is presupposed and stands fast as scientists develop, test, compare, and revise their various theories. Insofar, then, as eliminativism presupposes that our ordinary mentalistic vocabulary is nothing but a theory for explaining and predicting behavior, it is mistaken. The *practice* of scientific research is no less important than its results. Scientific results depend on scientific practice; and scientific practice hinges on various language games, some of which are inseparable from what eliminativists disdainfully call "folk" psychology.

What's important here are not the specific *sounds* we utter, but the *uses* that give them their meanings (chapter 2, pp. 39–40). So long as we continue to engage in the embodied social practices that give words like 'doubt', 'belief', 'toothache', and so on their current meanings, commonsense psychology will remain, regardless of the words we employ. Replacing 'goodbye' with 'ciao' or 'au revoir' makes no difference to the language game of leave-taking. Neither will replacing the words 'I have a toothache' with 'My C-fibers are firing,' so long as eliminativists don't forbid us to say "My C-fibers are firing" in circumstances in which we would formerly have said "I have a toothache." A rose by any other name is still a rose, and an expression of a (folk) psychological state is still such a state regardless of the words we use so long as we employ them according to the same rules in the same contexts. There is, then, nothing philosophical to be gained by replacing the words 'I have a toothache' with 'My C-fibers are firing' so long as one uses the latter in the same ways and contexts in which one used the former—and there is something to be lost.

What will be lost is, first, the *usefulness* of a term ('toothache') that identifies what you and I have in common when, despite the fact that my C-fibers are firing and your D-fibers are firing, we each moan and hold our jaw and say that it hurts in the same way at the same place. What will also be lost is the univocal meaning of 'C-fibers firing'. If expressions like 'My C-fibers are firing' are used in the same language games in which we currently say "I have a toothache," they will acquire a new—and "mentalistic"—meaning. Insofar as meaning is a function of use, we will have given a new and mentalistic meaning to 'C-fibers firing'. Rather than eliminating the mental, we will have mentalized the physical. Finally, if we were to replace 'pain' with the words of a matured neuroscience, we would risk doing grave harm to sentient beings whose "hardware" differed from ours. Suppose, for example, we were to encounter extraterrestrials or beings like C-3PO who experience and display pain much as we do. Would we be able to recognize and properly respond to our causing them pain? Not if we had replaced the word 'pain' with one or more terms describing states in the (human) brain.

So what went wrong? Why have eliminativists tried to deny the undeniable? There are, it seems to me, four closely related explanations. First, eliminativists are prepared to go to almost any length to distance themselves from Cartesian dualism. What more decisive way to avoid the problems of dualism, one might think, than to show that there are no such things as distinctively mental states or events? If beliefs, desires, intentions, hopes, wishes, and fears are little more than elements of a discredited theory for explaining and predicting behavior, there is no problem of explaining how they are related to the body or brain. This, however, as I suggest below, is not only to go from one implausible extreme to the other, but it ironically assumes on behalf of eliminativism the same untenable spectator point of view as Cartesian dualism.

Second, impressed by advances in science, eliminativists succumb to the seductions of *scientism*. Science has advanced because it has restricted itself to the impersonal perspective and emphasized systematic data collecting, quantitative analysis, theory construction, experimental testing, and so on. Confined to questions for which this perspective and these methods are appropriate, science greatly enhances our understanding and capacity for prediction and control. Science is one thing, however; scien*tism* is quite another. Scientism is a *philosophical doctrine* that dubiously privileges the impersonal perspective and denies the value or reality of anything that cannot figure into scientific theories or methods. By themselves, however, science and the scientific method are no more suited to answering our most important philosophical questions than are religion and theology. A conception of mind that denies the reality of mental states and experiences (as distinctively mental) makes insufficient contact with what James calls "this finite world of actual human lives." The capacity to ask and answer scientific questions hinges on the certainty that we and others are subjects of various distinctively mental (subjective, conscious, phenomenal, experiential, intentional, etc.) states. We should drink deeply of science, but not to the point of intoxication. The condescending expression "folk psychology" is a symptom of scientistic intemperance. Among the terms of "folk" psychology, P. F. Strawson wryly observes, are those of "such simple folk as Shakespeare, Tolstoy, Proust, and Henry James."[4]

Third, and related to scientism, eliminativists overintellectualize the mind by restricting their viewpoint to the third person (or spectator or impersonal) point of view. When they focus on the explanatory and predictive functions of mentalistic language they are thinking about the minds of others, not their own. A scientific view of the mind views it from outside, the view from nowhere or a God's-eye point of view, rather than from one's own point of view, that of the embodied social agent. Granted, the impersonal perspective is essential for fully understanding the mind. But what people sometimes say about New York City might also be said of the impersonal perspective: "It's a nice place to visit, but I wouldn't want to live there." Note that the impersonal perspective is, in one important respect, even less accommodating than New York. Though you might not want to live in New York, you could do so if you wanted to (and if you could afford it!). But you couldn't live your life from the impersonal perspective, even if you wanted to. *Leading* a life requires the personal perspective of an agent—tempered and informed, to be sure, by the scientific or impersonal standpoint—but not fully replaced by it. The main problem is that eliminativists seem to forget that an adequate philosophical understanding of the mind must account for *their own* minds and mental lives as well as those whom they study. If you think of yourself as a disembodied, lone spectator hovering above the earth with no other aim but to observe, explain, and predict the physical movements of human beings, you might well imagine replacing "folk psychology" with the vocabulary of a "matured neuroscience." (The extent to which this aspect of eliminativism resembles or tacitly buys into the idea of the Cartesian subject is a revealing [and, to my mind, delicious] irony.) If, however, you also think of yourself as *one of us*—an embodied social agent *in* the world as well as a spectator *of* it—you will come to see the implausibility of such replacement.

Finally, eliminativists seem to assume that the principal function of mentalistic language is to describe an independent reality and that the main question is whether either folk psychology or neuroscience offers the most accurate description. "In the idealized long run," eliminativist Patricia Churchland writes, "the completed [neuro]science is *a true description of reality*, there is no other Truth and no other Reality"[5] (italics added). But why assume that the principal function of commonsense psychology is to give a "true description" of reality? Why ignore the variety of nondescriptive uses of mentalistic language, especially those associated with the first-person or personal perspective? Are you mainly concerned with describing reality when, for example, you say, "Ouch!" or "I wonder what I should do?" or "I love you" or "I promise to be there"? If we understand our various language games as serving different, occasionally overlapping, purposes, we may not have to choose, once and for all, between them. Accommodation between different language games with different purposes is not contradiction. The appearance of contradiction assumes that the sentences "Ronna has a toothache" and "Ronna's C-fibers are firing" are *competing* descriptions of a singular reality and that there is a neutral vantage point for determining which description is true and which false. But, as pointed out in chapter 2, there are many uses of language besides pure description, and there is no neutral vantage point for comparing what we say about the world with the way the world is apart from any language-mediated understanding of it. Moreover, choosing once and for all between the two language games will, as I show below, leave us worse, rather than better, off.

Pragmatic Physicalism

A pragmatic conception of the mind hopes to avoid the pitfalls of both Cartesian dualism and reductive or eliminative physicalism. Like dualism, it acknowledges the reality and causal power of feelings, beliefs, and desires; but it does not attribute them to a ghostly, self-subsistent, mental substance. Like physicalism, it acknowledges the physical basis or realization of feelings, beliefs, and desires; but it does not seek to reduce them to or replace them with brain states. Here's a simple illustration.

You and I are complex biological organisms. Whenever we are in certain mental states two general kinds of stories can in principle be told: (1) a *personal* story that includes one or more terms from our ordinary psychological vocabulary and (2) a *physical* story that describes and explains what's going on in terms of a "matured neuroscience." Suppose, for example, you have a severe toothache. The personal story might include your having eaten large amounts of candy, neglecting to brush your teeth, and so on. The physical story would include the corrosive effects of large amounts of sugar on the enamel of your tooth, the subsequent stimulation of the nerve endings, and the resulting excitation of the C-fibers in your brain. The two stories are about the same biological organism, but they are told in different vocabularies with different purposes. The first emphasizes your history as an embodied agent, including, in this case, how you feel, your responsibility for your toothache, and what you might do to prevent similar occurrences in the future. The second emphasizes your history as a biological organism, including in this case the physical causes of the state of your tooth, its effects via the nervous system in your brain, and the possible mechanisms for cure. Serving different, but related, purposes, the two accounts are not *for all practical purposes* rivals. That the personal account requires no reference to an immaterial mental substance avoids the Scylla of Cartesian dualism. There's only one kind of stuff and that's physical stuff. The toothache is a state of you—and you're a complex, sentient biophysical organism. That the personal account serves important purposes not served by the physical account avoids the Charybdis of reductive or eliminative physicalism. We cannot, without significant loss, categorically replace the one story with the other. The toothache and the tooth decay are both states of an embodied social agent—you. The same is true of more complex conditions, such as depression and the activity of certain neurotransmitters, and others that remain to be understood.

This is, on the face of it, all the physicalism we need to avoid the pitfalls of Cartesian dualism. Human beings are complex biophysical organisms differing in degree, but not kind, from other biophysical organisms. Dogs, cats, pigs, horses, and many other nonhuman animals have a measure of sentient life, but there is no temptation to ascribe Cartesian minds to them. Just as a chimpanzee's mental life is more varied and complex than that of a squirrel, your mental life is more varied and complex than that of a chimpanzee. In both cases the difference is a function of natural selection and resulting differences in brain structure. Language-using animals like you and me are—in terms of a rhetorically revealing tautology—animals. We differ from other animals because of the size and complexity of our brains and our resulting linguistic capacity, not because we have Cartesian minds.

If pragmatic physicalism is superior to both Cartesian dualism and reductive or eliminative physicalism, however, it wins by default, not hands down. It's not that it's perfect or flawless, but that its difficulties are less intractable or incapacitating than those of its rivals. Like all current forms of physicalism, for example, pragmatic physicalism still needs to explain how certain brain states are related to conscious experience. Some have seized on the gap between physical understanding of the brain and the reality of conscious experience to argue that some form of dualism must, despite the difficulties with Descartes's version, be true. Whether pragmatic physicalists can fill this "explanatory gap" better than reductive or eliminative physicalists is an open question. Still, it is a problem that needs to be solved or explained away. Pragmatic physicalism must also acknowledge that the two general kinds of vocabularies—the personal/psychological and the physical—do not neatly mesh. There are situations where each, if true, seems to require conduct incompatible with the other. Nowhere is this clearer or more dramatic than with respect to the will.

WILL

Morality and law presuppose that we are generally accountable for what we do. In tracing the causes of morally or legally significant action, the buck often stops with us. If the consequences are good, we may take credit and are eligible for commendation, praise, or reward. If the consequences are bad, we may acknowledge fault and are eligible for criticism, blame, or punishment. The presumption of responsibility is, however, overridden when such factors such as severe mental illness, inculpable ignorance, external coercion, or duress are the principal causes of our conduct. If what we do is not ultimately "up to us," we cannot be credited or blamed for it. We are only responsible for actions we freely will.

The problem with this picture is its conception of causation. The idea of a "free will" is that of a cause that is neither random ("out of the blue") nor the outcome of a prior chain of causation. From a purely physicalist point of view this is impossible. Our actions are physical events. All physical events are the outcomes of prior (physical) causes, which are themselves the outcomes of prior (physical) causes, which are themselves the outcomes of prior (physical) causes, and so on ad infinitum. There is no such thing in the physical world as an uncaused cause, which is exactly what is presupposed by the idea of a free will.

Everything we do is, according to physicalism, determined by a complex chain of physical causation that ranges well beyond our control. Free will is, therefore, a myth or superstition, an outmoded legacy of a prescientific understanding of human beings.

This exposes a conflict internal to pragmatic physicalism. One part, commonsense psychology, presupposes that some of the things you and I and others do we do of our own free will and that we ought to be treated accordingly. The other part, neurobiology, presupposes both that everything we do is determined by causes over which we have no control and that we ought to be treated accordingly. How, then, can anyone accept pragmatic physicalism?

A Mediating Way of Thinking

If there were a contest for the best one-sentence definition of philosophy, it would be hard to beat Wilfrid Sellars's characterization of philosophy as an attempt to "understand how things in the broadest possible sense of the term hang together in the broadest possible sense of the term."[6] How do we hook up our understanding of the mind with our understanding of the brain? How does each of these hook up with ethics and law? What do we do when ethics conflicts with law? What do we do when liberty conflicts with equality? Justice with mercy? How do we reconcile our partiality to family, friends, and lovers with the impartial demands of basic human rights? How do our religious convictions square with the scientific picture of the world? How do freedom and responsibility "hang together" with neuroscientific explanations of human behavior? And, whatever the answers to these questions, how does each answer hook up with all the others?

Philosophers have generally adopted two strategies for answering these and similar questions. The first is to show that one of the polar positions is, when push comes to shove, right or real and the other wrong or illusory. In political philosophy, for example, libertarians argue that conflicts between liberty and equality ought always to be resolved in favor of the former, while radical egalitarians argue just the opposite. The second strategy is to show that the polar positions are, when properly analyzed or understood, actually compatible. Once we understand what liberty and equality "really mean," on this view, we will see they do not actually conflict. Both these strategies are employed in traditional responses to the free will question. Some people argue for free will and against determinism;

others argue for determinism and against free will. Still others argue that properly understood, free will and determinism are compatible, not conflicting. If, for example, 'freedom' means nothing but 'absence of *external* constraint' (such as not being tied up or in jail), an act's being free *in this sense* may be compatible with its being causally determined.

The aim of each strategy is to show that, appearances to the contrary, "things, in the broadest possible sense of the term, [really do] hang together, in the broadest possible sense of the term." If showing this requires either (1) denying the reality of either freedom or determinism or (2) radically redefining one or the other, it is, philosophers often assume, a small enough price to pay for an intellectually satisfying, coherent *picture* of the world (as Sellars's emphasis on "seeing" how things hang together may suggest).

This does not, however, sit well with the pragmatic temperament. Accounts of how things hang together must square with our vital *practices* as well as our perceptions—with what we *do* as well as with what we see. If either radically redefining freedom or determinism or denying the reality of one or the other does not square with unavoidable human practices, neither is acceptable. Pragmatism, as James once put it, is a "mediating way of thinking."[7] It seeks "what fits every part of life best and combines with the collectivity of experience's demands, nothing being omitted."[8] Applied to free will, this mediating way of thinking seeks accommodation with both freedom and determinism—even if they do not mesh or "hang together" as neatly as we would like. The *entire person* who, as James puts it, "feels all needs by turns"[9] is rightfully reluctant to make a once-and-for-all choice between freedom and responsibility, on the one hand, and causal determination, on the other. Nor, at this point at least, is there a way to fully integrate them. The vocabulary of freedom and responsibility and the vocabulary of causal determination both play important roles in our lives. To embrace one at the expense of the other is to endorse a simple (and simplistic) consistency at the expense of wholeness. Pragmatic mediation, in this instance, aims at striking a delicate balance between two perspectives, each of which captures part, but *only* part, of what is likely a more complex, if only partially understood, whole. If forced to choose between a practically incapacitating, but simple and intellectually satisfying extreme, on the one hand, and a practically empowering, but complex and intellectually disconcerting accommodation, on the other, the pragmatic temperament favors the latter.

Pragmatic Freedom

Among the pragmatic certainties that stand fast for us as we inquire into the nature of ourselves and our world is that many of the things we think and do are somehow "up to us." Living as if we were never free to choose one thing rather than another is not a genuine or live option. It is hard to imagine getting through a day, let alone *leading* a life, without thinking that it is sometimes up to ourselves and others whether to do one thing rather than another. Why else do we spend so much time deliberating about whether to go to college, take this job or that, get married, become a parent, buy a house, buy *this* house, and so on? That these and similar choices are up to us is part of the basic framework that stands fast as we seek a more impersonal understanding of the world. It's important to know about the world, reason well, understand others' points of view, and so on because we think we're more likely to choose, judge, and act correctly if we do. Even eliminative physicalists, while choosing which questions to investigate and how best to do so, cannot help believing that the choices they make are, in some reasonably robust sense, "up to them."

There is, however, an important difference between the pragmatic certainty that particular choices and decisions are up to us and the pragmatic certainties discussed in chapter 3. In many cases, hindsight may reveal that choices we thought were "up to us" were actually not. They were determined by factors outside our conscious control. The first time I saw my father play with our infant daughter, I was struck by the similarity between his way of playing with her and mine. "Where," I thought, "did he learn how to do that?" Then, of course, it dawned on me: the real question was, "Where did I learn how to play with an infant?" The answer, of course, is from my parents. What I had naively thought was fully attributable to my free will—my way of playing with a child—was, in large part, the result of (unconscious) memories that had been packed away in my mind (or brain) for nearly twenty-eight years.

Reductive physicalists seize upon this and related examples to argue that nothing we do is really "up to us." All our choices, they argue, are in reality determined by physical states and events outside our control. But this is too simple. My story is not over. After I learned that my "choice" of how to play with my daughter was not as free as I had thought, I had another decision to make. Should I continue playing with her like this or not? There were certain respects in which I wanted to be different from my father. Should this be among them? At the time I could not help believing the decision was "up to me." For learning of the causal antecedents of certain patterns of behavior often generates a new opportunity for choice.

In a remarkable book on autism, Temple Grandin, a professor of animal science who has designed one-third of all the livestock-handling facilities in the United States and who is herself autistic, talks about how an understanding of her own brain chemistry has expanded her freedom. After a hysterectomy she lost her feelings of empathy and gentleness and was "turning into a cranky computer." So she started taking low doses of estrogen supplements. This worked for a while, but after a year she began having a number of nerve and colitis attacks that, she determined, were probably due to too high a dose of estrogen. So, she tells us, she reduced the dosage:

> Now I fine-tune my estrogen intake like a diabetic adjusting insulin doses. I take just enough so I can have gentle feelings of empathy but not enough to drive my nervous system into hypersensitivity and anxiety attacks. I think the reason my panic attacks started at puberty was that estrogen sensitized my nervous system. . . . Now that I am closely regulating my estrogen intake, the nerve cycles are gone. . . .
>
> Manipulating my biochemistry has not made me a completely different person, but it has been somewhat unsettling to my idea of who and what I am to be able to adjust my emotions as if I were tuning up a car. However, I'm deeply grateful that there is an available solution and that I discovered better living through chemistry before my overactive nervous system destroyed me. . . . I am one of those people who are born with a nervous system that operates in a perpetual state of fear and anxiety. Most people do not get into this state unless they go through extremely severe trauma, such as child abuse, an airplane crash, or wartime stress. I used to think it was normal to feel nervous all the time, and it was a revelation to find out that most people do not have constant anxiety attacks.[10]

In learning of the causal determinants of various types of disconcerting feelings and behavior, Temple Grandin was confronted with a new choice: whether, with the aid of medical science, to alter them.

That her having this capacity may itself be causally determined does not, in itself, undermine her responsibility in exercising it. Whether or not we have a capacity for reflective choice may depend largely on factors beyond our control; for example, on our not being born severely mentally disabled, not incurring a brain-damaging head injury, not being severely neglected or abused as children, and not becoming severely mentally ill. We are not responsible for acquiring the capacity for reflective choice, but if we are lucky enough to have it, we may then be held (and hold ourselves) responsible for the way we exercise (or squander) it.

Søren Kierkegaard, in a passage paraphrased by James, writes, "It is perfectly true, as philosophers say, that life must be understood backwards. But they forget the other proposition, that it must be lived forwards."[11] The point, in the present context, is this. Looking backward, the impersonal or scientific perspective is useful for understanding the causal determinants of our own and other people's past behavior. We are then, however, presented from the personal or pragmatic perspective with a new, forward-looking choice. "What do we *make* of what we have learned? What should we *do* in the light of our newly acquired causal understanding?" These are open, forward-looking questions that cannot be conclusively answered by backward-looking considerations. "What would it be like," we ask, "if we were to do this?" "What would be the consequences of doing that?" We have, at least at this point, no reasonable alternative but to think of the choice as up to us, even if we also believe there is a sense in which (to be confirmed later by backward-looking considerations) it is not. This unsettling juxtaposition of the personal and impersonal perspectives is, to those whose philosophizing seeks "what fits every part of life best and combines with the collectivity of experience's demands, nothing being omitted," a formidable barrier to a clear, consistent resolution to the free will problem. There is currently no such resolution.

Limits to Understanding

There are two possible explanations for this. One is that our present concepts and theories are simply not up to providing a clear and complete, intellectually and pragmatically satisfying account of the relationships between mind and brain, freedom and determinism. It's not simply that the empirical factors are too many or the mathematics too complex. No, the questions are, *in their present terms,* unanswerable. What we need is a conceptual and theoretical revolution similar to, but larger and more radical than, the Copernican Revolution in astronomy and the Darwinian Revolution in biology. A radically new way of conceptualizing mind and brain, freedom and determinism, may result in a seamless integration of theory and practice. Until then, however, we must simply acknowledge the tensions and incongruities of our current conceptions of mind and brain, freedom and determinism, and do the best we can at fitting them together.

A second possibility is, perhaps, more pessimistic. Our inabilities to fully understand how mind and body, freedom and determinism "hang together" may be due to a built-in limitation of the human mind. Maybe, writes Steven Pinker, the mind of *Homo sapiens* "lacks the cognitive equipment to solve" this and related problems.

> We are organisms, not angels, and our minds are organs, not pipelines to the truth. Our minds evolved by natural selection to solve problems that were life-and-death matters to our ancestors, not to commune with correctness or to answer any question we are capable of asking. We cannot hold ten thousand words in short-term memory. We cannot see ultraviolet light. We cannot mentally rotate an object in the fourth dimension. And perhaps we cannot solve conundrums like free will and sentience.

Just as you and I can easily solve problems that are impossible for people who are severely brain-damaged or suffering from certain mental disorders, there may be, Pinker adds, "creatures with *more* cognitive faculties than we have, or with *different* ones. They might readily grasp how free will and consciousness emerge from a brain. . . . They could try to explain the solutions to us, but we would not understand the explanations."[12]

Whether we await the revolutionary insights of a new Copernicus or Darwin or whether the complex relationships between freedom and determinism are beyond human understanding, we ought to own up to our present limitations. We do not fully understand how mind and brain, freedom and determinism, fit together. It's better to admit this than to amputate one or another limb of this complex reality so as to fit it into an undersized Procrustean bed. (In classical mythology Procrustes was a robber who amputated the limbs of travelers too big to fit the length of his bed.) On the bright side, however, is the fact that the tension between our current understandings of freedom and determinism is dynamically creative.

A Creative Tension

There are, for example, many more questions in neuroscience than can be investigated by finite beings like ourselves. Choices must be made about where to focus our limited time, energy, and resources and where not. How can we make such decisions except by determining which possible results would be more useful or best serve our most important values and purposes? The impersonal vocabulary of empirical science can neither answer these questions nor even formulate them. Neuroscientists looking for research projects and panels allocating the funds for them cannot make and justify their decisions without employing a vocabulary that presupposes freedom and responsibility. Thus the vocabulary of freedom and responsibility exercises some influence on what has come to be known as the truths of (deterministic) science.

On the other hand, the results of neuroscience sometimes restrict and sometimes expand the scope of freedom and responsibility. The development of language games involving such terms as 'kleptomania', 'compulsion', 'addiction', 'brain lesion', 'serotonin re-uptake inhibitors', and so on has induced us to retract attributions of freedom and responsibility in some contexts. In other contexts, to learn more about the causal determinants of some kinds of undesirable behavior is to acquire new powers and a correspondingly new responsibility to prevent such behavior in the future. When, for example, we learn that a student's inattentiveness in school is the result not of his or her choice, but rather of the effects on the brain of beatings, malnutrition, or lead poisoning, the vocabulary of responsibility is extended to an area where it had previously had no footing. Who is morally or legally responsible, we now ask, for the student's being beaten, malnourished, or poisoned by lead? How can we prevent this from happening to other children?

Thus the two kinds of vocabulary creatively play off each other in mutually enriching ways. We use the vocabulary of freedom and responsibility to decide which of many possible directions we should follow in expanding scientific understanding. We use the vocabulary of scientific understanding to refine and expand the reach of the vocabulary of freedom and responsibility. Judicious tacking between the two vocabularies (chapter 1, pp. 23–24) optimizes reflective self-direction and contributes to meaningful survival.

Hard Choices

Still, there are situations in which the two kinds of vocabularies both seem applicable, yet they require opposing courses of action. Too often these days we come across articles about thirteen- and fourteen-year-olds charged with murder. (Two days after first writing these words, I read of an eight-year-old girl charged with attempting to murder her great-grandmother. Two months after writing them, I read of a five-year-old who brought a handgun to school to kill another student.) How should we respond? Is the vocabulary of freedom and responsibility rightly applied to a thirteen- or fourteen-year-old in such cases? Or do we describe and explain what he or she has done in the vocabulary of causal determination alone? Questions like these arise whenever, in a court of law, the prosecution's case, expressed in terms of the vocabulary of freedom and responsibility, is met by a defense couched in terms of causal determination. Though less momentous, they also arise in normal child-raising, as parents have to decide at what point to begin holding a developing youngster responsible for what he or she has done, and in personal relationships, as we have to decide whether to blame a coworker for poor performance or excuse him or her because he or she has just been diagnosed with depression.

One thing we can't do in such circumstances is to peek behind what we might call the "veil of words" to *see* which of the two vocabularies— freedom and determinism—actually corresponds to bare, nonlinguistic reality. As argued in chapter 2, there is no way to do this, no way to apprehend the "facts" or "reality" directly and nonlinguistically and then compare them with what we say. Rather we must ask ourselves such questions as: Which vocabulary would, *in this situation*, be a better overall fit with other things we know, do, and say? Which language game, if employed, would be likely to lead to the best overall, long-term consequences? Is it better, all things considered (including everything we know about psychology and neuroscience, this particular fourteen-year-old, and the circumstances in which he or she acted), to say he or she could have done otherwise and is therefore morally and legally responsible for the death? Or is it (on the same sorts of considerations) better to say that because of past beatings or undeveloped impulse control, he or she could not have done otherwise and is therefore not morally and legally responsible for the death? Since questions like this arise in a large variety of contexts with many complex variations, there is no "one size fits all" answer to them. Instead of a single, abstract, theoretical free will problem to be solved in one fell swoop, we are faced with a large number of concrete free will problems—problems requiring complex, context-dependent, ambivalent choice between the vocabularies of freedom and determinism. We make such choices in the light of past experience and are prepared to revise or replace them in the light of future experience.

In concrete cases, conflicts that appear sharp in the abstract may often, on inspection, be softened. In one particular case, for example, careful review of the evidence together with consideration of possible consequences may favor the vocabulary of freedom and responsibility. In another, it will favor the vocabulary of determinism. In yet another, the alternatives will seem perfectly, and maddeningly, balanced. The point is that careful examination of the context-dependent complexities of concrete cases—for example, Gitta Sereny's *Cries Unheard*, an exhaustively researched, highly nuanced account of eleven-year-old Mary Bell's murder of two small boys in Newcastle upon Tyne, England, in 1968—will go farther in answering our practical questions than the abstract theories of armchair philosophers.[13]

CONCLUSION

The mind–body and free will problems are among the most vexing in philosophy. I have no simple solution to them. On the contrary, I have suggested that in their present forms they are not fully resolvable. My aim, therefore, has been to outline a pragmatic approach to them—one that's true to their and to our complexity, and to the *demands of practice*. Philosophical questions, as James points out in the quotation at the beginning of the chapter, are raised by the *whole person*—the embodied social agent faced with a variety of hard choices in a complex, occasionally hostile environment who, at the same time, has the capacity to approximate a more detached or scientific understanding of self and others. Answers to philosophical questions must satisfy, insofar as possible, the demands of both perspectives. What James calls the "absurd abstraction" of an intellect formulating a purely scientific answer to a complex philosophical question is "as inept as it is impossible."[14] The result is often a scientistic doctrine like eliminative physicalism or determinism. Such doctrines may be defended by the spectator in us, but they do not, by themselves, answer to the demands of the agent. They are therefore unsatisfactory. An adequate solution to the mind–body and free will problems must speak to the whole person—agent as well as spectator.

Let us then acknowledge that there are no perfect or flawless answers to the mind–body and free will questions. Someday, perhaps, radical conceptual or theoretical revolution will either eliminate the questions or provide seamless solutions. In the meantime, however, we've got to cobble together and make do with the best answers we can find—answers that straddle the divide between the practical demands of agency and the theoretical demands of the intellect. Pragmatic physicalism together with context-specific mediation between freedom and determinism, I hope to have shown, satisfies these twin, and occasionally competing, demands better than any available alternative.

NOTES

1. Paul Churchland, *Matter and Consciousness*, 2d ed. (Cambridge, Mass.: MIT Press, 1988), 43.

2. Steven Pinker, *How the Mind Works* (New York: Norton, 1997), 148.

3. Avrum Stroll, *Moore and Wittgenstein on Certainty* (New York: Oxford University Press, 1994), 175.

4. P. F. Strawson, *Skepticism and Naturalism: Some Varieties* (New York: Columbia University Press, 1985), 56.

5. Patricia Churchland, *Neurophilosophy* (Cambridge: MIT Press, 1986), 249.

6. Wilfrid Sellars, "Philosophy and the Scientific Image of Man," in *Science Perception and Reality* (London: Routledge & Kegan Paul, 1963), 1.

7. William James, *Pragmatism*, in *William James: Writings 1902–1910*, ed. Bruce Kuklick (New York: Library of America, 1987), 504.

8. James, *Pragmatism*, 522.

9. James, "The Sentiment of Rationality," in *William James: Writings 1878–1899*, ed. Gerald E. Myers (New York: Library of America, 1992), 508.

10. Temple Grandin, *Thinking in Pictures* (New York: Vintage, 1995), 117–18.

11. Søren Kierkegaard, *The Journals of Søren Kierkegaard*, ed. and trans. Alexander Dru (London: Oxford University Press, 1938), 127. Paraphrased by James in *Pragmatism*, 584.

12. Pinker, *How the Mind Works*, 561, 562.

13. Gitta Sereny, *Cries Unheard: Why Children Kill; The Story of Mary Bell* (New York: Henry Holt, 1998).

14. James, "Sentiment of Rationality," 525.

Chapter 5

Ethics

Doubtless the greatest dissolvent in contemporary thought of old questions, the greatest precipitant of new methods, new intentions, new problems, is the one effected by the scientific revolution that found its climax in *Origin of Species*.

—John Dewey, "The Influence of Darwinism on Philosophy"

[T]here is no such thing possible as an ethical philosophy dogmatically made up in advance. . . . In other words, there can be no final truth in ethics any more than in physics, until the last man has had his experience and said his say.

—William James, "The Moral Philosopher and the Moral Life"

The problem of restoring integration and cooperation between man's beliefs about the world in which he lives and his beliefs about the values and purposes that should direct his conduct is the deepest problem of modern life. It is the problem of any philosophy that is not isolated from that life.

—John Dewey, *The Quest for Certainty*

In the dramatic opening scene of Ian McEwan's novel *Enduring Love*, five men race from different directions to the center of a large field where the pilot of a hot air balloon is struggling to keep it from being swept away by strong winds. The pilot—a fifty-five-year-old advertising executive— is incompetent and exhausted. In the balloon's basket is his frightened, incapacitated ten-year-old grandson. Grabbing various ropes, the five would-be rescuers (only two of whom know each other) are initially able to restrain the balloon. Then a couple of strong wind gusts lift the balloon into the air toward a steep escarpment. The men hold on to the ropes, though they too are aloft, their feet treading the air. If one of them were to lose his grip as the balloon rises over the escarpment, his fall could be fatal. If he were to let go now, he would suffer only bumps and bruises. The loss of one-fifth of the balloon's human ballast would, however, reduce the likelihood of success and increase the risk to those who remain. If one lets go, the others will rise higher and have to hang on longer; if two let go, the remaining three will rise even higher and have to hang on even longer. There is no time for reflective thought or discussion. Each man's conduct depends on the balance of two deeply embedded and, in this instance, conflicting instincts.

On the one hand, each of the rescuers is motivated by a wish to aid and cooperate with others. Why else would he have dropped what he was doing to dash across the field and join in the impromptu rescue effort? There was, one of the five (the novel's narrator) later writes, a deep "covenant, ancient and automatic, written in our nature. Cooperation— the basis of our earliest hunting successes, the force behind our evolving capacity for language, the glue of our social adhesion." The dictates of this instinct were to hang on for the sake of the boy and the other rescuers. On the other hand, the narrator adds, "[L]etting go was in our nature too. Selfishness is also written on our hearts. This is our mammalian conflict: what to give to the others and what to keep for yourself. Treading that line, keeping the others in check and being kept in check by them, is what we call morality. Hanging a few feet above the Chilterns escarpment, our crew enacted morality's ancient, irresolvable dilemma: us, or me."[1]

Each instinct—aiding and cooperating with others to benefit the group ("us") and looking out for oneself ("me")—is, as the narrator puts it, "written on our hearts." But how did these instincts come to be written there? And on what basis do we, in less pressing circumstances, reflectively decide between them?

In this chapter I address these and related questions. First, what is the origin of ethics? How did human beings acquire an inclination to aid and cooperate with others, in some cases at serious cost or risk to themselves? Are such inclinations a gift from God? A dictate of reason? Or are they, perhaps, the outcome of millions of years of evolution by natural selection? Second, how do we resolve conflicts between "us" and "me" and various other ethical choices? Are there fixed, objective standards— for example, God's commands—for distinguishing right from wrong, good from bad? Are ethical standards based on little more than varying subjective considerations such as personal preference or social convention? Or is there a third possibility—one that mediates between the two extremes? If ethical standards are neither prior to and independent of human thought nor merely a reflection of personal or social preference, exactly what is their nature and justification?

ORIGINS

Rational Fools

Before Darwin, most philosophers distinguished sharply between mind and body, reason and emotion, human and animal. The distinctions were related: humans, in virtue of their minds (or souls) and capacity for reason, were thought to differ in kind, not degree, from nonhuman animals, whose bodily behavior was thought to be mechanical or driven by feeling or emotion. Variations of this gulf between human and animal nature figure prominently in Plato, Descartes, and Kant and those who accept their respective starting points. Ethics, on this view, is restricted to humans and based entirely on mind or reason.

This sharp split between mind and body, reason and emotion, and human and animal is no longer tenable. Recent work in neurobiology, for example, suggests the emotions are essential to good moral decision making. In 1848 an explosion accidentally drove a pointed steel rod into the left cheek of construction foreman Phineas Gage. Three feet, seven inches long and weighing more than thirteen pounds, the rod pierced the base of Gage's skull, passed through the front of his brain, and exited the top of his head at high speed. Astonishingly, Gage could talk and walk immediately after the accident, and his doctors pronounced him physically cured in less than two months. There was, however, a marked change in his character. Though his linguistic, perceptual, and abstract reasoning capacities were fully intact, he had lost the capacity to make personal or social *decisions*. Before the accident, Phineas Gage had a strong sense of personal and social responsibility and was highly regarded by his bosses and fellow workers. After the accident, he could no longer observe social conventions or ethical rules. He was inappropriately profane, disrespectful, impatient, obstinate, capricious, and indecisive. He could no longer make good choices. "So radical was the change in him," writes neurologist Antonio Damasio, "that friends and acquaintances could hardly recognize him. They noted sadly that 'Gage was no longer Gage'."[2] The cause of the change was damage from the rod. The most reasonable explanation is that some part of the brain unrelated to language, perception, and impersonal rationality is necessary for personal, social, and ethical decision making.

Damasio has seen a number of patients whose incapacities closely resemble those of Phineas Gage. A man he calls "Elliott" was at one time a responsible husband and father and a highly effective corporate lawyer. Then he was diagnosed with a large, fast-growing brain tumor just behind the forehead. Surgery was performed and the (nonmalignant) tumor successfully removed. "As is usual in such cases," Damasio writes, "frontal lobe tissue that had been damaged by the tumor had to be removed too" (p. 36).

The operation was regarded a complete success. Elliott's linguistic, reasoning, and motor skills were unimpaired. Still, his life soon fell apart. He could no longer hold a job; he made several inexplicably poor business decisions; his wife left him; he married and divorced another woman against the advice of family and friends; and he ended up living in a spare bedroom in his brother's home. Damasio and his colleagues administered a number of intelligence tests (including tests of *general* moral reasoning) to Elliott, which he passed with flying colors. At first, Damasio was puzzled. Elliott was quite rational and nothing appeared wrong with his emotions. "On a more probing analysis, however," Damasio adds, "something was missing, and I had overlooked much of the prime evidence for this: Elliott was able to recount the tragedy of his life with a detachment that was out of step with the magnitude of the events. He was always controlled, always describing the scenes as a *dispassionate, uninvolved spectator*. Nowhere was there a sense of his own suffering, even though he was the protagonist" (p. 44, italics added). Elliott's emotional detachment, what Damasio characterizes as the "cold-bloodedness" of his reasoning, greatly impaired his personal decision making. His poor judgment and pathological indecision were due to an incapacity to assign different values to different options. He could no longer identify emotionally with any course of action because the surgery had inadvertently damaged the connection between the part of the brain connected with emotion and the part connected with rational thought. In Elliott and other patients whose brain damage is similar to that of Phineas Gage, Damasio concludes, "Some part of the value system remains and can be utilized in abstract terms, but it is unconnected to real-life situations" (p. 11).

The cases of Phineas Gage, Elliott, and others like them show that ethical thought and decision making cannot be separated from (embodied) feeling and emotion. Individuals who lose their capacity to integrate reason and emotion are, to adapt a term coined by Amartya Sen, "rational fools."[3] We cannot, in thinking about ethics, draw a sharp line between reason and emotion.

Underlying the philosophical split between mind and body, reason and emotion, and human and animal is the idea of a Cartesian subject of thought and reflection. Humans are identified with intellect and ethics with impersonal reason. This is, however, as the cases of Phineas Gage and Elliott suggest, mistaken. Once we reject a broadly rationalistic or Cartesian conception of ethical reflection—a disembodied, spectator conception—we can acknowledge our continuity, as embodied social agents, with other kinds of animal life. This, in turn, leads to a new and more promising understanding of the origins of ethics and the sources of moral motivation: evolutionary biology.

Moral Animals

Recall the narrator's exact words as he describes the dilemma of the would-be rescuers as they hang on to the ropes of the rising balloon: "This is our *mammalian* conflict: what to give to the others and what to keep for yourself" (italics added). Did you pause over the word 'mammalian' when you first read the passage? What, exactly, does the narrator mean when, in the next sentence, he says, "Treading that line, keeping the others in check and being kept in check by them, is what we call morality"? The book gives us a clue when we learn the narrator earns his living by writing about science for the general reader. He is, in this capacity, familiar with recent work on the biological origins of ethics. I can, in what follows, provide only a brief sketch of this work. Readers interested in this fascinating subject will find a number of sources in the accompanying bibliographical essay.

As animals, human beings have evolved over the course of millions of years through a process involving random mutation, heritability, and natural selection. Until fairly recently, however, social behavior remained a puzzle. Why, if nature selects for survival, do some organisms come to the aid of others, occasionally at considerable risk or cost to themselves? Shouldn't an instinct to risk oneself for others be a ticket to extinction?

The answer lies, in part, in looking at natural selection from the "standpoint" of the gene. Of course, genes aren't sentient and don't literally have standpoints. If, however, we conceive the gene as what is selected for by nature and the larger organism as a "vehicle" for nurturing and reproducing genes, we can construct a fairly plausible explanation of self-sacrificial behavior among biological organisms. From the standpoint of the gene, it doesn't matter whether its survival is mediated by one particular organism or another. What counts is survival of the largest number of copies of that type of gene.

Take the case of a young ground squirrel that, upon sighting a predator, emits a loud alarm. This act, while enabling other ground squirrels to escape, increases the likelihood of the noisy ground squirrel's death. Why then haven't such "altruistic" ground squirrels become extinct? The answer is that this ground squirrel is likely to have some close relatives who are alerted by the warning. Half of its siblings, for example, are likely to share the gene for sounding an alarm in the presence of predators. "If," as Robert Wright explains,

> the warning saves the lives of four full siblings that would otherwise die, two of which carry the gene responsible for it, then the gene has done well for itself, even if the sentry containing it pays the ultimate sacrifice. This superficially selfless gene will do much better over the ages than a superficially selfish gene that induced its carrier to scurry to safety while four siblings—and two copies of the gene, on average—perished. The same is true if the gene saves only one full sibling, while giving the sentry a one-in-four chance of dying. Over the long run, there will be two genes saved for every gene lost.[4]

This is what has come to be known as *kin selection*. If by random mutation an organism acquires a gene that causes the organism to take risks or to sacrifice itself for the sake of other organisms containing a copy of the same gene (its kin), then *the gene may proliferate*, even though the outcome for some individual organisms carrying that gene may be death.

Kin selection operates among species lower and higher than squirrels. We find it in colonies of ants, termites, and bees; and we find it in humans. Anyone who says individual human beings are basically selfish, caring about no one but themselves, is forgetting the vulnerability of the human infant and the extent to which the vast majority of parents sacrifice their own immediate interests for those of their children. Nearly all parents have an instinctive, self-sacrificing regard for the welfare of their children. The children of those of our most distant ancestors lacking genes for this trait were unlikely to survive infancy. Infants that did survive were likely to possess the genes for this instinct and to pass copies of it to their children, and so on. Similar, though successively weaker, bonds exist among siblings, first cousins, second cousins, and so on.

As animals, then, you and I have evolved from repeated cycles of random mutation and natural selection. Had our distant human ancestors not acquired genes inclining them to sacrifice their own short-run interests to feed, shelter, clothe, defend, guide, and educate their children, they would probably have had no descendants. In fact, they did make such sacrifices, and the resulting proliferation of genes inclining parents to sacrifice for their children led, over thousands of generations, to the birth of your parents and mine. Had our parents not been inclined, for reasons of culture as well as biology, to sacrifice their own short-run interests to feed, shelter, clothe, defend, guide, and educate us, we would not be here. Since we share our parents' genes and have been socialized by them, the vast majority of us are inclined to do the same for children of our own. Nature selects for genes whose "vehicles" are inclined to sacrifice for their close kin.

There is, however, more to the story than this. The five men who come to the aid of the hapless balloonist and his grandson are not related to them. Indeed, they've never even seen them before. Why are they inclined, at some cost and risk to themselves, to come to the rescue of total strangers? Why does the narrator characterize what motivates them as a "covenant, ancient and automatic, written in our nature"? The answer is found in another feature of evolutionary biology: *reciprocal altruism.*[5]

As organisms became more complex, a selective advantage accrued to the genes of individuals that, regardless of blood-relatedness, aided each other in time of need. Vampire bats, for example, go out each night in search of blood from sleeping horses or cows. This sort of bloodsucking is, however, a chancy business. Some nights a bat gets plenty to drink; other nights it gets nothing. A bat who goes more than sixty hours without blood is in danger of starving to death. But bats who luck out and get more blood than they can use generally return to the nest and regurgitate some of it into the mouths of bats who come home empty, regardless of whether they are kin. Bats who pair up for this purpose—who at the end of a given night share their good fortune—are more likely to survive and pass on their genes than those who do not. Genes that contribute to this "You feed me, I'll feed you" pattern of behavior thus have a distinct advantage with respect to survival. Vampire bats who share food are more likely to survive and pass on their genes (and the behavior they *gene*rate) than those who do not.

Suppose a bat gladly accepted food from others when it needed it, but refused to share when it did not. Shouldn't it do even better? As soon as it drinks enough for itself, this egoistic bat could return to the nest for additional rest and safety. On nights it finds no food it would return to the nest and obtain it from bats ("suckers" in two senses of the word) whose luck has been better. If this were to happen, the genes of egoistic bats would eventually predominate, even if it were to threaten the survival of the species. Apparently this does not happen. Vampire bats tend to nest in the same places and have long lives. They also have relatively large brains that enable them to identify and get to know each other as individuals. This, in turn, lets them pair up and monitor their behavior. Pairs of vampire bats groom each other, especially around the stomach, permitting them to detect the distended belly that is the sign of a good meal. Nonreciprocators, egoists, are therefore identifiable. Bats that donate blood will receive it when they need it; bats that do not donate blood will in turn be refused.

The food-sharing of vampire bats is said to be *altruistic* because it involves doing something for others at some cost to oneself, even if reasonably small. It's *reciprocal* because bats share food only with those who share food in return. The conditions for reciprocal altruism include a shared environment, stable relationships, some sense of time, and a good memory for keeping track of who has done what for whom. This last is necessary for detecting cheaters—individuals who take without giving. Altruists unable to distinguish reciprocators from cheaters are likely to do less well, in terms of survival, than those whose aid is more conditional. Among bats, vampires have the largest neocortex, which, presumably, generates the mental capacity to identify individuals and remember what they've done. Given the cognitive requirements of reciprocal altruism, it's not surprising that it's found mainly in higher mammals, especially primates.

When McEwan's narrator refers to cooperation in terms of a "covenant, ancient and automatic, written in our nature," he seems to be referring to reciprocal altruism. In self-conscious, self-determining, language-using animals like you and me, this biologically based instinct is strongly reinforced and extended by culture. It also generates a certain ambivalence. Though we want to help others, we know that doing too much for them, especially for nonreciprocators, may come at a very high cost to ourselves. Though we are inclined to favor ourselves, we know that doing too little for others, especially for discriminating reciprocators, may also come at a very high cost to ourselves. "This," the narrator adds, "is our mammalian conflict: what to give to the others and what to keep for yourself. Treading that line, keeping the others in check and being kept in check by them, is what we call morality." Human beings are, as the title of Robert Wright's book puts it, "moral animals."

Among primates, reciprocal altruism is most highly developed in humans, where it is often reinforced and extended by culture. In Tolstoy's *The Death of Ivan Ilych*, the dying Ivan Ilych takes great comfort from his servant Gerasim, who assumes the role of sick nurse. Unlike Ivan Ilych's family, friends, and physicians, Gerasim can acknowledge that his master is dying and try to comfort him. Ivan Ilych seems to feel better when Gerasim holds up his legs. Sometimes Gerasim would stay up all night with Ivan Ilych's legs on his shoulders. "Don't you worry, Ivan Ilych," he would say. "I'll get sleep enough later on." Or, "If you weren't sick it would be another matter, but as it is, why should I grudge a little trouble." Gerasim, Tolstoy writes, feels sorry for his "emaciated and enfeebled master."[6] "Once when Ivan Ilych was sending him away he even said straight out: 'We shall all of us die, so why should I grudge a little trouble?'—expressing the fact that he did not think his work burdensome, because he was doing it for a dying man and hoped someone would do the same thing for him when his time came" (p. 138). Though Gerasim does not expect the dying Ivan Ilych to reciprocate his kindness, he lives in a culture in which he can reasonably hope some third person will do the same for him when he is dying, and this third person can reasonably hope some fourth person will later do the same for him or her, and so on. Here teaching and culture supplement instinct and biology, extending the power and reach of reciprocal altruism among human beings. No longer is it restricted to particular times and individuals. Incorporated into a culture, reciprocal altruism directs each of us to aid others in need or in danger, provided we can do so without excessive risk or loss to ourselves. This, I think, partly explains the sacrifice and generosity witnessed in the United States in response to the attacks on the World Trade Center and the Pentagon on September 11, 2001.

There is a difference, however, between what motivates people to aid others, on the one hand, and what causally explains and philosophically justifies their being so motivated, on the other. In holding up Ivan Ilych's legs, Gerasim is motivated by his feeling sorry for the dying man. Seeing Ivan's suffering makes Gerasim want to help him. He doesn't calculate that it is in his interest to do so. That an evolutionary explanation of his motive turns on its having served the "interests" of his ancestor's genes, and that it may later serve his own interests if it reinforces a cultural norm of aiding and keeping company with the dying, is not Gerasim's principal motivation for doing what he does. Gerasim himself knew nothing about genes. So even if genes and natural selection are part of the causal story of how we come to have our motives, it doesn't follow that they are our motives. Nor may Gerasim be explicitly aware of the fact that it is in everyone's interest to live in a society in which people help others in need if they can do so at little risk or loss to themselves. Gerasim, the person, is *moved* to help Ivan mainly because he empathizes with him and wants to help. That both the full explanation of how he came to have this motivation and the justification for his retaining it refer in part to forms of self-interest does not mean that Gerasim is himself directly motivated by self-interest.

The five men who race to the aid of the balloonist and his grandson may never ride in a hot air balloon nor would they expect to be aided by either the balloonist or his grandson if, for example, any one of them were to take a nasty spill while riding a bicycle. Nor, in their split-second responses to the balloonist's shout for help, are they calculating that coming to his aid is in their long-run interest. There is no time for that. As the narrator, who was picnicking with his wife and preparing to open a bottle of wine when he heard the shout, put it: "We turned to look across the field and saw the danger. Next thing, I was running toward it. The transformation was absolute: I don't recall dropping the corkscrew, or getting to my feet, or making a decision, or hearing the caution Clarissa called after me."[7] The rescuers do, however, live in a culture where they can reasonably hope that someone—a perfect stranger—would come to their aid if they could do so at little risk or loss to themselves. Whether they know it or not, the benefits of this aspect of their culture greatly outweigh its occasional burdens.

This, however, raises two difficult questions. First, what counts as "excessive risk or loss to ourselves"? In coming to the rescue of the endangered balloon, there is no doubt in the minds of the would-be rescuers that they ought to interrupt what they are doing (working in a field, enjoying a picnic, hiking) to help hold the balloon down. Whether they are also obliged to risk their lives by hanging on to the balloon as the wind lifts it in the direction of the escarpment is, however, a debatable question (though under the circumstances the rescuers had no time for reflection). Second, how large is the class of those we ought to aid? The narrator talks of a conflict between "us" and "me." I interpret 'us' here as referring to one or more social groups of which the individual designated by 'me' is a member. Morality is also, however, characterized by conflicts between "us" and "them," where 'us' may refer to members of our own family, tribe, religion, culture, nation, and so on, and 'them' to those outside our family, tribe, religion, culture, nation, and so on. Is there a sense of "us" that includes all human beings, regardless of religious, cultural, or national identity? Could it also include members of distant future generations with whom we cannot enter reciprocal relationships? Is there a sense of "us" that includes, as well, all sentient beings—all beings capable of pain or sensation—regardless of species membership? Do we, for example, have a duty to remove a painful thorn from the paw of a harmless animal if we can do so at little risk or loss to ourselves? Is this animal one of "us"? Do we have a duty to withhold support from practices such as "factory farming" that cause significant pain to animals if we can do so at little risk or cost to ourselves?

The foregoing questions and others like them cannot be answered by evolutionary biology. They are philosophical questions to be answered by ethical reflection. Such reflection is likely to have emerged as our ancestors acquired the time and capacity to discuss and debate choices between "us" and "me" and various other conflicts of value. From kin selection to reciprocal altruism to reflective moral consciousness, ethics is, however, grounded firmly in our identities as moral animals—embodied social agents.

Insofar as we are (biologically) *embodied*, the legacy of kin selection and reciprocal altruism is, as a result of natural selection, wired into nearly all human brains. Insofar as we are *social*, the biological basis of morality has been supplemented and reinforced by culture. Our parents and our society explicitly teach us to sacrifice for our children and to help others when they are in need or jeopardy if we can do so without excessive risk or loss to ourselves. Insofar as we are (reflective) *agents* we cannot help asking, in certain contexts, the central question of philosophical ethics: "What, *all things considered*, should I do—*and why*?" Should I risk my life (and my children's having a father) to help the hapless balloonist's grandson? Should I buy my children "designer" bicycles or should I buy them less expensive bicycles and donate the difference to famine relief? Appeals to kin selection or reciprocal altruism cannot, alone, answer these and related questions. They are a matter of *normative* ethical reasoning, which is the topic of the following section. Before turning to it, however, I want to identify two important implications of an evolutionary account of the origins of ethics.

First, the subject of ethical thought and deliberation cannot be conceived in Cartesian terms. Ethics, as shown by the cases of Phineas Gage and Elliott, involves body as well as mind, emotion as well as reason, heart as well as head. A purely rational morality would, in practice, be a morality for fools. Yet there is no need to postulate a purely rational, immaterial subject of moral consciousness. Recent work in evolutionary biology shows how—from kin selection to reciprocal altruism to Socrates to you and me—morality is perfectly consistent with pragmatic physicalism and a pragmatic conception of the subject of ethical reflection.

Second, skepticism about ethics—whether there are good reasons for taking moral questions seriously—is not a genuine option for most of us. At least since Plato, philosophers have spent too much time on this sort of skepticism. Ethical skepticism asks, from a standpoint outside morality, whether there are good reasons for getting inside it—for concerning ourselves about what's morally right or wrong, good or bad. Once, however, we reject the mythical (and incoherent) idea of a Cartesian subject of philosophical reflection, moral skepticism is revealed as another philosophical parlor game. There is no such external standpoint for actual, embodied social agents like you and me. The biological legacy of kin selection and reciprocal altruism and the social legacy of our upbringings are part and parcel of who we are. Morality is not something those of us who are not psychopaths or otherwise seriously mentally disabled can really get outside of. It is, as Mary Midgley puts it, "like the air we breathe."

> Getting right outside morality would be rather like getting outside the atmosphere. It would mean losing the basic social network within which we live and communicate with others, including all those others in the past who have formed our culture. If we can imagine this deprived state at all, it would be a solitary condition close to that of autism or extreme depression—a state where, although intelligence can still function, there is no sense of community with others, no shared wishes, principles, aspirations or ideals, no mutual trust or fellowship with those outside, no preferred set of concepts, nothing agreed on as important.[8]

There's no way to get entirely outside of morality except by death or psychopathology.

Perhaps what people conceive as skepticism about morality *as such* is really skepticism about particular moral values or principles (or particular conceptions of morality). This, however, is a very different matter. It is raised from within, rather than outside, the moral point of view. Certain moral requirements or principles are subjected to doubt, on the basis of other, presumably more justifiable, moral requirements or principles. We may, for example, come to question traditional views about a doctor's duty to preserve and prolong life in the light of new circumstances and principles requiring respect for patient autonomy and reducing pain and suffering. The question, then, is not whether we ought to take morality seriously, but whether we ought to take *this* or *that* moral value or principle seriously. Skepticism about one moral requirement is based, in part, on commitment to others.

MORAL REASONING AND REFLECTION

The Ship of Morality

We do not choose our moral starting points. On the contrary, our initial understanding of right and wrong, good and bad, is dealt to us, much like a hand in a card game, by a combination of biology and socialization. From biology we acquire instincts for self-preservation, concern for kin, and reciprocal altruism. From our parents and our culture, we acquire a set of tacit attitudes (we come to love those who show love for us) and explicit "do's and don'ts" ("Help your brother." "Share your toys." Don't tease the cat."). With time we acquire the capacity to reflect critically on the moral outlook we've been dealt by our common biology and our particular upbringings and culture. As with Neurath's "ship of knowledge" (chapter 3), we learn from experience that the "ship of morality" on which we sail is not always as seaworthy as we would like it to be.

Neurath, you will remember, compared humans as knowers to "sailors who must rebuild their ship on the open sea, never able to dismantle it in dry-dock and to reconstruct it there out of the best materials."[9] The same metaphor applies to humans as moral agents. Some aspects of our inherited morality, we learn, are worn out. Others no longer serve any purpose. Still others are, in the light of new knowledge or circumstances, positively harmful. Finally, we face unprecedented choices and conditions for which our framework is ill-equipped. The "ship" on which we find ourselves, as we acquire the capacity for moral reflection, needs repair and rebuilding, but we can't do it all at once and from the bottom up. We are, after all, on the open sea. As a mariner must use and stand on some parts of a ship while examining, repairing, and improving others, we must rely on some (fallible) parts of our moral framework while testing, questioning, and revising others. As each part of a ship is subject to repair and replacement, no aspect of a moral framework is, in principle, immune to correction or improvement. On the open sea, however, an imperfect ship is better than no ship at all.

Wide Reflective Equilibrium

A working moral framework—what I'm characterizing as the "ship of morality"—is enormously complex; more complex, in fact, than anyone currently understands. A useful, though *highly simplified*, diagram identifies three main elements. In no particular order they are: (a) judgments about particular cases, (b) general rules or principles, and (c) background beliefs and theories.

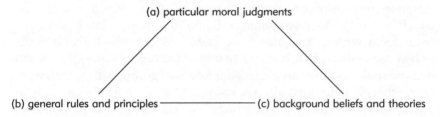

(a) particular moral judgments

(b) general rules and principles ——————— (c) background beliefs and theories

Each element consists of a set of presumptively true beliefs. *Judgments about particular cases* include beliefs like "Hitler's deliberately targeting civilians during the Blitz on London was wrong"; "It was wrong of Iago to falsely make Othello think Desdemona had been unfaithful"; "Huck Finn was right in helping Jim escape to freedom"; and "It's right to donate money to Oxfam or CARE." *General rules or principles* include beliefs like "Don't murder"; "Be truthful"; "Treat people as ends-in-themselves, not merely as means"; and "Maximize overall happiness (or welfare)." *Background beliefs and theories* include beliefs about such things as the nature of the world and of persons; the nature of morality, moral theories, and moral knowledge; and whether there is a God and, if so, God's role in human affairs.

The three elements of a moral framework are, as represented by the connecting lines in the diagram, interdependent and mutually supporting. Judgments about particular cases are, if challenged, supported by showing they cohere with general rules or principles and background beliefs and theories. For example, (a) Hitler's deliberately targeting civilians was wrong because it violated (b) the rule against murder and the principle that we ought to treat people as ends-in-themselves not merely as means and because (c) the awful consequences for the victims and their families eventually led to the Allies deliberately targeting German cities and their civilian inhabitants. Similarly, general rules or principles are supported by showing they cohere with highly secure judgments about particular cases and with our background beliefs and theories, and background beliefs and theories are supported by showing they cohere with highly secure judgments about particular cases and with our general rules and principles.

As we grow up, each of us is socialized by our parents, our religion, our socioeconomic group, and the larger society into a particular moral framework—a particular set of interrelated (a) beliefs about particular cases, (b) general rules and principles, and (c) background beliefs and theories. At some point, however, as we experience the world and acquire a capacity to think for ourselves, we may become aware of various shortcomings of our inherited framework (the "ship of morality" on which we find ourselves sailing). Some judgments about particular cases seem wrong. You may have been raised to think that atheists or homosexuals are bad, but you've met or learned of some atheists and homosexuals and they aren't, to your knowledge, any worse than most of the theistic heterosexuals you know and read about. Some rules or principles seem wrong. You may have been raised to think that life is sacred and ought to be prolonged no matter what, but that doesn't make much sense to you in the case of an infant born without a brain or an informed, mentally competent, terminally ill adult who refuses further life-prolonging treatment because the painful or undignified burdens of a high-tech, hospital-based existence are to him or her not worth the benefits. Some background beliefs seem wrong. You may have been raised to believe that black people, gay people, poor people, or rich people don't have the same *basic* hopes, fears, wishes, and values as you do, or that there can be no morality without God, but what you read and experience for yourself makes these seem quite doubtful. Your ship is leaking. What do you do? How do you make repairs?

You begin by identifying what, on reflection, are your most firmly fixed judgments about particular cases, general rules or principles, and background beliefs and theories. These are the convictions that, in a cool hour, seem to you most nearly certain, the ones you are least likely to revise or give up. If other judgments, rules, principles, or background beliefs and theories conflicted with one of these firmly fixed convictions, you would reject them before rejecting it. Some of these firmly fixed judgments seem pragmatically certain (chapter 3, pp. 61–64); for example: "It's wrong to cut off someone's arms to see what he'd look like without them" or "It's wrong to throw a child down a 300-foot well to hear what it sounds like when she hits bottom." Such judgments are so obviously true that you've probably never even thought of them before; they "go without saying." To adapt what Wittgenstein says about nonmoral pragmatic certainties, these and similar moral certainties are "the [nonpropositional] hinges" on which our entire system of morality turns, "the rock-bottom of our convictions," and the "inherited background against which [you and] I distinguish between" good and bad, right and wrong.[10] If these things aren't wrong, nothing is. A moral outlook or principle that directed us to cut off people's arms to see what they looked like without them or to throw little children down deep wells to hear what it sounds like when they hit bottom would be crazy—unhinged! Other fixed judgments, principles, background beliefs, and so on are not quite as certain, though we are still fairly confident about their rightness or wrongness—for example: igniting lighter fluid on a cat is wrong, and rescuing a toddler who has tumbled into the shallow end of a swimming pool is right.

Having identified a particular moral judgment in which we have great confidence, we then look for rules and principles to match or support it. Burning a cat, for example, is wrong because it violates a rule against torturing animals, which, in turn, may be justified by the principle of utility (one ought to maximize the net balance of good over bad, pleasure over pain, in the world). Rescuing a toddler from drowning in the shallow end of a pool is right because it complies with a rule requiring one to come to the aid of others if one can do so with little risk or loss to oneself, which, in turn, may be justified by such principles as the Golden Rule, the principle of utility, or Kant's Categorical Imperative (one ought to treat others as ends-in-themselves, not merely as means). These and other rules and principles serve to unify our particular moral judgments and to reveal their underlying rationale. We then do the same for general rules and principles in which we have great confidence.

If we were to go back and forth, trying to achieve a close fit between particular moral judgments and general rules and principles, we would achieve what John Rawls has called a "reflective equilibrium" between them.[11] General rules and principles and particular moral judgments are in *equilibrium* if they are mutually supportive. The equilibrium is *reflective* if it is based on a continuous dialectical interplay between the two. Such an equilibrium reinforces the presumptive validity of both particular judgments and general rules and principles, which can then provide guidance in cases and situations in which our initial convictions are less certain.

There is, however, a difficulty with this conception of reflective equilibrium. So long as we restrict ourselves to achieving coherence between particular moral judgments and general rules and principles, we run the risk of simply rationalizing preexisting prejudices.

Couldn't Nazis get a match between their particular moral judgments and a certain set of rules and principles? Couldn't racists, sexists, and homicidal maniacs do the same? The problem is that this sort of reflective equilibrium lacks a critical edge. There is no apparent check on the possibility of developing a narrowly coherent, but more broadly unacceptable, fit between preexisting judgments and principles.

The response (implicit in Rawls and explicit in the work of Norman Daniels) is to distinguish *wide* from narrow reflective equilibrium.[12] By adding a third element to the picture—background beliefs and theories—we obtain a semi-independent constraint on particular judgments and general rules and principles. Background beliefs and theories include beliefs about the nature of persons; the nature of the world as revealed by science and metaphysics (including whether there is a God and, if so, God's role in our lives); human psychology, sociology, and political and economic behavior; the nature of nonhuman animals; and so on. By insisting that a person's ethical framework cohere with plausible background beliefs and theories, we are able to expose the deficiencies in Nazi and overtly racist and sexist moral frameworks. Insofar as Nazis presuppose Aryan superiority and Jewish inferiority, their views fly in the face of well-grounded background beliefs and theories. It is demonstrably false that some people are "subhuman" or that the "Nordic blood" is superior, and so on. The same is true about racist and sexist presuppositions about the extent and significance of racial and sexual differences. A *wide* reflective equilibrium requires a consistent and coherent fit among particular moral judgments, general rules and principles, *and background beliefs and theories.* Particular moral judgments and general rules and principles inconsistent with well-grounded background beliefs and theories must be either revised or replaced by others.

Efforts to achieve such an equilibrium require going back and forth among the three elements, trying to achieve the most comprehensive and coherent fit we can among them. Sometimes we'll revise a particular judgment in the interests of coherence with more secure rules or principles or background beliefs and theories. Other times we'll revise a rule or principle to fit with a particular moral judgment and background belief or theory. In some cases, as I show below, we'll even revise a background belief or theory to square with particular judgments and rules or principles. The relations among the three types of elements are therefore dynamic, not static. None enjoys privileged status. Particular moral judgments, rules and principles, and background beliefs or theories are each subject to modification or replacement in the interest of achieving a more consistent, comprehensive, and coherent equilibrium, or overall "fit," with the others. For this reason, we should now modify our diagram by changing the straight connecting lines into bidirectional lines to indicate the dynamic relationships among the three main elements:

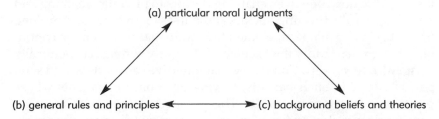

(a) particular moral judgments

(b) general rules and principles ◄──────────► (c) background beliefs and theories

"There is nothing in WRE [wide reflective equilibrium]," as Kai Nielsen puts it, "that is basic or foundational."

> Instead we weave and unweave the fabric of our beliefs until we get, for a time, though only for a time, the most consistent and coherent package which best squares with everything we reasonably believe we know and to which we, on reflection, are most firmly committed. There are some extensively fixed points, points which we *may* always in fact obtain anywhere, anywhen, but they are still, logically speaking, provisional fixed points which are not, in theory at least, beyond question, if they turn out not to fit in with the web of our beliefs and reflective commitments, commitments which will not be extinguished when we take them to heart under conditions of undistorted discourse.[13]

Once we've obtained wide reflective equilibrium among the elements of our moral framework (made initial repairs to the "ship of morality" on which we found ourselves), we then apply it to new or previously unconsidered cases or to cases in which we are unsure what our particular judgments ought to be. In some instances our newly secured rules or principles will provide straightforward guidance. In other instances we can, with a little work, find close analogies between the new situation and cases in which our judgments are confident or we can modify our rules or principles to handle the new situation. If, however, the new or previously unconsidered case cannot be accommodated by our framework—if, indeed, it reveals flaws or limitations in the framework—we may, in Nielsen's terms, have to reweave the fabric of our beliefs. This may require modifying or replacing one or more of our judgments about particular cases, general rules or principles, or background beliefs and theories. Here's an example.

In the late 1960s, advances in medical knowledge and technology were beginning to allow physicians to maintain the lives of patients whose brains had been completely and irreversibly destroyed. In the past, the patients' hearts would have stopped within minutes and they would have been declared dead; modern respirators and other technology were now, however, enabling doctors to prolong breathing and heartbeat. A rule directing doctors and nurses to preserve and prolong life, at (b) in our diagram, seemed to require that treatment be continued. But to many this now seemed intuitively wrong, economically wasteful, or even silly. Could it be that intensive care units would soon be teeming with such patients, leaving no room for patients whose prognosis was more favorable? This prospect clashed with more secure judgments about particular cases at (a) in our diagram. Two fairly obvious ways of eliminating the disequilibrium, either weakening the duty to preserve and prolong life or adopting the judgment that continued treatment for such patients is right, were rejected in favor of a third: the modification of one of our widely held background beliefs at (c) in the diagram.

An interdisciplinary committee at Harvard Medical School proposed criteria for identifying respirator-dependent unconscious patients whose brain function had been wholly and irreversibly lost.[14] It then suggested that we modify our beliefs about what constituted a living human person. Individuals whose brain function had been totally and irreversibly lost should no longer be considered living persons, despite the presence of respirator-assisted breathing and heartbeat. They are actually, the committee reasoned, (brain) dead. And the duty to preserve or prolong life does not apply to those who are already dead. Thus a new problem generated by a conflict between the application of (b) an entrenched moral rule and (a) a strong particular judgment was resolved by a relevant modification of (c) background beliefs and theories. Equilibrium was restored without either relinquishing an important rule or accepting what seemed to be a counterintuitive application of it. In other cases, it will be the rule or principle that will be modified or the particular moral judgment.

As a form of practical knowledge or know-how, knowledge in ethics is passed by parents and communities from one generation to the next. Like other types of practical knowledge—for example, medical, legal, or agricultural knowledge—it is then modified as concrete experience reveals the need for correction and improvement. "In a changing world," James D. Wallace writes, "no body of practical knowledge can be said to be complete, nor can it be known to be adequate as it stands for any test it may have to face in the future."[15] Practical knowledge must be able to accommodate changes in the world as well as in our understanding of it. Thus a distinct advantage of the method of wide reflective equilibrium is that it incorporates the wisdom of the past while remaining responsive to a changing future.

Though the label "wide reflective equilibrium" may be new to you, the process is probably not. If you've deliberated about real-life ethical problems, my hunch is you've already engaged in this kind of thinking, even if you were not explicitly aware of it. The method of wide reflective equilibrium is just Wilfrid Sellars's characterization of philosophy—"an attempt to see how things, in the broadest possible sense of the term, hang together, in the broadest sense of the term"—applied to ethics.[16] We try to get a coherent fit between what we *do* in particular cases and (a) moral judgments about other cases, (b) ethical rules and principles, and (c) background beliefs and theories. Moreover, the method of wide reflective equilibrium mediates between the implausible extremes of objective absolutism and subjective relativism (chapter 1, pp. 13–16).

Objective absolutist approaches to ethics argue that moral standards must be not only objective (or independent of what people *happen* to value), but absolute (or invariant with respect to time and place). Moral standards, they maintain, are somehow prior to and independent of human thought. Subjective relativist approaches, by contrast, hold that moral standards are nothing but expressions of personal taste or the mores of a particular society, culture, or subculture. What some individuals or societies regard as right will be regarded as wrong by others. And there is no independent or external standpoint for saying that one is better than the other. Moral judgments are internal to and inseparable from the personal, cultural, and historical circumstances and orientation of those who make them; and there is no neutral or objective way to show that one set of values or assessments is better than another.

Objective absolutists are right in holding out for objectivity, but wrong in linking it with absoluteness or something entirely outside human thought and experience. First, as shown in chapters 2 and 3, there is no getting out of human thought and experience. "The trail of the human serpent," as William James puts it, "is . . . over everything."[17] Like law and medicine, ethics is a living body of practical knowledge designed to address a certain set of practical human problems. Second, it is, with respect to basics like prohibitions against murder, rape, and genocide, no less objective than law or medicine. By 'objective' I mean what Hilary Putnam calls "objectivity humanly speaking." To say that something is objective *humanly speaking* is, as Putnam puts it, to say it is "objective from the point of view of our best and most reflective practice."[18] In medicine, for example, our best and most reflective practice for comparing the efficacy of two or more treatments is the randomized clinical trial. A particular medical treatment is objectively (though not absolutely or eternally) better than others if impeccably designed and conducted, randomized clinical trials clearly reveal it to be so. That it is generally the best treatment is not a matter of a particular physician's subjective preference; it is (humanly speaking) an objective fact. Still, our knowledge is fallible. It's possible we've made a mistake or that a new treatment will be discovered that is objectively better than this one. In ethics our best and most reflective practice is the method of wide reflective equilibrium. As shown by the foregoing criticism of Nazi morality, the method of wide reflective equilibrium has the capacity with respect to the most basic questions to distinguish objective from subjective moral beliefs and theories. If what some individuals or groups *happen* to value cannot be supported in *wide* reflective equilibrium, it is not "from the point of view of our best and most reflective practice" objective. We can, then, reject the stagnant ideal of ethical absolutism without, at the same time, rejecting objectivity.

Subjective relativists are right to emphasize a certain kind of relativism in ethics, but wrong to link it with subjectivism. Ethical judgments, principles, and theories are indeed relative to the best available background beliefs and nonmoral theories at our disposal. This is, however, simply to say that they, like medical and legal judgments, principles, and theories, are fallible. It is always possible that new knowledge or changes in the world will induce us to revise or replace various ethical judgments, principles, or theories. Yet it hardly follows that they are "merely" subjective, little more than matters of taste or naked preference. As objective absolutists mistakenly link objectivity with absoluteness, subjective relativists mistakenly link relativism with subjectivity. We can, in endorsing the method of wide reflective equilibrium in ethics, *combine objectivity*, in the sense of "what is objective from the point of view of our best and most reflective practice," *with relativism*, in the sense of being relative to various other beliefs about the world which are themselves fallible.

The method of wide reflective equilibrium captures what James is getting at when he writes: "[T]here is no such thing possible as an ethical philosophy dogmatically made up in advance. . . . In other words, there can be no final truth in ethics any more than in physics, until the last man has had his experience and said his say."[19] Insofar as they are fallible, our particular judgments, rules and principles, and background beliefs and theories are always open to revision. Only when the world stops changing or people stop learning and experiencing it will we arrive at "final truth in ethics." The method also responds to what Dewey characterized as the "deepest problem of modern life," namely, "restoring integration and cooperation between man's beliefs about the world in which he lives and his beliefs about the values and purposes that should direct his conduct. It is the problem of any philosophy that is not isolated from that life."[20] The interplay, in wide reflective equilibrium, between background beliefs and theories at (c) and particular moral judgments and general rules and principles at (a) and (b), respectively, connects scientific and other beliefs about the world in which we live with beliefs about values and purposes. There is, in the method, no hard and fast line between facts and values, science and ethics. Values are revised in the light of facts and facts are revised in the light of values (as illustrated by the example of "brain death").

Though ethics has its origins in the facts of evolutionary biology, it is not held hostage by them. Language, as Dewey points out, "grew out of unintelligent babblings, instinctive motions called gestures, and the pressure of circumstance. But nevertheless language once called into existence is language and operates as language. It operates not to perpetuate the forces which produced it but to modify and redirect them."[21] The same may be said about the relation between ethics and its origins. Ethics grew out of genetically directed instincts toward kin selection and reciprocal altruism in unreflective animals. But nevertheless reflective morality once called into existence is reflective and operates in that way. It operates not to perpetuate the forces that produced it but to modify and redirect them. Thus if we have certain evolutionarily understandable inclinations—such as, perhaps, nepotism in government or stronger inclinations among males than females to marital infidelity—this does not mean that ethics must endorse such practices. On the contrary, reflective morality may, while acknowledging the strength of such inclinations, rightly work to modify and redirect them.

The five men who come to the aid of the balloonist and his grandson find themselves in what the narrator characterizes as "morality's ancient, irresolvable dilemma: us, or me." How much, in cases of conflict, do we give to others and how much do we keep for ourselves? There is in the case of the runaway balloon no time for reflection and discussion. Other cases, however, afford more time. Should I do what's best for my family or what's best for me alone? Should I give some of my money to famine relief or should I spend it on myself? Should I support higher taxes for Head Start programs and better schools for poor children or should I oppose all taxes that do not directly benefit myself? Should I support an increase in the foreign aid budget (for the sake of them) or should I oppose any governmental aid to other countries (for the sake of us)? Is abortion (physician-assisted suicide, capital punishment, affirmative action, and so on) right or wrong? These and many other ethical questions invite moral reasoning and reflection. And the best way to do this is to employ the method of wide reflective equilibrium.

Our aim, as we discuss and debate these and other difficult questions, is personal and interpersonal coherence. By personal coherence, I mean answers that, from your own point of view, satisfy the conditions of wide reflective equilibrium better than any alternative. By interpersonal coherence, I mean that your answers and the answers of others strive for as much agreement or congruence with each other as can be obtained. Insofar as we can, through mutually respectful, give-and-take discussion, use the method of wide reflective equilibrium to attain personal and interpersonal coherence, we have a basis for reasonable agreement. Is it possible that the method of wide reflective equilibrium will eventually lead to agreement on all ethical questions? Is interpersonal moral harmony a realistic possibility? Or is a certain amount of ethical conflict and disagreement a permanent feature of human life? These and related questions are the topic of the following chapter, "Democratic Pluralism."

NOTES

1. Ian McEwan, *Enduring Love* (New York: Doubleday, 1997), 15.

2. Antonio R. Damasio, *Descartes' Error: Emotion, Reason, and the Human Brain* (New York: Putnam, 1994), 8.

3. Amartya Sen, "Rational Fools," *Philosophy and Public Affairs* 6, no. 4 (Summer 1977).

4. Robert Wright, *The Moral Animal: The New Science of Evolutionary Psychology* (New York: Vintage, 1994), 158.

5. Matt Ridley, *The Origins of Virtue: Human Instincts and the Evolution of Cooperation* (New York: Viking Penguin, 1996), 62–63, 69; Gerald Wilkinson, "Reciprocal Sharing in the Vampire Bat," *Nature* 308, no. 5955 (March 8, 1994): 181–84; Lisa K. Denault and Donald A. McFarlane, "Reciprocal Altruism between Male Vampire Bats, *Desmodus Rotundus*," *Animal Behavior* 49 (1955): 855–56.

6. Leo Tolstoy, *The Death of Ivan Ilych*, in *The Death of Ivan Ilych and Other Stories*, trans. Aylmer Maude (New York: New American Library, 1960), 138.

7. McEwan, *Enduring Love*, 1.

8. Mary Midgley, *Can't We Make Moral Judgements?* (Bristol, U.K.: The Bristol Press, 1991), 15.

9. Otto Neurath, "Protocol Sentences," in *Logical Positivism*, ed. A. J. Ayer, trans. George Schick (Chicago: Free Press, 1959), 201.

10. Ludwig Wittgenstein, *On Certainty*, ed. G. E. M. Anscombe and G. H. von Wright, trans. Denis Paul and G. E. M. Anscombe (New York: Harper & Row, 1969), §341, §246, §94.

11. John Rawls, *A Theory of Justice*, rev. ed. (Cambridge, Mass.: Harvard University Press, 1999), 18–19, 42–45.

12. Rawls, *A Theory of Justice*; Norman Daniels, "Wide Reflective Equilibrium and Theory Acceptance in Ethics," in *Justice and Justification: Reflective Equilibrium in Theory and Practice* (Cambridge: Cambridge University Press, 1996), 21–46.

13. Kai Nielsen, "Relativism and Wide Reflective Equilibrium," *Monist* 76, no. 3 (July 1993): 318.

14. Ad Hoc Committee of the Harvard Medical School to Examine the Definition of Death, "A Definition of Irreversible Coma," *Journal of the American Medical Association* 205, no. 6 (August 5, 1968): 337–40.

15. James D. Wallace, *Ethical Norms, Particular Cases* (Ithaca, N.Y.: Cornell University Press, 1996), 64.

16. Wilfrid Sellars, "Philosophy and the Scientific Image of Man," in *Wilfrid Sellars, Science, Perception and Reality* (London: Routledge & Kegan Paul, 1963), 1.

17. William James, *Pragmatism*, in *William James: Writings 1902–1910*, ed. Bruce Kuklick (New York: Library of America, 1987), 515.

18. Hilary Putnam, "Pragmatism and Moral Objectivity," in *Hilary Putnam, Words and Life*, ed. James Conant (Cambridge, Mass.: Harvard University Press, 1994), 177n.

19. William James, "The Moral Philosopher and the Moral Life," in *William James: Writings 1878–1899*, ed. Gerald E. Myers (New York: Library of America, 1992), 595.

20. John Dewey, *The Quest for Certainty*, in *John Dewey: The Later Works, 1925–1953*, Vol. 4: 1929, ed. Jo Ann Boydston (Carbondale: Southern Illinois University Press, 1988).

21. John Dewey, *Human Nature and Conduct*, in *The Middle Works of John Dewey*, Vol. 14: 1922, ed. Jo Ann Boydston (Carbondale: Southern Illinois University Press, 1983), 56–57.

Chapter 6

Democratic Pluralism

Neither the whole of truth, nor the whole of good, is revealed to any single observer, although each observer gains a partial superiority of insight from the peculiar position in which he stands.

—William James, "On a Certain Blindness in Human Beings"

Many people believe all good things and all right actions must ultimately fit together in a single harmonious scheme of morality and that as we acquire more knowledge and improve our reasoning we will eventually agree on a single set of rules and principles that support one, and only one, right answer to each ethical question. Even if prejudice, ignorance, or bad reasoning keeps us from achieving this goal, it is, in principle, reachable. Stuart Hampshire calls this the "doctrine of moral harmony."[1]

In the first part of this chapter I show this doctrine is mistaken. So long as individuals and groups enjoy a certain amount of freedom to think and act for themselves, there will be conflicts between good and important moral values and principles that cannot be resolved by reason. This is a *fact* about ethics—the fact of *moral pluralism*—that must be included among our background beliefs and theories in reflective equilibrium.

Moral pluralism creates a certain ambivalence. As agents, we are inclined to act on our particular values and principles. As spectators, we are inclined to respect those who act on opposing, but nonetheless reasonable, values and principles. Political theorist Joshua Miller calls the capacity to combine these aspects of the self the "democratic temperament."[2] The idea of a democratic temperament is, according to Miller,

William James's principal contribution to political theory. I discuss and explore the implications of a democratic temperament in the second part of this chapter.

James, we have seen, thinks of pragmatism as a "mediating way of thinking." Combined with moral pluralism and the democratic temperament, a mediating way of thinking suggests a willingness to compromise in cases of rationally irreconcilable ethical conflict. Compromise in ethics, however, raises troubling questions about integrity. If you really believe your position is ethically preferable to the opposing position, how can you compromise without compromising (or betraying) your integrity? I address this question in the last part of the chapter by developing and defending the idea of an integrity-preserving moral compromise. In some cases, I show, seeking or endorsing a compromise is actually more integrity-preserving than using force, rank, or deception to impose what you regard as the ethically superior position on others. I conclude by using the issue of physician-assisted suicide to illustrate the interlocking ideas of *moral pluralism*, the *democratic temperament*, and *integrity-preserving compromise*.

MORAL PLURALISM

Moral pluralism holds that a number of *good and important* ethical values and principles are inherently incompatible. They cannot be combined into a single harmonious scheme of morality for all. I have emphasized 'good and important' to distinguish what John Rawls, following Joshua Cohen, calls pluralism *as such* from "reasonable pluralism."[3] Pluralism as such includes (a) plural and conflicting values resulting from selfishness, prejudice, ignorance, bad reasoning, and so on together with (b) plural and conflicting values that remain even when selfishness, prejudice, ignorance, bad reasoning, and so on have been overcome. Reasonable pluralism is restricted to (b). Pluralism is reasonable when plural and conflicting values are not the result of selfishness, prejudice, ignorance, bad reasoning, bias, or other deficiencies. Even when we exclude obvious "bad guys" like Nazis and hit men, there will be a certain amount of ethical conflict between informed, clear-thinking, well-meaning "good guys" like you and me.

Moral pluralism—understood now as *reasonable* pluralism—is a general *fact* that (like facts about biology and psychology) must be included among our background beliefs and theories in wide reflective equilibrium. It is, as Rawls puts it, "a permanent feature of the public culture of democracy."[4] So long as people enjoy free association and the capacity to think and act for themselves, there will be conflicts between good and important values and principles that are not due to selfishness, prejudice, ignorance, poor reasoning, and so on. Everyone's adhering to a single, unified conception of right and wrong, good and bad, can be maintained, as Rawls adds, "only by the oppressive use of state power."[5]

Why is this so? First, as Isaiah Berlin has persuasively pointed out, many good and important values and principles are logically incompatible:

> Justice, rigorous justice, is for some people an absolute value, but it is not compatible with what may be equally ultimate values for them—mercy, compassion, as arises in concrete cases.
>
> Both liberty and equality are among the primary goals pursued by human beings through many centuries: but total liberty for wolves is death to the lambs, total liberty of the powerful, the gifted, is not compatible with the rights to a decent existence of the weak and less gifted. . . . Equality may demand the restraint of the liberty of those who wish to dominate; liberty—without some modicum of which there is no choice and therefore no possibility of remaining human as we understand the word—may have to be curtailed in order to make room for social welfare, to feed the hungry, to clothe the naked, to shelter the homeless, to leave room for the liberty of others, to allow justice or fairness to be exercised.[6]

And that's just the beginning:

> Spontaneity, a marvelous human quality, is not compatible with capacity for organised planning, for the nice calculation of what and how much and where—on which the welfare of society may largely depend. . . . Should a man resist a monstrous tyranny at all costs, at the expense of the lives of his parents or his children? Should children be tortured to extract information about dangerous traitors or criminals?[7]

These and other conflicts between good and important values, Berlin argues, are unavoidable. It is a *conceptual* truth that unrestrained liberty for the wealthy and powerful is incompatible with social welfare for the poor and weak, that absolute justice is incompatible with mercy, that spontaneity is incompatible with planning, and so on.

Good and important values are so complex and so many, that any individual or group must, if it is to be reasonably unified, emphasize one reasonably coherent set at the expense of others. There is not room enough in any single life or single group for a full measure of all good and important values and principles. Different individuals and groups—with different histories and in different circumstances—will therefore acquire, develop, and order their lives around different, though nonetheless reasonable and coherent, bundles of values and principles. And these will in some cases put them at odds.

Philosophers have generally resisted the idea of moral pluralism. From Plato to Kant to Bentham and Mill, they have devised elaborate theories designed to show that at some level and from some perspective what we see and experience as agonizing conflicts between good and important values is readily resolved. R. M. Hare, a contemporary utilitarian, asks us to imagine a "being with superhuman powers of thought, superhuman knowledge and no human weaknesses." Hare calls this being "the archangel."[8] The archangel is, for Hare, the ideal moral reasoner. When confronted with a conflict of values or principles, the archangel takes them all into account and translates them into the morally neutral vocabulary of "preferences." Then with perfect knowledge of the intensity of the preferences of all parties involved in the conflict, the archangel impersonally identifies the course of action that will result in the greatest overall preference satisfaction. Assuming the right thing to do is that which maximizes overall preference satisfaction, this action, whatever it turns out to be, resolves the conflict, without remainder. So, Hare says, when confronted with a real-life conflict of values and principles we each ought to approximate the standpoint and reasoning of the archangel. Insofar as we are successful, we will all agree on the same resolution. "[A]rchangels, at the end of their critical thinking," Hare writes, "will all say the same thing . . . on all questions on which moral argument is possible . . . ; and so shall we, to the extent that we manage to think like archangels."[9]

The problem with this and similar comprehensive theories is not only that we lack the perfect knowledge and reasoning powers of an archangel, but that the archangel represents only the impersonal or spectator standpoint while we also, and inevitably, identify ourselves as particular agents with *specific* values and principles associated with *specific* personal viewpoints. The archangel differs from us not merely in degree (of knowledge and reasoning powers), but in kind. To reduce our values and principles to the common currency of preferences eliminates our identity as particular people with particular conceptions and ideals of right and wrong, good and bad. The qualitative moral differences between Hitler and Mother Teresa are, for example, entirely erased when their values and principles are translated into the morally neutral, but quantifiable, currency of preferences. Referring not specifically to Hare's theory, but to theories like it, Berlin writes,

> If we are told that these contradictions [between good and important values] will be solved in some perfect world in which all good things can be harmonised in principle, then we must answer, to those who say this, that the meanings they attach to the names, which for us denote the conflicting values, are not ours, that the world in which what we see as incompatible values are not in conflict is a world altogether beyond our ken; that principles with which, in our daily lives, we are acquainted, if they are transformed, it is into conceptions not known to us on earth. But it is on earth that we live, and it is here that we must believe *and act.*[10] (italics added)

Unsurprisingly, Hare provides no detailed illustration of his theory's capacity to resolve interesting and important real-life problems. The illustrations on which he carries through—for example whether I should move someone's bicycle in order to park my car—are fairly trivial. When it comes to the question of whether a racist organization should be permitted to meet in a public hall where its incitements to racial hatred are likely to cause violence, Hare bails out just when real work has to be done. He tells us his method is likely to issue a principle that "guarantees freedom of speech but qualifies it by restrictions on what may be said." So far, so good, but this is a principle that most of us would come up with without the benefits of Hare's theory. When it comes to the nitty-gritty—determining what these restrictions are and how they are to be justified—Hare seems to lose interest. "This is not the place," he says in the very next line, "to discuss precisely what those restrictions should be; for example, how to draw the line between incitement to violence and the expression of political dissent."[11] On the real-world questions that really trouble us, then, Hare and other abstract, comprehensive theorists have disappointingly little to offer.

How, then, *do* we contend with the actual multiplicity of good and important conflicting values and principles? To simultaneously embrace all these values and principles is to invite a kind of madness, a moral schizophrenia that undermines unity and cripples agency. To embrace only a *single dominant* value from which others may possibly be derived is to invite a different kind of madness, a monomaniacal narrowness that borders on fanaticism and repudiates the richness and complexity of human life. A more plausible (and mediating) possibility is to embrace a useful, relatively rich and coherent, but occasionally conflicting, *subset* of good values and principles while acknowledging the reasonableness of certain alternative subsets.

Different cultures, Berlin points out, are organized and identified in terms of different clusters or subsets of values.[12] The values, virtues, and ideals unifying the Roman Republic—emphasizing aggression, worldliness, domination, opportunism, and so on—were quite different from those unifying the early Christians—humility, acceptance of suffering, unworldliness, the hope of salvation in an afterlife, and so on. These clusters of more or less compatible values structured the internal identity and integrity of the cultures as well as most of the individuals comprising them. While the defining virtues and values of the Roman Republic are incompatible with those of Christianity, each by itself is reasonably coherent and sufficiently comprehensive to provide its members with a rich and distinctive *worldview* and corresponding *way of life*.

A worldview is a complex, often unarticulated (and perhaps not fully articulable) set of deeply held and highly cherished beliefs about the nature and organization of the universe and one's place in it. Normative as well as descriptive—comprising interlocking general beliefs about knowledge reality and values—a worldview so pervades and conditions our thinking that it is largely unnoticed.[13] A way of life is a set of patterns of living, admired ideal types of men and women, ways of structuring marriage, family relationships, governance, educational and religious practices, and so on.[14] Worldviews and ways of life are dynamically interrelated. A worldview helps to structure a way of life; a way of life presupposes and embodies a particular worldview. Deep changes in one are likely to occasion related changes in the other.

A distinctive and easily recognized contemporary worldview and way of life is that of the Amish. Many worldviews and ways of life are, however, more difficult to delineate in rapidly changing, multicultural, secular societies like ours, which permit, if not encourage, the exercise of individual choice. A complex amalgam of a wide variety of reasonably coherent beliefs, attitudes, values, ideals, and practices, an individual's worldview and way of life will, in a contemporary liberal democracy, often be highly individualized. Think here of pro-choice or outwardly gay Catholics, pro-life feminists, Jews for Jesus, and so on. Think also of reasonably coherent combinations of beliefs, attitudes, values, ideals, and practices that, perhaps like your own, are too individualized to fit neatly into any single conventional category.

The point is that like Homeric Greece, classical Athens, the Roman Republic, and the early Christians, individuals in contemporary liberal democracies organize their lives around different, occasionally

conflicting, *reasonably coherent subsets* of values and principles corre-
lated with particular worldviews and ways of life. We do not, however, invent them out of whole cloth. We begin, as we must, with reasonably coherent subsets of values and principles, worldviews and
ways of life, inherited from our parents and the larger culture in which
we are born. As we acquire the capacity to think for ourselves, however, and put our inherited values and principles, worldviews and
ways of life, to the test of experience, we modify them by employing
the method of wide reflective equilibrium (as described in chapter 5).

Rawls identifies a number of sources or causes of reasonable disagreement.[15] First, in considering difficult issues like affirmative action, economic justice, global warming, and abortion, the relevant empirical and scientific evidence is complex and hard to evaluate.
Different individuals will, in some cases, draw different, yet nonetheless reasonable, conclusions from the same evidence. Second, even
when we agree about relevant factors, we may reasonably disagree
about their weight, and thus arrive at different conclusions. On abortion, for example, you may put more weight on the sanctity of pre-
sentient human biological life than I do. Third, in many cases our concepts will be vague and subject to different interpretations. Think here
of concepts like "nature," "justice," "welfare," "life," and so on. Different reasonable interpretations may lead to different moral conclusions. Fourth, the way we assess evidence and weigh moral and political values is often shaped by what Rawls calls "our total experience,
our whole course of life up to now; and our total experiences must always differ." The world is large and complex and each of us can only
experience a small part of it—from a particular standpoint and with a
particular set of concepts and expectations. As we address questions
characterized by conflicting empirical and scientific evidence, factors
to which different weights can be assigned, and vague and ambiguous
concepts, our differing past experiences may reasonably lead to differing conclusions. Sociologist Kristin Luker's illuminating description of the differing backgrounds and experiences of pro-life and pro-
choice activists on the abortion question provides an excellent
illustration.[16] Finally, contemporary moral and political problems are
often characterized by different kinds of values and principles on different sides of an issue and there is, as yet, no common vocabulary
into which they can be translated and then measured. Two of the most
plausible general principles of morality, Kant's Categorical Imperative
and Mill's Principle of Utility, seem indispensable to moral reflection,
yet they occasionally give conflicting guidance. The upshot of all this

is that informed, thoughtful individuals will not always agree about complex moral and political issues. A number of important conflicts will have no clear resolution.

Nor, as some might think, are advances in knowledge likely to contribute to convergence on a single worldview and way of life. New knowledge brings new possibilities—possibilities that create or aggravate as many conflicts as they eliminate or reduce. Think of how better understanding of human reproduction and the development of various reproductive technologies have provided new and conflicting conceptions of motherhood and the family. Who, for example, is *the* mother of a child when (1) Ann provides an egg that is fertilized *in vitro* with Robert's sperm; (2) the embryo is then transplanted into Bettina, who becomes pregnant and gives birth; and (3) Carrie, who is married to Robert, takes the infant home from the hospital, and raises it? Different thoughtful individuals with different experiences and different worldviews and ways of life will take different reasonable positions. This is only one among many ethical conflicts generated by advances in knowledge and technology.

These considerations and others support the *fact* of reasonable moral pluralism. As we continue to apply and refine our moral outlooks in wide reflective equilibrium, we must therefore incorporate this fact into our background beliefs and theories. Someday, perhaps, someone will come up with radically different moral concepts and ways of reasoning that will be both useful and acceptable to everyone and converge on one, and only one, answer to all ethical questions. This is analogous to the possibility, mentioned in chapter 4 (pp. 94–95), of a theory describing and explaining human behavior that dissolves the mind–body and free will problems. It faces, however, the same formidable obstacles. Such a theory may be beyond the capacities of finite minds like ours. But, as Berlin reminds us, "it is on earth that we live and it is here [and now] that we must believe and act." In the meantime, then, and perhaps for all time, we will have to muddle through without the benefits of such a theory. This means acknowledging the fact of moral pluralism as a provisional fixed point among our background beliefs and theories in wide reflective equilibrium.

DEMOCRATIC TEMPERAMENT

Suppose you and I are members of a hospital ethics committee. You're a prestigious physician, medical director of the hospital, and chair of the committee. I'm a nurse. Our committee is developing a policy for blood transfusions involving Jehovah's Witnesses, whose religious understanding forbids blood transfusions even if necessary to save life. We agree that conscious, competent, adult Jehovah's Witnesses generally have a right to refuse blood transfusions, but we are divided on the thorny question of whether that same right applies to pregnant women. You argue that the presence of a "second patient"— the fetus—sets this case apart. Though a woman may have the right to refuse a lifesaving blood transfusion for herself, she does not have a right to do so for the fetus. Since her refusal will, in this case, lead to the death of the fetus, it cannot be honored. I disagree. A pregnant Jehovah's Witness, I maintain, should have the same right to personal autonomy as other Jehovah's Witnesses.

As a prestigious physician, medical director, and chair of the committee, you have the power to see that your position prevails. You can make life very difficult for me and for others who oppose your position. In fact, however, you resist this temptation. You acknowledge the complexity of the issue, the fact of reasonable moral pluralism, and the reasonableness of my position. As an individual you make the best case you can for your view. As chair of the committee, however, you strive to be scrupulously fair to each member supporting an opposing, yet reasonable, view. You acknowledge your fallibility—the inevitable limitations of your own experience—and are prepared to revise or even relinquish your view in the light of new understanding. Thus you foster mutually respectful give-and-take discussion, hoping to persuade others to agree with you, while remaining genuinely open to the possibility of being persuaded to agree with them. If, after sustained deliberation, the committee cannot reach consensus or devise a mutually acceptable compromise, the matter may be put to a vote or left undecided. In refraining from pulling rank or using your prestige and power to impose your position on those who share mine, you exhibit a democratic temperament. (In the published account on which this example is based, the committee, after two years of deliberation and numerous reversals, eventually concluded that it could not reach a decision on specific guidelines for pregnant Jehovah's Witnesses. "Reluctantly," Ruth Macklin reports, "the committee adopted the suggestion that it not even attempt to dictate a policy but limit its task to describing the competing principles, leaving the decision-making process to the patient and clinician."[17])

A democratic temperament combines support for particular positions on moral and political issues with respect for those holding opposing, yet reasonable, positions on the same issues. As agents, each of us identifies with a particular set of values and principles related to a particular worldview and way of life. These, in turn, give shape and meaning to our lives and provide a basis for personal choice and action. Though subject to revision in the light of new knowledge or experience, our values and principles, worldviews and ways of life, have a more or less definite, identity-conferring structure. We can also, however, approximate a more detached or impersonal point of view, that of a spectator. From this standpoint we understand the sources of reasonable disagreement and acknowledge the fact of moral pluralism; there are, we can see, a number of occasionally conflicting, but nonetheless reasonable, worldviews and ways of life of which ours is only one. There are, moreover, no neutral criteria for determining that one reasonable worldview and way of life is in all respects superior to the others. Balancing personal conviction with respect for reasonable differences, the democratic temperament combines the standpoints of both agent and spectator. The trick—and part of being human—is being able to retain both standpoints while judiciously tacking between them.

The democratic temperament, as the example of the hospital ethics committee suggests, is not restricted to politics or government. Dewey distinguished a broader conception of democracy—"democracy as a social idea"—from a narrower conception, "political democracy as a system of government."[18] The broader conception, Dewey maintained, applies not only to government, but to various forms of social life including, where appropriate, the family, the school, the workplace, and so on. Whatever the context of reasonable disagreement, the democratic temperament inclines us to share the power to shape and make decisions with those affected by them.

Democratic participation of those affected by various decisions increases the likelihood that their (reasonable) perspectives and concerns play a role in making them. Human beings, James points out, suffer from a "certain blindness" with regard to "creatures and people different from ourselves."

We are practical beings, each of us with limited functions and duties to perform. Each is bound to feel intensely the importance of his own duties and the significance of the situations that call these forth. But this feeling is in each of us a vital secret, for sympathy with which we vainly look to others—the others are too much absorbed in their own vital secrets to take an interest in ours. Hence the stupidity and injustice of our opinions, so far as they deal with the significance of alien lives. Hence the falsity of our judgments, so far as they presume to decide in an absolute way on the value of other persons' conditions or ideals.[19]

Awareness of this type of "blindness" and other sources of fallibility should incline us to share the power to shape and make decisions with those affected by them. "[N]either the whole of truth," as James adds, "nor the whole of good, is revealed to any single observer, although each observer gains a partial superiority of insight from the peculiar position in which he stands."[20] The reasonable perspectives of individuals affected by a decision are more likely to be taken into account if they participate (directly or indirectly) in shaping and making it.

COMPROMISE

The fact of moral pluralism means that some ethical disagreements cannot be resolved by reason. But if reason cannot resolve a particular disagreement, it does not follow that it cannot, through compromise, help to contain it. "If the old perennial belief in the possibility of realizing ultimate harmony is a fallacy," Isaiah Berlin writes,

> if we allow [that] Great Goods can collide; that some of them cannot live together, even though others can—in short that one cannot have everything, in principle as well as in practice—and if human creativity may depend upon a variety of mutually exclusive choices: then, as Chernyshevsky and Lenin once asked, "What is to be done?" How do we choose between possibilities? What and how much must we sacrifice to what? There is, it seems to me, no clear reply. But the collisions, even if they cannot be avoided, can be softened. Claims can be balanced, *compromises can be reached*: in concrete situations not every claim is of equal force—so much liberty and so much equality; so much for sharp moral condemnation, and so much for the full force of the law, and so much for the prerogative of mercy; for feeding the hungry, clothing the naked, healing the sick, sheltering the homeless [italics added].[21]

Historically, philosophers have had little to say about compromise. One possible reason is the understandably high regard they have for integrity. Compromise and integrity are, on the face of it, among the "Great Goods" that Berlin suggests "cannot live together."

Central to compromise is the idea of mutual concessions for mutual gain. Here 'compromise' refers both to a characteristic process for accommodating conflict and to the outcome of this process. Compromise raises no special problems when restricted to conflicts of nonmoral interests among equals. Examples include buyers and sellers compromising on the final price of a house or an automobile. *Moral compromise*—where opposing positions are each grounded in an ethical conviction or principle—is, however, more controversial. To compromise your ethical convictions, it seems, is to betray them and yourself (or others). A central question for ethics, then, is whether moral compromise is compatible with retaining one's integrity (or wholeness) as a person.[22]

Moral Compromise

It is important, in this connection, to distinguish a strict from a loose sense of 'compromise'. If, after mutually respectful, give-and-take discussion, parties initially holding opposing ethical positions, *A* and *B*, jointly embrace a third position *S* (a synthesis that combines the strengths of each *A* and *B* while avoiding their weaknesses), the outcome is not, strictly speaking, a compromise. Neither party concedes anything. Each relinquishes what it now regards as a defective view (*A* or *B*) for a better one (*S*). The outcome may be called a compromise in a loose sense of the term—something intermediate between two poles—but it is more accurately characterized as a synthesis.

Suppose, for example, you and I initially disagree about economic justice. You're a libertarian. You think people have a fundamental right to do with their property, including their money, as they see fit. Government has no right to tax some people in order to provide benefits (food, shelter, clothing, education, or health care) for others. This is a violation of the (sacred) right to property. The only justification for government is to protect individuals from domestic or international force or aggression. Taxation, then, can be justified for the police, court and prison systems, and the military, but not for a welfare system, educational system, or health care system. If people want food, shelter, clothing, education, and health care, they should earn their own money and buy them.

I, on the other hand, am a radical egalitarian. Thus I think government should see to it that everyone has roughly the same amount of food, shelter, clothing, education, and access to health care. If this requires very heavy taxes on the well-off, so be it. People are basically equal and thus have an equal right to the necessities and goods of life. No one should have three cars, while others have none. So we should tax the rich and give to the poor until everyone has roughly the same amount of money.

Both of these views are, of course, highly problematic. Suppose as you and I go back and forth, each trying to convince the other of the rightness of his or her view and the wrongness of the other's, we each come to appreciate previously undetected weaknesses in our own view and strengths in the opposing view. As the discussion continues we each find ourselves gravitating toward a third, more moderate, position; one that appears to synthesize the strengths of both libertarianism and radical egalitarianism, while eliminating their obvious weaknesses. Citizens are taxed to ensure that everyone has a certain decent minimum of food, shelter, clothing, education, and access to health care, but there is no effort to bring all citizens to a level of equality. After a while, you relinquish your libertarianism for this middle-of-the-road position. I, too, abandon my original commitment to radical egalitarianism and embrace the same moderate synthesis or consensus. This is not, strictly speaking, a compromise. Compromise involves mutual *concessions* for mutual gain. In this case neither of us concedes anything. Each of us forsakes what we now regard as a defective view (libertarianism in your case, radical egalitarianism in mine) for a better one (some sort of middle-of-the-road position combining both liberty and equality).

If, however, the parties to a disagreement remain wedded to their opposing ethical positions but find themselves in circumstances requiring a nondeferrable joint decision, mutually respectful give-and-take discussion may eventually lead to a compromise position, C, which more or less splits the difference between them. Each party will, in this event, make concessions for the sake of agreement on a single course of action that seems to have some independent validity and to capture as much of one polar position as it does of the other. The matter is not, however, fully settled; there is no closure, no final harmony. Strictly speaking, moral compromise is not resolution. It makes the best of what both parties regard as a bad situation; each may subsequently try to persuade the other of the superiority of its initial position or to see that the same situation does not arise again. It is the discrepancy between the belief in the superiority of A or B and then acting in accord with C that raises philosophical difficulties. If my attachment to either A or B is a matter of ethical principle or conviction, how can I compromise without compromising my integrity?

In 1984, for example, the British Parliament appointed a Committee of Inquiry into Human Fertilization and Embryology, chaired by philosopher Mary Warnock.[23] Among the issues addressed by this group of physicians, lawyers, theologians, social scientists, and ordinary citizens was the question of biomedical research on human embryos. Moral opinion on this matter was at the time (and still is) deeply divided. At the root of the controversy are opposing views of the moral status of the embryo. People who believed human life begins at conception considered the human embryo to have the same status as an adult human being, and they were strongly opposed to embryo research. People who regarded the moral status of the embryo as significantly lower than that of an adult supported the research because it promised to advance understanding and treatment of infertility, miscarriage, congenital defects, and related problems. In 2002, with an emphasis on embryonic stem cells, this list has been expanded to include Parkinson's disease, Alzheimer's disease, and spinal cord injuries. The Warnock Committee was charged with making a recommendation at the national policy level on this highly controversial question. Although moral views on this matter were divided, a policy embodied in law would necessarily be singular and binding on all.

The committee's central recommendation on this question seems to have been a compromise between the two opposing positions. Such research would be permitted, but only for up to fourteen days from fertilization. It would, after this point, be unconditionally forbidden. As Mary Warnock put it: "In the end the Inquiry felt bound to argue, *partly* on Utilitarian grounds, that the benefits that had come in the past from research using human embryos were so great (and were likely to be even greater in the future), that such research had to be permitted; but that it should be permitted only at the very earliest stage of the development of the embryo."[24] Thus each party to the disagreement obtained part, but not all, of what it was after. And each made certain concessions. Those opposed to embryo research gained an absolute prohibition after a period of fourteen days, but had to acquiesce to research up to that time. Those wanting unrestricted embryo research gained permission to do research for up to fourteen days of development, but had to acquiesce to an absolute prohibition after that point.

Suppose you were a member of the Warnock Committee who believes, on reflection, that the embryo is a living human being entitled to all the rights and protections of any other human being. At the same time, however, you have a democratic temperament, affirm the reasonableness of the opposing position, recognize the need for a uniform national policy on embryo research, and acknowledge the importance of the committee's speaking with one voice on the matter. Days of debate and examining and responding to expert testimony and position papers have brought the committee to an impasse. You are now resigned to the fact that the full committee will not endorse your position; but at the same time it is clear that you and those of similar mind will never agree to the opposing position—one favoring little or no restriction on embryo research. Finally, someone proposes that research be permitted only until the formation of the primitive streak (fourteen days from fertilization). If all members of the committee come to agree that the occurrence of the primitive streak marks an independently valid, morally significant difference, one that trumps the emphasis on the sanctity of human life underlying the one polar position and the utilitarian considerations underlying the other, they agree on the independent superiority of a moderate or synthesis position. There is, in this instance, no compromise and no problem about preserving integrity. If, however, you and those sharing your view are still morally opposed to all embryo research, but are prepared, for the sake of agreement, to permit it for up to fourteen days, you are endorsing a moral compromise. The question is whether you can do this while retaining your integrity.

Circumstances of Compromise

The circumstances of compromise are those conditions that provide both the motivation and the grounds for moral compromise. They include factual and metaphysical uncertainty; moral complexity; a continuing cooperative relationship among the contending parties; an impending, nondeferrable decision; and limited resources.

Factual and Metaphysical Uncertainty

Central to the controversy over embryo research is uncertainty about the status of the embryo. Is a human embryo a living human being with the same rights as any other human? Is it, at best, only a potential human being, worthy of a measure of respect, but not to the same degree as full or actual human beings? Or is it, especially in its earlier stages, simply a clump of cells? The answer to this set of questions is not at all clear. In other contexts uncertainty may be less metaphysical, more empirical. Making an accurate prognosis for seriously ill, low-birthweight infants in newborn intensive care units is, for example, fraught with empirical uncertainty. As advances in medical knowledge and technology allow physicians to sustain the lives of younger and smaller newborns, knowledge of the long-range outcomes for such infants diminishes. Such uncertainty is endemic to the practice of medicine. In the case of embryo research, for example, there is uncertainty as to whether the proposed studies will in fact yield significant benefits.

Moral Complexity

The debate over embryo research is compounded by moral complexity. Both sides appeal to morally relevant considerations to support their views. Those opposed to further research place a theological or a Kantian emphasis on the respect owed to human life, while those favoring research stress the utilitarian value—in terms of sustaining and preserving future human lives—of the research. Neither party can, therefore, be accused of indifference to human life. Ethically, there is much to be said for both positions. At worst, each emphasizes certain important values while downplaying or placing less weight on others. Moral complexity of this sort is a function of the fact of (reasonable) pluralism. It is unlikely to be eliminated, at least in the near future, by advances in ethical theory.

Continuing Cooperative Relationship

Members of the Warnock Committee were involved in a continuing, cooperative relationship. As individuals each was free to take and defend the position most congenial to his or her worldview and way of life. To fill their communal charge to Parliament, however, they were under pressure to speak with one voice. For each to go his or her separate way, issuing a series of individual opinions, would be to admit failure of the collective project. Parliament knew public opinion was divided. One of the reasons for assembling the committee was to see if a highly informed, deliberative body representing all reasonable positions could come to some sort of reasonable agreement on the matter.

Impending Nondeferrable Decision

A policy on embryo research was needed soon. Unlike a seminar on moral philosophy, the committee did not have the luxury of endless debate or an inconclusive result. Committee members could not defer making a recommendation until factual and metaphysical uncertainty and moral complexity were fully resolved without abrogating their responsibilities as members of such a committee. In other situations, too, practical choice must often be made without philosophical certainty.

Limited Resources

A final circumstance of compromise is limited resources. Even if we are not limited by factual or metaphysical uncertainty and moral complexity, a compromise recommendation might be the best course of action when what is at issue is a distribution of scarce resources. Although not prominent in the debate over embryo research, it plays a role in various budgetary controversies and disputes over such limited resources as land and access to goods (for example, transplantable organs) and services (for example, access to health care). Another limited resource is time. Given sufficient time for reading, reflection, and discussion, a particular group might reach consensus on a particular issue. If, however, the situation is urgent and time for deliberation quite limited, it might in the meantime seek compromise.

Factual and metaphysical uncertainty, moral complexity, the need to maintain a continuing cooperative relationship, the need for a more or less immediate decision, and limited resources constitute the circumstances of compromise. If, in situations characterized by these circumstances, two or more parties to a moral conflict are unable to reach agreement, they should consider the possibility of compromise.

Integrity

Suppose now you were a member of the Warnock Committee and you are personally convinced that one or the other polar position on embryo research is morally correct—either such research should be absolutely forbidden or it should be permitted so long as the research is well designed and likely to add to clinically significant knowledge. You have a democratic temperament and acknowledge factual and metaphysical uncertainty and moral complexity. Could you, in these circumstances, agree to the compromise eventually endorsed by the committee without compromising your integrity? I think you could.

To see how compromise may be integrity-preserving, it is important to distinguish (1) what you believe to be correct, leaving aside for the moment your position on the committee and the fact that the circumstances of compromise apply, from (2) what you judge the committee ought to recommend, *all things considered*, when among the things to be considered are (a) your role as a committee member; (b) the rationally irreconcilable nature of the conflict; and (c) the circumstances of compromise.[25] As an individual you have a particular position on the ethics of embryo research. As a member of the committee with a democratic temperament, however, you must consider the extent to which the issue admits of reasonable differences, the need for a singular policy on the matter, and the importance of virtual unanimity if the committee's recommendation is to be credible and persuasive. In your capacity as committee member, these considerations reflect values and principles that you endorse and that partially determine who you are and what you stand for. You are committed to resolving the *policy* question on terms that pay equal respect to the contending reasonable positions and that stand a chance of public acceptability. Agreeing to the proposed compromise—that research be permitted for up to fourteen days but forbidden thereafter—may not, under such circumstances, constitute a threat to your integrity. On the contrary, taking into consideration *all* your values and principles, not simply those underlying your personal moral position, the compromise may be more integrity-preserving than any plausible alternative. The same will be true of those holding the opposing personal moral position.

The main point is that your identity is constituted in part by a complex constellation of occasionally conflicting values and principles. Your democratic temperament leads you to believe both in the superiority of your particular position *and* in the value of arriving at some sort of agreement on the policy question that reflects the complexity of the question and pays equal respect to those holding the opposing reasonable position on what seems, at least for now, to be a rationally irreconcilable conflict. In such cases of *internal* as well as external conflict, preserving integrity requires that you pursue that course of action that seems on balance to follow from the preponderance of your central and most highly cherished and defensible values and principles. In this case, I'm assuming your democratic temperament occupies a more central position in the constellation of your values and principles than holding out for your personally preferred moral position at the expense of a mutually respectful settlement on an issue involving reasonable disagreement and the circumstances of compromise. Endorsing the compromise position under such conditions is not to betray your integrity; it is rather to preserve it.

Yet there is no closure. Although the question of public policy may, for the time being, be settled, the ethical question remains open, and you are free, as an individual, to continue to make the case for the truth as you see it. Perhaps, if you and others are successful in this endeavor, public opinion will eventually swing in your favor and the compromise will be replaced by a policy more in line with your personal moral convictions.

PHYSICIAN-ASSISTED SUICIDE

The debate over legalizing physician-assisted suicide provides a useful illustration of the interlocking ideas of moral pluralism, the democratic temperament, and integrity-preserving compromise. First, there are reasonable positions on both sides of this complex issue. Second, whatever our particular position, a democratic temperament should incline us to seek a mutually respectful resolution. Third, the possibility of a patient's refusing food and water while receiving medical relief for pain and discomfort may be a bedside compromise—one worked out by doctors, nurses, and patients and their families—that can be accepted by those on both sides of the debate without compromising their integrity.

Moral Pluralism

Physician-assisted suicide (PAS) involves a doctor's providing a terminally ill patient with the means for ending his or her own life. This may, for example, involve a prescription for a large dose of barbiturates together with information about how to take them. In the vast majority of cases, terminally ill patients afforded the benefits of high-quality palliative care will have no desire to end their lives. In a small, but significant, number of cases, however, even the best palliative care will be ineffective or unacceptable to some dying patients. It will be unacceptable if, despite pain control, psychological suffering (due to loss of meaning, dignity, mobility, or independence) renders the patient's continued existence intolerable. PAS is thus, in the words of physicians Timothy Quill and Bernard Lo and philosopher Dan Brock, an option "of last resort for [the very small number of] competent, terminally ill patients who are suffering intolerably in spite of intensive efforts to palliate and who desire a hastened death."[26]

The argument for legalizing PAS turns on the same values and principles supporting the right to refuse life-extending medical treatment: respect for autonomy and patient well-being. Conscious, mentally competent, adult patients currently have a legal right, based on self-determination, to refuse any and all life-extending medical treatment if, in *their* informed judgment, the burdens of living with that treatment outweigh the benefits. The same basic values, the argument goes, should apply in the case of informed, conscious, competent, terminally ill patients whose pain or suffering is, despite high-quality palliative care, intolerable and who desire to end their lives. Physicians are legally required to "assist" patients who deliberately end their lives by refusing life-extending treatment by removing or refraining from administering such treatment. Physicians should also be *permitted* (but not required if it violates deeply held ethical or religious convictions) to assist the very small number of "competent, terminally ill patients who are suffering intolerably in spite of intensive efforts to palliate and who desire a hastened death."

There must, however, be stringent safeguards against the possibility of error, abuse, or coercion. These may include (1) ensuring access to high-quality palliative care; (2) obtaining the patient's fully informed consent (and perhaps requiring a brief waiting period to ensure the patient's request is stable and enduring); (3) obtaining independent second opinions about the diagnosis and prognosis, the ineffectiveness of palliative care, and the absence of treatable depression; and (4) requiring documentation of (1), (2), and (3) to ensure accountability. Permitting PAS under such conditions, the argument goes, allows us to respect patient autonomy and relieve suffering while minimizing, if not eliminating, risks to others.

This is a reasonable position. The trouble is that the opposing position is, on the face of it, no less reasonable. First, the very idea of PAS violates the medical profession's traditional prohibition against intentionally contributing to a patient's death. Legalizing it will require a reconceptualization of the function of medicine that the profession has, to this point, been unwilling to undertake. Second, even if we can identify individual cases where a physician would be *ethically* justified in assisting a patient in suicide, there is a reasonable case against *legalizing* it. To permit physicians to intentionally contribute to death, many argue, is to take the first step on a "slippery slope" that may well lead from PAS to voluntary active euthanasia, and from voluntary active euthanasia to nonvoluntary active euthanasia. From here it's only a short step to physicians hastening the deaths of patients whose continued treatment poses a burden not to themselves, but to others. The risk of sliding to the bottom of this slippery slope, the argument goes, is so great that we ought not to take the first step. We ought, therefore, to retain the legal prohibition against PAS even if it comes at the cost of intolerable pain and suffering for the relatively small number of patients who could possibly benefit from its being legal. All things considered, the moral costs of legalizing assisted suicide are likely to outweigh the prospective benefits.

Each of these lines of argument is, though reasonable, inconclusive. Factual uncertainty and moral complexity, as I will show below, prevent each side from obtaining the sort of conclusive support that would reduce the opposition to a tiny minority of cranks. So the debate continues, as does the rancor. What should we do in the meantime?

Democratic Temperament

Personally, I favor legalization. It's possible, I think, to respect the rights of the small number of people for whom PAS would be justified while reducing the possibility of coercion, error, or abuse, and thus safeguarding those for whom it would not be justified. A law permitting PAS under restricted circumstances has been in effect in Oregon since 1997 with no ill effects. I appreciate the complexity of the matter, however, and respect the reasonableness of those opposing it. My democratic temperament inclines me to seek some sort of accommodation.[27] I'm unhappy with the status quo in all states but Oregon, because it gives everything to those who reasonably oppose legalization and nothing to those who no less reasonably support it. Is there some third, more or less coherent, possibility that splits the difference between the two? I think there is.

Integrity-Preserving Compromise

The debate over PAS is characterized by the circumstances of compromise. First, there is factual uncertainty about the consequences of legalizing assisted suicide. No one knows for sure whether legalization will ultimately result in sliding down the slippery slope to widespread abuse. Second, the issue is morally complex. Each party to the debate can point to morally significant values and principles to support its position. Third, there is an impending, nondeferrable decision. The status quo favors one side of the issue, but its victory is not democratic. Opinion polls often show more than 50 percent of the public favoring legalization. Until legislatures pay more attention to the reasonable positions on both sides, the issue will not go away. Fourth, as a matter of law in a democratic society, the issue involves citizens related in a continuing, cooperative relationship. Finally, limited resources are an issue insofar as one of the questions is whether the nation is willing to provide high-quality palliative care to everyone who could benefit from it irrespective of their insurance coverage or their ability to pay out-of-pocket. If the poor or uninsured are denied high-quality palliative care, they might elect assistance in suicide rather than suffering without such care. Such a choice, however, seems less than free. If, on the other hand, the nation fails to provide access to high-quality palliative care to all who could benefit from it, how can it, in good conscience, oppose assistance in suicide to terminally ill patients who are denied such care and for whom the prospect of continued pain and suffering renders death preferable to continued life? Granted, under more favorable conditions they might not elect PAS. But those conditions do not exist and this, the life they are living, is the only one they have. "It is on earth that we live," Berlin has said, "and it is here [and now] that we must believe and act."

A possible compromise, splitting the difference between the opposing positions and requiring no change in the law, would permit mentally competent, terminally ill patients for whom palliative care is either ineffective or unacceptable to hasten their deaths by refusing hydration and nutrition with the assistance of physicians and nurses who relieve associated pain and discomfort. An article on patient refusal of hydration and nutrition (PRHN) by physicians James Bernat and R. Peter Mogielnicki and philosopher Bernard Gert points out that death by starvation and dehydration need not be accompanied by intolerable physical suffering. Health care professionals may comfort the dying patient, they point out, "by physical presence as well as skillful treatment of symptoms, including pain, dyspnea, and dryness of mouth."[28] Depending on the patient's overall condition, the process will take one to three weeks or longer if he or she continues to take some fluids. Moreover, there is no need to change the law. The established ethical and legal right of competent informed patients to refuse life-prolonging medical interventions, including medically administered hydration and nutrition, may reasonably be interpreted as extending to "natural" drinking and eating as well. In an article in the *Journal of the American Medical Association*, physician David M. Eddy describes his eighty-four-year-old mother bringing her life to a close in just this way.[29]

PRHN may thus be a reasonable compromise between those favoring physician-assisted suicide and those opposing it. Each party makes concessions for the sake of respecting the other. Supporters of assisted suicide must accept a slower death, and perhaps more psychological suffering, than they would like. Many will also think PRHN undignified, especially if mental clarity is lost toward the end of the process. Still, it should from their standpoint be better than the status quo and accommodates many of the concerns of those opposed to assisted suicide. Opponents of PAS must agree to the provision of comfort care to individuals engaging in PRHN. Still, the mechanism of death is provided and controlled by the patient alone. Doctors and nurses make no causal contribution to the patient's ending his or her life. They simply provide the same sort of comfort and care that they would provide to a patient who has refused one or another form of life-extending medical treatment. Because PRHN requires considerable and extended patient resolve, health professionals can be reasonably sure of the act's voluntariness, and the possibility for abuse is greatly diminished. In agreeing to comfort care in such circumstances, however, opponents of PAS acknowledge and respect some of the reasonable concerns of those who support it.

The compromise is integrity-preserving for individuals on both sides because it permits them to retain much of what is central to their respective positions on PAS while acknowledging (a) their status as mutually respectful democratic citizens, (b) the reasonableness of the opposing position, and (c) the circumstances of compromise. As democratic citizens each of us must consider the extent to which the issue admits of reasonable differences and the value of mutual respect and informed, unforced reasonable agreement. Each of these considerations reflects values and principles that we endorse and that partially determine who we are and what we stand for. We value resolution of the disagreement on terms that pay equal respect to the contending reasonable positions. As with the Warnock Committee's position on embryo research, then, whatever our particular position on PAS, compromising on PRHN may, in the light of all our values and principles, be more integrity-preserving than any alternative. Preserving and respecting a democratic temperament in ourselves and those with whom we disagree may be more important than "winning" on this particular issue.

Although there is a small literature on PRHN, more work must be done if it is to serve as an acceptable compromise position. It needs to be explicitly discussed and debated by the public and by health care professionals. And a set of procedural safeguards, similar to those proposed for PAS, may have to be devised and put into effect.

Finally, though I have focused on plausible examples of compromise, I don't want to leave the impression that every reasonable moral conflict can be settled by an integrity-preserving compromise. Tragic conflict, like reasonable disagreement, is also a part of human life. Still, acknowledging the fact of moral pluralism, cultivating a democratic temperament, and engaging in mutually respectful give-and-take discussion may result in more integrity-preserving compromise than we might initially expect.

NOTES

1. Stuart Hampshire, *Morality and Conflict* (Cambridge, Mass.: Harvard University Press, 1983), 144.

2. Joshua Miller, *Democratic Temperament: The Legacy of William James* (Lawrence: University Press of Kansas, 1997).

3. John Rawls, *Political Liberalism* (New York: Columbia University Press, 1993), 36; Joshua Cohen, "Moral Pluralism and Political Consensus," in *The Idea of Democracy*, ed. David Copp, Jean Hampton, and John Roemer (Cambridge: Cambridge University Press, 1993), 270–92.

4. Rawls, *Political Liberalism*, 36.

5. Rawls, *Political Liberalism*, 37.

6. Isaiah Berlin, "On the Pursuit of the Ideal," in *The Crooked Timber of Humanity*, ed. Henry Hardy (Princeton, N.J.: Princeton University Press), 12.

7. Berlin, "On the Pursuit of the Ideal," 13.

8. R. M. Hare, *Moral Thinking: Its Levels, Method, and Point* (Oxford: Oxford University Press, 1981), 44.

9. Hare, *Moral Thinking*, 46.

10. Berlin, "On the Pursuit of the Ideal," 13.

11. Hare, *Moral Thinking*, 156.

12. Berlin, "On the Pursuit of the Ideal," 7–10.

13. Kristin Luker, *Abortion and the Politics of Motherhood* (Berkeley: University of California Press, 1984), 158.

14. Hampshire, *Morality and Conflict*, 6.

15. Rawls, *Political Liberalism*, 55–57.

16. Luker, *Abortion and the Politics of Motherhood*, 158–91.

17. Ruth Macklin, "Inner Workings of an Ethics Committee: Latest Battle over Jehovah's Witnesses," *Hastings Center Report* 18, no. 1 (February 1988): 25.

18. John Dewey, *The Public and Its Problems*, in *John Dewey: The Later Works, 1925–1953*, vol. 2: 1925–1927, ed. J. A. Boydston (Carbondale: Southern Illinois University Press, 1977), 325.

19. William James, "On a Certain Blindness in Human Beings," in *William James: Writings 1878–1899* (New York: Library of America, 1992), 841.

20. James, "On a Certain Blindness," 860.

21. Berlin, "On the Pursuit of the Ideal," 17.

22. This paragraph and much of the remainder of this section are adapted from Martin Benjamin, *Splitting the Difference: Compromise and Integrity in Ethics and Politics* (Lawrence: University Press of Kansas, 1990); and Martin Benjamin, "Philosophical Integrity and Policy Development in Bioethics," *Journal of Medicine and Philosophy* 15 (June 1990): 375–89.

23. Mary Warnock, *A Question of Life: The Warnock Report on Fertilisation and Embryology* (Oxford: Basil Blackwell, 1985).

24. Mary Warnock, "Moral Thinking and Government Policy: The Warnock Committee on Human Embryology," *Milbank Memorial Fund Quarterly* 63, no. 3 (Summer 1985): 517.

25. Arthur Kuflik, "Morality and Compromise," in *Compromise in Ethics, Law, and Politics*, ed. J. Roland Pennock and John W. Chapman (New York: New York University Press, 1979), 51.

26. Timothy Quill, Bernard Lo, and Dan W. Brock, "Palliative Options of Last Resort," *Journal of the American Medical Association* 278, no. 3 (December 17, 1997): 2099.

27. David Wong, "Coping with Moral Conflict and Ambiguity," *Ethics* 102, no. 4 (July 1992): 763–84.

28. James Bernat, Bernard Gert, and R. Peter Mogielnicki, "Patient Refusal of Hydration and Nutrition: An Alternative to Physician-Assisted Suicide and Voluntary Euthanasia," *Archives of Internal Medicine* 153, no. 24 (December 27, 1993): 2724.

29. David M. Eddy, "A Conversation with My Mother," *Journal of the American Medical Association* 272, no. 3 (July 20, 1994): 179–81.

Chapter 7

Determining Death

The individual has a stock of old opinions already, but he meets a new experience that puts them to a strain. . . . The result is an inward trouble to which his mind till then had been a stranger, and from which he seeks to escape by modifying his previous mass of opinions. He saves as much of it as he can, for in this matter of belief we are all extreme conservatives.

—William James, *Pragmatism*

What serious men not engaged in the professional business of philosophy most want to know is what modifications and abandonments of intellectual inheritance are required by the newer industrial, political, and scientific movements. They want to know what these newer movements mean when translated into general ideas. Unless professional philosophy can mobilize itself sufficiently to assist in this clarification and redirection of men's thoughts, it is likely to get more and more sidetracked from the main currents of contemporary life.

—John Dewey, "The Need for a Recovery of Philosophy"

Debates over the determination of death illustrate these observations by James and Dewey. From about 1850 to the 1960s, there was general agreement about the determination of death. An individual was pronounced dead when breathing and heartbeat had permanently ceased. In the mid-1960s, however, advances in medical knowledge and technology were enabling physicians to maintain respiration and circulation in patients with *total* loss of brain function. This new experience, as James might have put it, together with a growing need for transplantable organs, was placing considerable strain on our old opinions about the determination of death. The result was an "inward trouble" of mind from which physicians sought to escape by modifying our "previous mass of opinions." This modification—declaring patients with heartbeat and respiration but total loss of brain function *dead*—saved as much of the previous mass of opinions as possible, confirming James's observation that "in this matter of belief we are all extreme conservatives."

Yet the change has not remained stable. Debate over when someone is dead continues to this day. An explanation is suggested by the passage from Dewey. Adopting new criteria for death required certain "modifications and abandonments of intellectual inheritance" that were not at the time adequately considered. Those in the forefront of change gave insufficient attention to the philosophical question of what these modifications and abandonments meant when translated into general ideas. This question ranged beyond the more or less immediate practical concerns of physicians. Thus, to adapt Dewey's words, *until* serious men and women not engaged in academic philosophy attend fully to the philosophical dimensions of the determination of death and *until* academic philosophers adequately assist in this clarification and redirection of our thought, the debate is likely to continue.

This chapter has two aims. The first is to identify and resolve the main philosophical question raised by the debate over the determination of death. I begin by tracing the historical development of the debate. I turn then to what Dewey called the general ideas—the possible alterations of our intellectual inheritance—at stake in it. I conclude by proposing a clarification and redirection of our thinking about death and defend it on pragmatic grounds. The second aim is to reinforce and relate various points made in previous chapters. The debate over the determination of death illustrates some of the advantages of a practical or pragmatic approach to philosophical questions.

BACKGROUND

In the not-so-distant past, respiration and circulation were the principal signs of human life. Individuals were pronounced dead when they had permanently stopped breathing or their hearts had stopped beating. In the mid-1960s, however, developments in mechanical respiration (together with related supportive measures) gave physicians the capacity to maintain respiration and circulation in patients who had undergone total and permanent loss of brain function. Such patients—patients who were totally and permanently unconscious—were, according to the prevailing understanding, living human beings.

In 1968 a landmark article published by an ad hoc committee of the Harvard Medical School identified reliable clinical criteria for identifying respirator-dependent patients who have lost *all* brain functions, including primitive brain stem reflexes. Patients satisfying these criteria, the committee said, were in "irreversible coma."[1] The committee then proposed that patients in irreversible coma be declared dead and removed from the respirator. The publication of this article gave currency to the misleading term 'brain death'.

'Brain death' in the first and most literal sense means the death of an organ, the brain. But death of an *organ* is one thing and death of the *organism of which it is a part* quite another. Yet the term 'brain death' soon came to be used to refer to the latter as well. That is, a patient pronounced dead by use of the so-called Harvard criteria for irreversible coma was often said to be "brain dead." The result was a misleading impression that there were now *two kinds* of death—ordinary (heart-lung) death and "brain death." The confusion may be avoided by scrupulously restricting the expression 'brain death' to the death of the brain and using the term 'brain criteria' to refer to the criteria for pronouncing a respirator-dependent patient with absolutely no brain function *dead*. Such a patient should be considered dead in the same way, and for the same basic reasons, as a patient whose heartbeat and respiration have permanently ceased. This important clarification, however, required taking account of certain philosophical considerations that, in the late 1960s, were given insufficient attention.

The motivations for the ad hoc Harvard committee's recommendation that "irreversible coma" (or the death of the brain) be accepted as a criterion for determining the death of the patient were clinical, not philosophical. First, the increasing number of respirator-dependent patients meeting the Harvard criteria were becoming a burden on limited medical, technological, and financial resources. This seemed wasteful insofar as physicians believed such patients could no longer benefit from treatment. Second, the development of organ transplantation was increasing the demand for kidneys, hearts, and other organs. Transplant surgeons wanted permission to remove healthy organs from irreversibly comatose, respirator-dependent patients without being accused of murder. And third, waiting to pronounce such patients dead according to traditional heart-lung criteria was exacting a high emotional toll on friends and family members awaiting the inevitable.

After publication of the Harvard criteria, states began reconsidering their statutes on death. By 1980, twenty-four states had incorporated brain criteria. Then in 1981 a Presidential Commission undertook a comprehensive review of the medical, legal, and ethical issues in the determination of death. The commission eventually endorsed brain criteria and, together with the American Medical Association and the American Bar Association, recommended adoption by all states of a model statute, the Uniform Determination of Death Act (UDDA):

> An individual who has sustained either (1) irreversible cessation of circulatory and respiratory functions or (2) irreversible cessation of all functions of the entire brain, including the brain stem, is dead. A determination of death must be made in accordance with accepted medical standards.[2]

Brain criteria for the determination of death have now been incorporated into the law of all states. Health professionals, lawyers, legislators, and the public at large generally agree that a patient who has permanently lost all brain function is, despite respirator-assisted breathing and heartbeat, dead.

Yet the debate has not ended. As specified by the UDDA, the new criteria require "irreversible cessation of *all* functions of the *entire* brain, *including the brain stem*" (italics added). But beginning with the case of Karen Ann Quinlan in 1976, the condition now dubbed "persistent vegetative state" has become both more prevalent and widely known. Patients in a persistent vegetative state are unconscious because the parts of the brain necessary for thought and consciousness are no longer functioning. If and when a neurologist determines that the patient will *never* recover consciousness, the condition is called "permanent vegetative state." Patients in this condition are totally and *permanently* unconscious. Yet they do not satisfy the current criteria for death. They have not lost *all* brain function. Because their brain stems continue to function and because the brain stem can regulate respiration, blood pressure, and a number of other vegetative functions, in the absence of cerebral function, patients in a permanent vegetative state are often able to breathe and maintain heartbeat without the assistance of a respirator.[3] Are such patients living or dead?

According to the law, they are alive. The general criteria for death proposed by the ad hoc Harvard committee, endorsed by the President's Commission, and adopted by the states explicitly require the permanent loss of *all* brain function, *including the brain stem*—and patients in a permanent vegetative state have functioning brain stems. But a number of bioethicists have recommended that such patients be pronounced dead. Total and permanent loss of consciousness, and not total and permanent loss of *all* brain function, they maintain, is what marks the line between life and death for the likes of you and me.

The controversy is usually characterized as a debate over the "definition" of death. Defenders of the status quo are said to accept a "whole-brain" definition of death, while their opponents propose we adopt a "higher-brain" definition. This characterization is, however, misleading. The disagreement is not, at bottom, a matter of definition, but a question of what Dewey described as the "general ideas" underlying the "modifications and abandonments of intellectual inheritance" required by a "new scientific movement." The new scientific movement is, in this instance, the capacity to diagnose total and permanent loss of consciousness in patients for whom respiration and heartbeat may be medically maintained (in some cases, for over thirty years). The underlying general idea is whether being alive is, for the likes of you and me, solely a matter of biology or whether it also involves consciousness (or the potential for consciousness). This is a far-reaching philosophical question, not simply a matter of definition.

THE MAIN QUESTION

We have no trouble understanding what people mean when they speak or write of the death of a human embryo, a lawn, a dog, a language, or an entire culture. In each case, the entity to which the word 'dead' (or one of its cognates) is applied has ceased to exist as a thing *of that kind*. The conditions of existence and death of any entity—be it a human embryo, a lawn, a dog, a language, or a culture—are determined by the *kind* of thing that it is, which is in turn determined by the rules of the language games within which it is used. 'Death' is the cessation of life, the ceasing to be. When we are puzzled over what it means to say "Karen Ann Quinlan is dead," the problem centers not on the meaning of 'dead', but rather on the entity to which we refer—exactly what *kind* of entity is it, and what are the conditions of its existence? Are we referring to a human biological organism or are we referring to something else, something whose conditions of existence include consciousness or at least the potential for consciousness?

The so-called definition of death debate, then, is really a debate over how we should *conceive* the individual subject to which the words 'is dead' are applied. Exactly what *sort* of thing *ceases to exist* when we say someone like you or me is dead? This is the difficult, unavoidable philosophical question generated by the capacity of modern medicine to sustain respiration and heartbeat in patients who are totally and permanently unconscious.

We owe the misplaced emphasis on definition, I suspect, to the fact that the terms of the debate were set by those who first encountered and addressed it—members of the medical community. Physicians are understandably more comfortable talking about definitions than they are about opposing philosophical conceptions of the human individual. But the philosophical questions are now unavoidable. What exactly is it that loses life or ceases to be when we say that someone like you or me is dead? What's so important about whatever has been lost when we pronounce death to justify the enormous difference between our treatment of the living and the treatment of the dead? These are not, on reflection, easy questions. And there may be no single answer to them that ought, at this time, to be embraced by all of us, insofar as we are informed and rational. Still, we will not reach closure on the determination of death until we can satisfactorily resolve them.

Death of the Organism as a Whole

Though the ad hoc Harvard committee did not address these questions, eleven years later the President's Commission did. Essential to human life, the commission argued, is the integrated functioning of the circulatory system, the respiratory system, and the central nervous system.

> Three organs—the heart, lungs, and brain—assume special significance . . . because their interrelationship is very close and the irreversible cessation of any one very quickly stops the other two and consequently halts the integrated functioning of the organism as a whole. Because they were easily measured, circulation and respiration were traditionally the basic "vital signs." But breathing and heartbeat are not life itself. They are simply used as signs—as one window for viewing a deeper and more complex reality: a triangle of interrelated systems with the brain at its apex.[4]

The subject of life and death is, then, "the organism as a whole." The organism as a whole is alive when there is the integrated functioning of the circulatory, respiratory, and central nervous systems. The organism dies when the integrated functioning of these three systems is permanently disrupted. Permanent loss of any corner of the "triangle" soon leads to permanent loss of the other two.

According to the commission, adoption of brain criteria does not require a change in philosophical understanding. The subject of life and death has always been the organism as a whole, conceived as the integrated functioning of the circulatory, respiratory, and central nervous systems. Each set of criteria—heart-lung and brain—represents a different "window" for viewing the same state, death of the organism as a whole. "On this view," the commission writes, "death is that moment at which the body's physiological systems cease to constitute an integrated whole. Even if life continues in individual cells or organs, life of the organism as a whole requires complex integration and without the latter, a person cannot properly be regarded as alive." The commission considered and explicitly rejected "higher-brain" criteria because, among other things, even if it could be shown that higher brain function is necessary for consciousness, the cessation of higher brain function "often cannot be assessed with the certainty that would be required in applying a statutory definition [of death]."[5]

Finally, the commission acknowledged with some pride that its proposal is "deliberately conservative." The UDDA incorporates legal recognition of a new way to diagnose death, but it does not put forth a new philosophical conception of death. Brain criteria identify the very same thing heart-lung criteria have traditionally identified—death of the organism as a whole. Thus, in modifying our old opinions to accommodate a new experience that puts them to a strain, the commission sought to save as much of our previous mass of opinions as it could. "For in this matter of belief," as James put it, "we are all extreme conservatives."

Death of the Person

But, advocates of higher-brain criteria contend, the capacity to sustain biological life long after an individual becomes totally and permanently unconscious requires more extensive revision of our previous mass of opinions than the President's Commission was willing to acknowledge. A "person"—where the word 'person' designates the kind of being whose continued existence is generally of the utmost importance to us—may be dead even though the organism as a whole is alive. What really matters to us, when we consider our own lives and the lives of others, is continued existence as subjects of consciousness, *persons*, not continued existence as *personless* biological organisms.

Imagine, for example, the following situation. In one part of a large urban hospital, infant Andrew is born with anencephaly. Anencephaly is a rare congenital condition marked by absence of a major portion of the brain, skull, and scalp. Anencephalic infants have a functioning brain stem, but because they lack functioning cerebral hemispheres, they do not and never will experience any degree of consciousness. Andrew, though "alive" by current criteria, is totally and permanently unconscious. Without highly aggressive care, Andrew is likely to satisfy the UDDA's criteria for death within a few days, if not hours. Even with aggressive care, he is unlikely to live for more than a week or two.

In a nearby hospital lies infant Helen. Helen has hypoplastic left heart syndrome, a congenital malformation very likely to lead to an early death. Apart from her seriously defective heart, Helen is healthy. Her brain is fine. Apart from his seriously defective brain, Andrew is healthy. His heart, in particular, is fine. Suppose, as may in reality be the case, it is surgically possible to replace Helen's defective heart with Andrew's healthy one. Such an operation is likely to significantly extend Helen's life. The surgeon cannot, however, wait until Andrew is pronounced dead. By the time Andrew satisfies the current criteria for death, his heart will have seriously deteriorated. So the question is whether, if both Helen's and Andrew's parents give their informed consent, it would be wrong for a surgeon to remove Andrew's heart and transplant it to Helen.

If by 'wrong' we mean *illegal*, the answer is clear. Under current law, removing Andrew's heart would be an act of murder. Andrew is a living human being and the cause of death would be the surgeon's cutting into his chest and removing his heart. But is removing Andrew's heart to save Helen's life a significant *moral* wrong? Indeed, might it not be wrong *not* to do the operation—wrong not only for Helen and her parents, but also for Andrew's parents? (Parents of anencephalic infants often want to donate their child's organs to retrieve some measure of good from an otherwise ill-fated pregnancy.) How, if Andrew is totally and permanently unconscious, would he be wronged by removing his heart? Removing his heart will not cause him pain or suffering, nor will it deprive him of a valuable future. As far as pain or prospects for future experience go, Andrew is no different than any cadaver organ donor. Why, then, should it be okay to save a life by transplanting the heart of a patient satisfying "whole-brain" criteria for death, but wrong to save a life by transplanting Andrew's heart?

The Council on Ethical and Judicial Affairs of the American Medical Association reports that "in a survey of leading medical experts in ethics, two thirds of those surveyed stated that they consider the use of organs from anencephalic infants 'intrinsically moral,' and more than half stated their support for a change in the law to permit such use."[6] I'm inclined to agree; and when I ask *why* the law should be changed, the answer that springs to mind is that there is an important sense in which Andrew is *already* dead. Though Andrew is certainly a living human organism, something central to my understanding of the wrongness of killing is missing in this and similar cases.

Exactly what this is comes into sharper focus when we shift from anencephaly to *permanent* vegetative state. Both anencephalic infants and patients in a permanent vegetative state are totally and permanently unconscious. The main difference is that total and permanent unconsciousness is *congenital* in the former and *acquired* in the latter. Thus if anencephalic infants are to be pronounced dead because they are totally and permanently unconscious, we shall have to do the same with patients in a permanent vegetative state. Is there good reason to consider these patients dead?

Imagine you have just been diagnosed with a terrible disease that will soon ravage your body and end your life. A surgeon then comes along who offers the possibility of a dramatic new operation guaranteed to stop the disease in its tracks. There is, however, a hitch. The operation is very long and the anesthetic very powerful. One of the unfortunate side-effects is that although the disease will be cured, you will emerge from the operation in a permanent vegetative state. But, the surgeon cheerfully emphasizes, at least you'll be alive! The operation will cure the disease and your life will have been saved. Finally, let us suppose, the operation is very expensive. To cover its costs you will have to use up your life savings and sell most of your possessions. The question now is whether you'd agree to undergo the operation.

When I put this question to myself, the answer is clear. Whether or not I have the operation, it seems to me that *I* will be dead. That is, I—the being whose motivation for having the operation is to live to watch my grandchildren grow, finish the book I'm working on, enjoy conversation and travel with my wife, and see the Chicago Cubs win the World Series—will not survive in either case. Whether I have the operation or forego it, I—whatever exactly 'I' refers to here—*will be dead*. Though my body will survive the operation, I—the person whose body it is—will not. The only difference from my perspective is whether the doctors get my money or whether it goes to my family. And there's no question that I'd want it to go to my family.

The same general point can be made from a third-person perspective. Suppose someone develops a permanent vegetative state drug— a tasteless chemical compound that makes anyone who ingests it totally and permanently unconscious. Then someone deliberately places this drug in the drink of one of your dearest friends or relatives. Soon after drinking it, your friend or relative becomes totally and permanently unconscious. The heinous perpetrator is then caught. How should he or she be charged? Should the charge be *murder*? If you (not unreasonably) answer "yes," isn't this because you believe that your friend or relative (the person you loved, whose well-being and future you valued, and whose company you cherished) is now *dead*? How persuaded would you be by a defense attorney arguing for a lesser charge by pointing out that your friend or family member still enjoys integrated functioning of the circulatory, respiratory, and central nervous systems and therefore (on no less authority than the report of a Presidential Commission) is alive?

As these examples suggest, there may be an important difference between a living human biological organism and whatever it is we regard as the subject of life and death when we say of ourselves or others that we are living or dead. What, then, is the subject of the predicates 'living' and 'dead' when applied to the likes of you and me? What, in other words, does X refer to when we say of beings like ourselves, "X is alive" or "X is dead"? Does it refer principally to a biological organism (the class of which includes you and me *together with* anencephalic infants and permanently vegetative patients) *or*, as my examples suggest, does it refer to what I am calling a *person*, where in a small number of cases a person may be dead while its body—a biological organism—remains alive? There will be no closure on the determination of death until there is closure on this fundamental question.

THE SUBJECT OF LIFE AND DEATH

Whatever the answer, it will not be discovered in a fixed, external reality that is somehow independent of and prior to human aims and interests. As argued in chapters 2 and 3, the idea of such a reality does no real work for us. All efforts to apprehend the world directly and nonlinguistically and then compare it with what we say about it have ended in failure. We cannot make cognitive contact with the world (or reality or the facts) apart from the way we talk about it, and there is no way to separate how we talk about the world from our various aims and interests. What is at issue, in determining whether, for the likes of you and me, the subject of human life and death is a biological organism or a person is a far-reaching choice among language games.

As with past choices among language games—between, for example, a Ptolemaic (or geocentric) and a Copernican (or heliocentric) way of thinking and talking about the universe—we must look to our overall aims, the comparative usefulness of different ways of talking, thinking, and acting, and the extent to which certain ways of talking, thinking, and acting usefully cohere with other ways of talking, thinking, and acting. On such grounds, educated people largely agree that the Copernican conception of the universe is preferable to the Ptolemaic conception. The one is true, we say, and the other false. So too, whether we conceive the subject of human life and death as a biological organism or a person is a question of comparative usefulness and coherence with other things we say, think, and do rather than a question of accurate representation.

Which conception of the human individual—and its related existence conditions—best coheres with the complex network of actions and beliefs giving shape and meaning to our lives? Which conception is a better overall fit with other background beliefs and theories, judgments about particular cases, and general rules and principles in wide reflective equilibrium (as discussed in chapter 5)? Which conception yields a better overall account of "how things in the broadest possible sense of the term hang together in the broadest possible sense of the term"? Is it principally a biological conception, centering on the integrated functioning of the organism as a whole? Or is it a social/psychological conception, centering on consciousness? To fix this question pragmatically—to bring it "down to earth," as it were—we must ask ourselves such further questions as: What really matters to us with respect to questions of life and death? Are we, when push comes to shove, really concerned with the continued existence of the integrated functioning of the circulatory, respiratory, and central nervous systems, *independent of its contribution to consciousness*? Are we, when push comes to shove, willing to sacrifice other important values and principles, not to mention economic and social resources, to sustain the integrated functioning of a human organism as a whole irrespective of consciousness or potential for consciousness? What conception of the subject of life and death provides the most practical and unified

approach to the largest number of bioethical issues? And, most generally, what conception best *presently* coheres with the largest number of things we are, on reflection, strongly inclined to *do and believe*?
Though detailed and complete answers to these and related questions are beyond the scope of this chapter, my hunch is that conceiving the subject of life and death in terms of personhood provides a more satisfactory answer to this family of questions than
conceiving it in terms of biology alone.

First, when we ask what really matters to us with regard to human
life and death—why, for example, we believe murder is so very
wrong—the most plausible answer, it seems to me, turns on the loss
to the individual of all the valuable experiences, enjoyments, plans,
and actions that would otherwise have constituted his or her future.
This is why we are inclined to think that someone who slips someone else a "permanent vegetative state drug" should be charged with
murder. Killing in general and murder in particular are wrong because they inflict the greatest possible loss to the victim. But neither
anencephalic infants nor those in a permanent vegetative state can
be deprived of all of the valuable experiences, enjoyments, plans,
and actions that would otherwise have constituted his or her future
because they are, due to the absence or permanent loss of cerebral
functioning, incapable of experiencing, enjoying, planning, or doing
anything. If the loss of all possible experience, enjoyment, plans, and
actions is what makes killing prima facie wrong, murder victims are
best conceived as biological *persons*, not simply as biological organisms. (Note that this also accounts for why in some cases death may
be considered a benefit. If unmitigable pain and suffering permanently deprive an individual of all valuable experience, enjoyment,
plans, and actions, death may no longer be the worst thing that can
happen to him or her. He or she, as we sometimes put it, may be
"better off dead.")

Second, acceptance of the UDDA has not entirely eliminated the "inward trouble" of mind to which the Harvard criteria and the UDDA
were a response. Many of us are troubled by the prohibition against
transplanting hearts from anencephalic infants like Andrew in order
to save the lives of infants with hypoplastic left heart syndrome like
Helen. We also question spending over a billion dollars per year for an
increasing number of permanently vegetative patients while millions
of Americans are denied access to genuinely beneficial health care because of limited funds. And we are disturbed by the fact that each year
hundreds of persons in need of a new heart or liver die on waiting lists

while the hearts and livers of patients in a permanent vegetative state keep on going until they satisfy the UDDA, at which time their organs are no longer biologically suitable for transplantation. To what extent should we be willing to trade off the lives of infants like Helen, together with the extensive financial and human resources used to maintain permanently vegetative patients and the life-saving potential of their organs, for the sake of the integrated functioning of various sets of circulatory, respiratory, and central nervous systems? Can defenders of a biological conception of the subject of life and death show why the continued existence of a totally and permanently unconscious living human organism is more valuable than the lives of infants like Helen, other medical uses for the resources necessary to maintain vegetative life, or the lives of those who die while awaiting transplantable organs?

Finally, a shift from a mainly biological conception of human life and death to a more social/psychological conception may lead to plausible and coherent resolutions to a wide range of bioethical issues—from abortion and embryo research, on the one hand, to euthanasia and assisted suicide, on the other. Exploring the ramifications of such a change—its overall human and economic costs, benefits, implications, and so on—may also lead to a better understanding of ourselves and of the value of our lives.

But what about the problem of diagnosing permanent vegetative state? One of the difficulties with identifying the subject of life and death with the person and using permanent vegetative state as a criterion of death is that permanent vegetative state cannot be assessed by *all* physicians with the same high degree of certainty as total and permanent loss of all brain function. A statutory definition of death, the President's Commission argued, requires that death be able to be diagnosed by all physicians with a high degree of certainty. Conceiving life in terms of the organism as a whole and death as the loss of integrated functioning of the respiratory, circulatory, and central nervous systems satisfies this requirement. Neither special equipment nor special training is required for reliably determining, in the words of the UDDA, "either (1) irreversible cessation of circulatory and respiratory functions or (2) irreversible cessation of all functions of the entire brain, including the brain stem." Irreversible cessation of all brain functions can be diagnosed shortly after it occurs and, in the words of neurologist Ronald Cranford, "with an extraordinarily high degree of certainty."[7] The diagnosis of permanent vegetative state is, however, another matter. It must be made over time and by specialists in neurology. It also, as the following passage from a task force of specialists reveals, varies with the cause of injury and is probabilistic:

> a persistent vegetative state can be judged to be permanent 12 months after a traumatic injury in adults and children; recovery after this time is exceedingly rare and almost always involves a severe disability. In adults and children with nontraumatic injuries, a persistent vegetative state can be considered to be permanent after three months; recovery does occur, but it is rare and at best associated with moderate or severe disability.[8]

Because, then, the diagnosis of permanent vegetative state is not as simple or certain as that of total loss of brain function, it cannot serve as a statutory criterion of death.

This presents a complication for conceiving the subject of life and death as a person, but not an obstacle. First, even if permanent vegetative state cannot, at this point, be determined as easily and as reliably as either (1) irreversible cessation of circulatory and respiratory functions or (2) irreversible cessation of all functions of the entire brain, including the brain stem, conceiving the subject of life and death as a person provides a more adequate rationale for (1) and (2) than does conceiving the subject of life and death as a biological organism. Why are (1) and (2) criteria of death? Because an individual meeting either (1) or (2) *is totally and permanently unconscious*. This is what really matters to us, not the disintegration of the integrated functioning of the respiratory, circulatory, and central nervous systems. Individuals undergoing irreversible cessation of circulatory and respiratory function were for centuries (rightly) said to be dead by people who had little or no understanding of the respiratory, circulatory, and central nervous systems and the relations among them. But they did know that individuals whose breathing and heartbeat had permanently ceased would never again be conscious. Disintegration of the integrated functioning of the respiratory, circulatory, and central nervous systems is significant not in and of itself but because it leads to total and permanent loss of consciousness.

Second, in the vast majority of cases it is currently as easy to diagnose the death of a person as it is the death of the organism as a whole *because they employ the same criteria*. A *person* is dead if he or she sustains either (1) irreversible cessation of circulatory and respiratory functions or (2) irreversible cessation of all functions of the entire brain, including the brain stem. Each is *sufficient* to determine total and permanent loss of consciousness, and hence death, of a person. What defenders of the personhood conception add, however, is that neither (1) nor (2) (nor both together) is *necessary* for determining that death has occurred. In a small number of cases, individuals may undergo total and permanent loss of consciousness even if neither (1) nor (2) is satisfied. These are individuals in a permanent vegetative state.

Third, we can therefore acknowledge that the subject of life and death is a person even if we are hesitant to accept permanent vegetative state as a criterion of death. A person is dead, we may say, when consciousness is totally and permanently lost. We know this has occurred when either (1) or (2) is satisfied. But diagnosis of permanent vegetative state is not, *at this point*, simple and reliable enough to serve as a third criterion of death (that is, total and permanent loss of consciousness). Until we can identify permanent vegetative state as easily and as precisely as we can identify irreversible cessation of circulatory and respiratory functions or irreversible cessation of all functions of the brain, including the brain stem, we should regard individuals in a vegetative state as living. It does not follow, however, that they must be treated indefinitely. Clear evidence that the patient would have wanted treatment withdrawn under such circumstances morally and legally justifies terminating it.

Finally, it is quite possible that more specific and reliable criteria for diagnosing permanent vegetative state will eventually emerge from further studies of large patient populations and/or the development and proliferation of more refined technology such as the PET (positron-emission tomography) scanner, which can detect decreases in cerebral cortical metabolism consistent with unconsciousness and deep anesthesia.[9] If, then, you are troubled by the fact that diagnosis of permanent vegetative state is not, at this point, as simple or certain as diagnosis of total loss of brain function, you can say: "Death is total and permanent loss of consciousness. At the moment we have two highly reliable ways of determining this has occurred: (1) irreversible cessation of circulatory and respiratory functions and (2) irreversible cessation of all functions of the entire brain, including the brain stem. In time we may have an additional, equally reliable, criterion for determining death: total and irreversible loss of higher brain function as determined perhaps by PET scan or in some other way. If and when this occurs, permanent vegetative state will become a third criterion of death."

Personally, I think the subject of life and death should be conceived as a person rather than a biological organism. My hunch is that with time and the development of handier, more reliable criteria for diagnosing permanent vegetative state, this position will enjoy widespread, well-grounded philosophical/moral/religious support. In the meantime, however, I realize a shift from a biological to a social/psychological conception of the subject of life and death is a far-reaching matter about which reasonable people can disagree. A person's conception of the subject of life and death is central to his or her worldview and way of life. Worldviews and ways of life are usually characterized by a certain identity-preserving conservatism. While not necessarily fixed or unchanging, worldviews and ways of life are often associated with particular traditions that give shape and meaning to our lives and, as a result, resist abrupt or radical change. Too much change too quickly poses a threat to our identity and integrity as particular selves. Thus worldviews and ways of life tend to evolve slowly, so as to give us time to adjust our sense of self to potentially disorienting new circumstances or conditions. (Compare, in this regard, the slow and reluctant accommodation of many people's worldviews and ways of life to the Copernican and Darwinian Revolutions.) Different people have different capacities to accommodate what Dewey calls the "modifications and abandonments of intellectual inheritance . . . required by the newer industrial, political, and scientific movements." This is a fact about human psychology that must be incorporated into our background beliefs and theories in wide reflective equilibrium. So while supporting the personhood conception on moral and philosophical grounds, my democratic temperament inclines me to support a pluralistic compromise for purposes of law and public policy.

LAW AND PUBLIC POLICY

The question of whether someone is dead turns on our conception of the subject of life and death and its conditions of existence. This is a matter on which there is a certain amount of reasonable disagreement. To this day a number of people refuse to accept irreversible cessation of all functions of the entire brain, including the brain stem, as a criterion of death. An individual, they maintain, does not die when the brain dies. An individual is dead only when heartbeat and respiration have irreversibly ceased. Many Orthodox Jews, for example, believe that where there is breath there is life. The Japanese have traditionally identified life with the entire body, not just the brain. Many Native Americans hold religious beliefs that oppose brain-based criteria of death. Some Fundamentalist Christians, worried about the implications of a brain-oriented conception of death for the question of abortion, press for a consistent pro-(biological) life position by opposing brain-oriented conceptions of death.[10] And some prominent bioethicists are now arguing for a return to the traditional heart-lung conception of death.[11]

The traditional conception of the subject of life and death is therefore still a part of a large number of reasonable worldviews and ways of life. In this light, the UDDA may be seen as using the coercive power of the state to impose a particular conception of death grounded in a particular set of worldviews and ways of life on individuals holding a different conception of death grounded in differing, yet reasonable, worldviews and ways of life. This is a serious matter. Imagine holding a traditional conception of death and having a doctor tell you that a close relative whom you regard as alive is dead because his or her entire brain is dead. You look on with horror as the doctor proceeds to remove the respirator. To you this is tantamount to killing your relative. That it is sanctioned by law makes it even worse.

The state of New Jersey is unique in including a conscience clause in its statute on death. The law, like that of most other states, recognizes the death of the (whole) brain as the death of the person. But it also explicitly permits those who object to this criterion on religious grounds to exercise a right to be declared dead on heart-lung criteria alone. Passed in 1991, The New Jersey Declaration of Death Act reads, in part:

> The death of an individual shall not be declared upon the basis of neurological criteria . . . of this act when the licensed physician authorized to declare death, has reason to believe, on the basis of information in the individual's available medical records, or information provided by a member of the individual's family or any other person knowledgeable about the individual's personal religious beliefs that such a declaration would violate the personal religious beliefs of the individual. In these cases death shall be declared, and the time of death fixed, solely upon the basis of cardio-respiratory criteria.[12]

Taking this as a starting point, bioethicist Robert M. Veatch makes a compelling case for what we might call a "pro-choice" approach to the legal determination of death.

The New Jersey law is good as far as it goes, Veatch points out, but it does not go far enough. First, there is no reason to restrict legitimate appeals to conscience to those based on religious conviction. "The only reason that the New Jersey Commission on Legal and Ethical Problems in the Delivery of Health Care and the New Jersey Legislature limited its provision to religious objection," Veatch writes, "was political."[13] What is important is that the person's convictions about death be part of a *deeply held* worldview and way of life, not that they be part of an explicitly religious worldview and way of life. Second, there is no reason to restrict appeals to conscience to the traditional (heart-lung) conception of death. Individuals like myself, whose deeply held worldviews and ways of life identify death with total and permanent loss of consciousness, should be accorded the same respect as those whose deeply held worldviews and ways of life identify death with irreversible cessation of respiratory and circulatory functions.

The result would be a statute that would include something like the UDDA as the centrist or default conception of death together with a conscience clause that would enable those for whom this position is too broad to request that they be declared dead *only* under the traditional (heart-lung) criteria and those (like myself) for whom this position is too narrow to request that they *also* be declared dead if they are reliably determined by a qualified neurologist to be in a *permanent* vegetative state. Individuals on both sides of the centrist or default position could incorporate their wishes in their advance directives ("living wills" or durable power of attorney documents). Next-of-kin may be allowed to express the wishes of such individuals who have not documented their wishes. Such a statute might look something like this:

An individual who has sustained either (1) irreversible cessation of circulatory and respiratory functions or (2) irreversible cessation of all functions of the entire brain, including the brain stem, is dead. A determination of death must be made in accordance with accepted medical standards.

However, no individual shall be considered dead on these criteria if he or she, while competent, has explicitly asked to be pronounced dead only in the event of irreversible cessation of circulatory and respiratory functions. Moreover, an individual shall be considered dead if he or she, while competent, has explicitly asked to be pronounced dead either by (1) or (2) or by (3) total and permanent loss of consciousness as determined by irreversible loss of higher brain functions. Individuals making such requests should be pronounced dead only on the requested criteria. If an individual has not, while competent, explicitly asked to be pronounced dead on either of these latter criteria, the next-of-kin may do so. The criteria selected by the next-of-kin shall determine death for all legal purposes.

A statute drafted along these lines respects reasonable differences and reflects a democratic temperament.

Endorsing such a statute does not, however, imply ethical indifference or subjectivism. I, for example, think one of these three positions is significantly better than the others. The subject of life and death, I believe, is the person, not the biological organism, and a person is dead when he or she is totally and permanently unconscious, even if an intact brain stem is able to maintain breathing and heartbeat without the aid of a respirator. I will argue for this position and believe it will eventually prevail. At some point in the future this position and it only will be recognized in the law. In the meantime, however, my democratic temperament inclines me to respect all reasonable views on this controversial and heartfelt matter. Insofar as a "pro-choice" political compromise, like the one proposed by Veatch, is workable, it ought, for the time being, to be implemented.

But is the proposed legislation really workable? Many claim it would lead to what Veatch calls "policy chaos."[14] Would health insurers pay for medical support of Orthodox Jews or Native Americans whose preferred conception of death would involve higher cost? Would life insurers pay beneficiaries of individuals like myself whose preferred conception of death might cost them more? Might next-of-kin be inclined to choose a higher-brain conception of death in order to gain an inheritance more quickly? Would a spouse opt for such a conception in order to become a widow/widower sooner and thus to remarry? Would the need for transplantable organs coerce individuals or next-of-kin into selecting a higher-brain conception of death? How would presidential succession be determined if different presidents embraced different conceptions of death? How will health professionals deal with the stress of treating some patients in a particular biological condition as alive and others, in the very same biological condition, as dead?

Veatch considers each of these potential difficulties and gives what, to my mind, are plausible responses to them.[15] Many of his responses point out that the question is not unique—that it already arises in contexts in which surrogates make decisions to continue or forgo life-sustaining treatment for still living patients—and that in similar circumstances the feared consequences have not come to pass. Another possible difficulty turns on determining which conceptions of death are reasonable—and thus worthy of respect—and which not. What if a person were to believe that he or she would be alive even if circulatory, respiratory, and central nervous functions have all completely and irreversibly ceased? What if a person were to believe that he or she would be dead even if all of these functions, including higher-brain function, remain intact? Here I think we can safely say that such bizarre beliefs are unreasonable because they fly in the face of pragmatic certainties on which the meanings 'living' and 'dead' are hinged (chapter 3, pp. 61–70). It *goes without saying* that an individual whose circulatory, respiratory, and central nervous functions have completely and irreversibly ceased is dead. It *goes without saying* that an individual, like yourself, who now enjoys full circulatory, respiratory, and central nervous system functions is alive. It's likely that no one ever told or taught you either of these. Indeed, it's hard to imagine contexts in which they'd actually be uttered or written. Anyone who denies either of them either doesn't know what the words 'dead' and 'alive' mean or else is crazy—*unhinged!*

Once we recognize the extent to which the debate over the determination of death is more a matter of philosophy than biology, we may be more amenable to a "pro-choice" or pluralistic response to questions of law and public policy. To incorporate one reasonable conception of the subject of life and death in law at the expense of others is undemocratic, especially if there is a way to accommodate, at relatively little cost or inconvenience, all reasonable positions. Veatch's pluralistic proposal is, to my mind, a plausible compromise that can be endorsed with integrity by all parties to the debate.

NOTES

1. Ad Hoc Committee of the Harvard Medical School, "A Definition of Irreversible Coma," *Journal of the American Medical Association* 205, no. 6 (August 5, 1968): 337–40.

2. President's Commission for the Study of Ethical Problems in Medicine and Biomedical and Behavioral Research, *Defining Death* (Washington, D.C.: U.S. Government Printing Office, 1981), 73.

3. Multi-Society Task Force on PVS (American Academy of Neurology, Child Neurology Society, American Neurological Association, American Association of Neurological Surgeons, American Academy of Pediatrics), "Medical Aspects of the Persistent Vegetative State," *New England Journal of Medicine*, Part I, 330, no. 21 (May 26, 1994): 1499–1508; Part II, 330, no. 22 (June 2, 1994): 1572–79.

4. President's Commission, *Defining Death*, 33.

5. President's Commission, *Defining Death*, 40.

6. Council on Ethical and Judicial Affairs, American Medical Association, "The Use of Anencephalic Neonates as Organ Donors," *Journal of the American Medical Association* 273, no. 20 (May 24–31, 1995): 1614. Though supporting the use of anencephalics as sources of organs, the council does not consider them dead.

7. Ronald Cranford, "Criteria for Death," in *Encyclopedia of Bioethics*, 2d ed., vol. 1, ed. Warren T. Reich (New York: Macmillan, 1995), 530.

8. Multi-Society Task Force, "Medical Aspects," Part II, 1575.

9. Multi-Society Task Force, "Medical Aspects," Part II, 1578.

10. Robert M. Veatch, "The Conscience Clause: How Much Individual Choice in Defining Death Can Our Society Tolerate?" in *The Definition of Death: Contemporary Controversies*, ed. Stuart J. Youngner, Robert M. Arnold, and Renie Schapiro (Baltimore: Johns Hopkins University Press, 1999), 141.

11. Robert D. Truog, "Is It Time to Abandon Brain Death?" *Hastings Center Report* 27, no. 1 (January/February 1997): 29–37.

12. Veatch, "Conscience Clause," 157n.

13. Veatch, "Conscience Clause," 144.

14. Veatch, "Conscience Clause," 149.

15. Veatch, "Conscience Clause," 149–55.

Chapter 8

Meaningful Lives

The things in civilization we most prize are not of ourselves. They exist by grace of the doings and sufferings of the continuous human community in which we are a link. Ours is the responsibility of conserving, transmitting, rectifying and expanding the heritage of values we have received that those who come after us may receive it more solid and secure, more widely accessible and more generously shared than we have received it.

—John Dewey, *A Common Faith*

In 1879 the great Russian novelist Leo Tolstoy became obsessed with whether his life could have a meaning that wouldn't be destroyed by death. "If not today then tomorrow," Tolstoy wrote,

sickness and death will come . . . to everyone, to me, and nothing will remain except the stench and the worms. My deeds, whatever they may be, will be forgotten sooner or later, and I myself will be no more. Why, then, do anything? How can anyone fail to see this and live? That's what is amazing! It is possible to live only as long as life intoxicates us; once we are sober we cannot help seeing that it is all a delusion, a stupid delusion![1]

It's an important question. If, no matter what we do, we all come to the same dismal end—dead, buried, and eventually forgotten—why do what's hard rather than easy, selfless rather than selfish, good rather than bad? Why, as Tolstoy asks, do anything?

After surveying and rejecting various answers, Tolstoy found only one he could accept: "However I may put the question of how I am to live," he wrote in his autobiographical *Confession*, "the answer is: according to the law of God. Is there anything real that will come of my life? Eternal torment or eternal happiness. What meaning is there which is not destroyed by death? Union with the infinite God, paradise."[2] Our finite lives, in other words, acquire meaning in the face of mortality by becoming part of the plan and purpose of an infinite God.

Must God and the supernatural be part of any adequate response to Tolstoy's question? Or are there also credible—and satisfying—secular or naturalistic answers? These and related questions provide an important test for practical philosophical inquiry.

The issue is not so much whether life *in the abstract* has any meaning, but whether individual *human* lives like yours and mine can, depending on how they are lived, be either meaningful or meaningless. The question of whether life *as such* has meaning—whether, for example, it makes a difference to the cosmos that it contains living as well as nonliving things—has little practical bearing. But if individual lives can be either meaningful or meaningless, it's important to know the difference and to try to lead our lives accordingly.

GOD, MEANING, AND MORTALITY

Seven years after describing his personal crisis, Tolstoy transformed it into art in *The Death of Ivan Ilych*. The fictional Ivan Ilych is an ambitious, reasonably well-off, prosecuting attorney "intoxicated" by the various pleasures of late nineteenth-century middle-class life. He insulates himself from anything that might intrude on these pleasures, including human suffering and death. As an attorney, for example, Ivan Ilych tries "to exclude everything fresh and vital, which always disturbs the regular course of business, and to admit only official relations with people, and then only on official grounds."[3] He does the same as a husband. When his wife's pregnancy disturbs his pleasant routine, he ignores her concerns and buries himself in his work. His relations with friends and family are "proper" but distant. His greatest satisfactions include decorating his home, giving pleasant dinner parties, and playing "a clever and serious game of bridge" with "good players, not noisy partners, . . . and then to have supper and drink a glass of wine" (p. 119).

For a number of years a life centered on these and similar diversions permits Ivan Ilych to deceive himself about human reality, including his own mortality. Then he develops an odd taste in his mouth and some discomfort in his left side. His visits to physicians are unsatisfying, partly because nineteenth-century doctors didn't know very much, but also because their professional detachment gives him a taste of his own medicine. Ivan Ilych's doctors are as impersonally professional and dismissive about what's really troubling him—is his case serious or not?—as he has been of the personal concerns of his clients.

As Ivan's condition worsens and he is confined to bed, he is abandoned by family and friends who systematically ignore his needs for understanding, compassion, and human touch as for years he has ignored theirs. His dying is in many ways an embarrassment to them—an interference with the pleasures of playing bridge, giving dinner parties, and attending the theater. It is also an unwelcome reminder of their own mortality. So they deceive themselves about the gravity of his condition: "The awful, terrible act of his dying was, he could see, reduced by those about him to the level of casual, unpleasant, and almost indecorous incident (as if someone entered a drawing-room diffusing an unpleasant odour) and this was done by that very decorum which he had served all his life long. He saw that no one felt for him, because no one even wished to grasp his condition" (pp. 138–39).

So long as we deceive ourselves about mortality, Tolstoy suggests, a life consisting of little more than a succession of pleasant experiences may seem satisfactory. But once we sober up—once, that is, we face up to mortality—we realize the intolerable emptiness of such a life. Insofar as our lives resemble that of Ivan Ilych—a life Tolstoy characterizes as "most simple and most ordinary and therefore most terrible"—they are utterly without meaning (p. 104).

As death closes in, Ivan Ilych undertakes a painful examination of his life. He admits to himself that since becoming an adult his whole life had been wrong. Everything about it—his pride and ambition, his prestigious job, the perfectly decorated home, the socially correct dinner parties and card games—rings hollow in the light of his impending death. Yes, he had squandered his life. But perhaps, he thinks, it is still possible to make amends, to "rectify" matters (p. 155). But how? How should he have lived? What kind of life has a meaning that cannot be destroyed by death?

Ivan is fortunate to have been cared for by Gerasim, the butler's assistant, who alone has been able to acknowledge Ivan's dying. "Only Gerasim," Tolstoy writes,

> recognized it and pitied him. And so Ivan Ilych felt at ease only with him. He felt comforted when Gerasim supported his legs (sometimes all night long) and refused to go to bed, saying: "If you weren't sick it would be an-

other matter, but as it is, why should I grudge a little trouble?" Gerasim alone did not lie; everything showed that he alone understood the facts of the case and did not consider it necessary to disguise them, but simply felt sorry for his emaciated and enfeebled master. (p. 138)

Gerasim, Tolstoy suggests, can acknowledge Ivan's mortality because he acknowledges his own; and he can acknowledge his own mortality because he believes in God and is living according to God's law. "It's God's will," he says of Ivan's death shortly after he has died. "We shall all come to it some day" (p. 103).

Gerasim, the simple peasant, knows more about what's really important in life than those he serves. Ivan learns from him—not from what he says, but by his example. Our lives, Ivan Ilych finally realizes, acquire meaning that transcends the boundaries of the finite self by becoming part of something larger and more permanent—God's law for how we should live. And this, as Gerasim reveals, means identifying with and caring for other human beings whose condition—joys, afflictions, and fate—we inevitably share. Rich or poor, young or old, man or woman, we are all equally mortal and equally subject to pain and suffering.

Shortly before he dies, Ivan sees his schoolboy son and his wife in a new light as they stand by the bedside. He senses their distress and for the first time feels more sorry for them than he does for himself. More importantly, he wants to spare them further hurt. "With a look at his wife he indicated his son and said: 'Take him away . . . sorry for him . . . sorry for you too . . .' He tried to add, 'forgive me,' but said 'forgo' and waved his hand knowing that He [God] whose understanding mattered would understand" (p. 155). Though Tolstoy is ambiguous about whether Ivan literally survives death, his more general and unmistakable point is that our finite lives acquire "a meaning that cannot be destroyed by death" by becoming part of the purpose and plan of an infinite God.

There is something right about this. But it also raises questions—at least for some of us. First, how can we reconcile the existence, goodness, and power of God with the abundance of pain, suffering, and premature death in the world? If philosophy is "an attempt to see how things, in the broadest possible sense of the term, hang together, in the broadest possible sense of the term," how does the existence of an all-knowing, all-powerful, perfectly good God hang together with, for example, the suffering and deaths of young children? This is a long-standing philosophical problem—the problem of evil. As David Hume puts it: "Epicurus' old questions are yet unanswered. Is he

[God] willing to prevent evil, but not able? then is he impotent. Is he able, but not willing? then is he malevolent. Is he both able and willing? whence then is evil?"[4] Second, the idea of God has often been used to explain natural patterns and events we don't otherwise understand. But advances in scientific knowledge are steadily eroding the explanatory role of a supernatural God. Darwin's account of evolution by natural selection has, for example, replaced God as the most plausible explanation of the appearance of design in the natural world. Similarly, astronomy and geology undermine the literal reality of Heaven and Hell, and contemporary neuroscience makes it increasingly difficult to identify the mind with an immortal soul. There just aren't as many gaps for the idea of God to fill as there were two thousand years ago. As the French mathematician and astronomer Laplace is reported to have responded when asked by Napoleon why his book about the universe made no mention of God, "I have no need of that hypothesis." If, then, we have no better reason for believing in God than the comfort it gives us, belief in God may be as self-deceptive as denying our mortality.

MEANING WITHOUT GOD

It's illuminating, in this connection, to compare *The Death of Ivan Ilych* with another masterpiece of philosophical fiction, Albert Camus's *The Plague*. Like Tolstoy, Camus asks whether our lives can have meaning in the face of mortality. Unlike Tolstoy, he cannot accept a theistic answer. For Camus, the suffering and death caused by plague—especially as it affects children—make it difficult to believe in a God worthy of worship. At one point Camus's main character, Dr. Rieux, says, "'[S]ince the order of the world is shaped by death, mightn't it be better for God if we refuse to believe in Him and struggle with all our might against death, without raising our eyes toward the heaven where He sits in silence?'"[5] Literary critic Rachel Bespaloff hits the mark when she says of *The Plague*, "Reduced to its simplest expression, Camus' thought is contained in a single question: *What value abides in the eyes of the man condemned to death who refuses the consolation of the supernatural?* Camus cannot take his mind off this question. All his characters bring an answer; one only has to listen to them" (italics added).[6]

The book is set in the 1940s in the Algerian port of Oran during an outbreak of bubonic plague. Taken literally, plague represents *natural evil*—pain, suffering, and death caused by earthquakes, floods, tornados, disease, and other occurrences over which we have no control. Symbolically, plague represents *moral* evil—pain, suffering, and death caused by murder, rape, war, genocide, and other terrible things people do to each other. It is no coincidence that Camus conceived and made notes for *The Plague* while active in the organized Resistance to the Nazi occupation of France.

As the death toll mounts, Dr. Rieux plays a leading role in resisting the plague, including persuading a reluctant government to place the town under quarantine. Then the Jesuit scholar, Father Paneloux, delivers a forceful sermon to a packed church. His opening sentence sets the tone for what follows: "'Calamity has come on you, my brethren,' he says in a powerful voice, 'and my brethren, you deserved it'" (p. 94). Plague, as Father Paneloux sees it, is God's punishment for the wicked, the impious, and the unjust. "'The just man need have no fear, but the evildoer has good cause to tremble. For plague is the flail of God and the world His threshing-floor, and implacably He will thresh out His harvest until the wheat is separated from the chaff'" (p. 95). As for secular efforts to ward off plague, the priest adds, "'No earthly power, nay, not even—mark me well—the vaunted might of medical science can avail you to avert that hand [of death] once it is stretched toward you. And winnowed like corn on the blood-stained threshing floor of suffering, you will be cast away with the chaff'" (pp. 96–97). Insofar as the plague has come from God as punishment for their sins, Paneloux concludes, people should take heart that God cares about them and wants them to change. "Never more intensely than today had he, Father Paneloux, felt the immanence of divine succor and Christian hope granted to all alike. He hoped against hope that despite all the horrors of these dark days, despite the groans of men and women in agony, our fellow citizens would offer up to heaven that one prayer which is truly Christian, a prayer of love. And God would see to the rest" (p. 99).

Shortly after Paneloux's sermon, Dr. Rieux is asked what he thought of it. "'I've seen too much of hospitals,' he responds, 'to relish any idea of collective punishment. But, as you know, Christians sometimes say that sort of thing without really thinking it. They're better than they seem'" (p. 125). The problem, he adds, is that "'Paneloux is a man of learning, a scholar. He hasn't come in contact with death; that's why he can speak with such assurance of the truth—with a capital T. But every country priest who visits his parishioners and has heard a man gasping for breath on his deathbed thinks as I do. He'd try to relieve human suffering before trying to point out its excellence'" (p. 126).

To supplement the government's understaffed and inefficient sanitary department, another character, Tarrou, organizes volunteer "sanitary squads" to help maintain cleanliness and dispose of corpses. When Tarrou informs Rieux that Father Paneloux has joined the sanitary squads, Rieux says, "'That's good. I'm glad to know he's better than his sermon'" (p. 150). To become a member of the sanitary squads is to resist rather than welcome the plague. What Paneloux *does* to combat plague as a member of the sanitary squads is, to Rieux's mind, more important than what he *said* about its causes in his sermon.

One evening, Rieux, Paneloux, Tarrou, and others gather at the bedside of a small boy to observe the effects of the first trial of a locally developed serum.

> They had already seen children die—for many months now death had shown no favoritism—but they had never yet watched a child's agony minute by minute, as they had now been doing since daybreak. Needless to say, the pain inflicted on these innocent victims had always seemed to them to be what in fact it was: an abominable thing. But hitherto they had felt its abomination in, so to speak, an abstract way; they had never had to witness over so long a period the death-throes of an innocent child. (p. 214)

As the boy suffers and wails, Paneloux, the scholar, experiences firsthand what Rieux said was known to every country priest. The abstract theology of his sermon gives way to firsthand experience of the painful reality of death and disease. Falling to his knees, Father Paneloux says in a hoarse, but clearly audible voice, "'My God, spare this child!'" (p. 217). But the child is not spared. Not only does he die, but, as Paneloux ruefully observes, the serum, which may eventually save the lives of others, serves only to prolong his suffering.

Leaving the boy's bedside, Rieux, recalling Paneloux's sermon, abruptly turns on the priest: "'Ah! That child, anyhow, was innocent, and you know it as well as I do.'" Moments later Paneloux responds, "'Why was that anger in your voice just now? What we'd been seeing was as unbearable to me as it was to you. . . . I understand. That sort of thing is revolting because it passes our human understanding. But perhaps we should love what we cannot understand.'" Rieux shakes his head. "'No, Father. I've a very different idea of love. And until my dying day I shall refuse to love a scheme of things in which children are put to torture'" (p. 218). Rieux's anger is, however, tempered by Paneloux's work with the sanitary squads. "'What I hate'," he says on parting, "'is death and disease, as you well know. And whether you wish it or not, we're allies facing them and fighting them together.' Rieux was still holding Paneloux's hand. 'So you see'—but he refrained from meeting the priest's eyes—'God Himself can't part us now'" (p. 219).

After watching the boy die, there is a noticeable change in Paneloux. His faith seems shaken. He tells Rieux he is working on an essay titled "Is a Priest Justified in Consulting a Doctor?" He adds that he will soon be giving another sermon and he hopes Rieux will attend.

The second sermon differs greatly from the first. After experiencing the effects of plague firsthand, Father Paneloux is no longer so sure of himself nor does he separate himself from those he is addressing. "He spoke," we are told, "in a gentler, more thoughtful tone than on the previous occasion, and several times was noticed to be stumbling over his words. A yet more noteworthy change was that instead of saying 'you' he now said 'we'" (p. 222). So far as plague is concerned, Paneloux now believes everyone, including himself, is in the same boat. And this boat, so far as the spiritual life is concerned, is the ultimate test of faith. "'My brothers,' he says, 'a time of testing has come for us all. We must believe everything or deny everything. And who among you, I ask, would dare to deny everything?'" (p. 224).

There are, he's saying, only two alternatives. The first is to believe in God and His ultimate wisdom and beneficence despite the presence of plague and the incomprehensible suffering it causes. "'[T]he Christian should yield himself wholly to the divine will, even though it passed his understanding'" (p. 226). There are, it is true, no guarantees. It is a matter of blind faith. But what else can we do? The second alternative is unthinkable. To deny everything is to deny God, and to deny God is to deny morality and that our lives and our suffering—and the suffering of children—have any meaning. This is nihilism. We cannot live as nihilists. We must have faith that somewhere, somehow, in a realm beyond empirical comprehension, the suffering and deaths of children are redeemed and given meaning by God. "'No,' Paneloux said, 'there was no middle course. We must accept the dilemma and choose either to hate God or to love God. And who would dare to choose to hate Him?'" (p. 228).

For Camus, though, there *is* a middle course—the course represented by Dr. Rieux. Rieux doesn't believe in God, but he's not a nihilist. Rieux's life achieves a degree of meaning and value larger than his biological existence by becoming part of the social practice of medicine. The practice of medicine is a project that began long before he was born and won't be completed, if ever, until long after he is dead.

As a medical student, Dr. Rieux acquired in a few years knowledge, skills, and techniques that took centuries to accumulate. No individual or no individual generation could produce, from the ground up, the complex combination of knowledge and skill that constitutes modern medicine. By becoming part of and contributing to this worthy historical project, Dr. Rieux transcends his own limited existence. He has learned to relieve pain, resist disease, and forestall death from generations of previous physicians; he uses what he has learned to benefit the sick while learning from experience and experiment; and he conveys what he has learned to future physicians who will, because of him and his colleagues and predecessors, become even more proficient in relieving pain and forestalling death. The project of medicine is, as a whole, bigger and more important than Dr. Rieux's limited lifetime. Still, in becoming part of this project—in resisting death and disease and linking medicine's past with its future—his life acquires meaning and value that transcends or outlives the self.

There are many ways of outliving the self apart from becoming a doctor, nurse, or other health professional. Many of us do it as parents—in learning certain values and ways of life from our parents, improving on them in our lifetimes, and then passing them on to our children, who, we hope, will improve them further and pass them on to their children, and so on, long after we are dead. As democratic citizens each of us can do the same in trying to build a more just society. We learn from those who preceded us (for example, Socrates, Immanuel Kant, John Stuart Mill, Elizabeth Cady Stanton, Mohandas Gandhi, Martin Luther King, Jr., and Cesar Chavez), we try to make our society more just during our lifetimes, and we raise our children and support forms of education and social organization that increase the likelihood that the struggle for social justice will continue and be more widespread and successful after we are gone. We can also "outlive the self" as teachers, scientists, architects, firefighters, artists, engineers, social workers, and so on.[7]

As a student I learned some of the accumulated wisdom of 2,500 years of philosophical inquiry. Then I became a teacher and began sharing what I had learned with my students. Philosophical inquiry and understanding, I believe, make significant contributions to a democratically pluralistic society and to the lives of its members. It is also an integral part of what's best in our culture. As I face up to mortality, I take some satisfaction in thinking that some of my former students will, as parents, citizens, health professionals, teachers, or scholars, continue the project of philosophical inquiry after I am dead—modifying, improving, and adding to what they have learned from me and my colleagues and then passing it on to their children, students, or readers, some of whom will do the same after my former students are dead, and so on.

Toward the end of *The Plague*, the narrator reveals himself to be none other than Dr. Rieux. As an *author*, Rieux (as a fictional stand-in for Camus) leaves an additional legacy to the future, the book itself. As the city of Oran celebrates the official end of the plague, the narrator, still referring to himself in the third person, writes, "Dr. Rieux resolved to compile this chronicle, so that he should not be one of those who hold their peace but should bear witness in favor of those plague-stricken people; so that some memorial of the injustice and outrage done them might endure; and to state quite simply what we learn in time of pestilence: that there are more things to admire in men than to despise" (p. 308). By focusing our attention not just on his characters but on all who have dedicated part of their lives to combating moral and natural evil, Camus keeps them alive in our memory. Insofar as we read, enjoy, and learn from books like *The Plague*, their authors exert a beneficial influence even after they are dead. The prospect of exerting a similar influence as parents, citizens, doctors, teachers, and so on gives meaning to our lives as well.

This, I think, is what Dewey is getting at in the passage that begins this chapter.[8] You and I are the beneficiaries of a wide variety of human projects (agriculture, government, fire fighting, medicine, engineering, philosophy, and so on) that extend thousands of years into the past. The things we prize most are not entirely of our own making, but the cumulative legacy of many others who came before us. We should, if we think about it, recall and be grateful to those men and women from various walks of life whose hard work, social practices, and personal sacrifice contribute to our well-being—our freedom, the best of our social and political institutions, our health and safety, our knowledge and understanding, and so on. As connecting links, we conserve, modify, and augment the best of what we have received from past generations and transmit it securely, generously, and widely to future generations. We can, in this way, *give* our lives meaning—meaning that transcends individual existence—without relying on God or the supernatural.

Contrary to Father Paneloux, then, we are not forced to choose between God and nihilism. There is a third possibility, one that combines the meaning implicit in the first alternative with the naturalism of the second. Our lives may acquire meaning and value that transcends the finite self by becoming part of and contributing to one or more worthwhile plans and projects that began before we were born and won't be finished, if ever, until long after we are dead. As with Father Paneloux, however, there are no guarantees. That our lives have meaning is ultimately, for believers and unbelievers alike, a matter of faith. In the one case it's faith in God. In the other it's what Annette Baier calls "secular faith"—"faith in the human community and its evolving procedures—in the prospects for many-handed cognitive ambitions and moral hopes."[9]

PRAGMATISM AND RELIGION

Camus's answer to the question of life's meaning is, to my mind, at least as plausible as Tolstoy's. Which of them is more compatible with the pragmatic temperament? Must pragmatists choose between them? Or can they accommodate both?

On the one hand, most pragmatists place a high value on scientific naturalism. If, for purposes of prediction and control, we want to know what the world is like, our best bet is to look to the fruits of scientific inquiry. And the increasing scope of scientific explanation leaves little room for appeals to the supernatural. If we want to stop plague, we'll be more effective joining the sanitary squads than becoming more pious. If plague is less worrisome now than it was in the past, it's because of improved sanitation and antibiotics, not because of improved church attendance. As for God, the problem of evil remains unsolved. How can we reconcile belief in a God worthy of worship with the great amount of natural and moral evil in the world? How can a presumably all-knowing, all-powerful, perfectly good God have permitted well over ten million children to die *each year* from 1965 to 1995 from readily preventable causes?[10]

On the other hand, belief in God is practically beneficial to many men and women. Only the most aggressive (and obtuse) atheist would pick an argument with a returned Kosovar Albanian I read about in the newspaper who, having learned that Serbs had killed every member of his family, said something like, "I couldn't continue living if I didn't believe in God." Think, too, of the "born again" former drug addict and alcoholic who has apparently pulled his life together with the help of Jesus. Can there be any doubt that belief in God plays a useful role in these and many other people's lives? When, for example, people's situations and prospects are so bleak as to afford no reasonable expectation of relief in this world, their only hope may be to look beyond nature and this life to the supernatural and an afterlife.

"On pragmatic principles," James writes, "we cannot reject any hypothesis if consequences useful to life flow from it."[11] How, in the light of this, can pragmatists categorically reject various life-sustaining, meaning-enhancing, religious beliefs?

Here as elsewhere the complexity of human life requires a pluralistic response. Pragmatists may be secular or religious. The secular middle ground between theism and nihilism represented by Dr. Rieux is fully compatible with pragmatism, as made clear by the passage from Dewey. Secular pragmatists replace Tolstoy's faith in "Union with the infinite God, paradise" with Dewey's faith in "the continuous human community in which we are a link." James, however, and contemporary pragmatists like Cornel West show that pragmatism may also be religious. Referring to "the theistic God," James writes, "On pragmatistic principles, if the hypothesis of God works satisfactorily in the widest sense of the word, it is true. Now whatever its residual difficulties may be, experience shows that it certainly does work, and that *the problem is to build it out and determine it so that it will combine satisfactorily with all the other working truths*" (italics added).[12]

Drawing on his research into the nature and extent of religious experience, James personally believes that "higher powers exist and are at work to save the world on ideal lines similar to our own."[13] He has no proof for this belief nor does he urge everyone else to embrace it. But, he maintains, each of us has a right to retain this or similar beliefs without apology, and we can do so without betraying the pragmatic temperament or our intellectual integrity. How? By conceiving God and religion as complementing, not opposing, our well-grounded scientific beliefs and by reaffirming our commitment to democratic pluralism.

It's possible, James points out, that there is a God and that He created the world in such a way that whether the world is "saved" or perfected is conditional on each of us doing our level best to contribute to its perfection. Whether we'll succeed is, however, an open question. "'I offer you the chance of taking part in such a world,'" James imagines God saying to us. "'Its safety, you see, is unwarranted. It is a real adventure, with real danger, yet it may win through. It is a social scheme of co-operative work genuinely to be done. Will you join the procession?'" God asks. "'Will you trust yourself and trust the other agents enough to face the risk?'"[14]

Such a world, James adds, "would be just like the world we practically live in." People may, if it suits their temperament, believe in such a God, conduct themselves accordingly, and hope that success will somehow bring them something unimaginably (perhaps even eternally) good. Day in, day out, however, the *public* conduct of such theistic pragmatists will differ little from that of secular pragmatists. In fact, day in, day out, there is little difference between the public conduct of most religious believers, pragmatic and nonpragmatic, and most secular pragmatists. This shouldn't be surprising. As embodied social agents we must all contend with the same hazards in the same (physical) world. Recall, in this connection, what Dr. Rieux says to Father Paneloux after the priest joins the sanitary squads: "'[W]hether you wish it or not, we're allies facing [death and disease] and fighting them together. . . . So you see . . . God Himself can't part us now.'" Dorothy Day, the deeply religious Catholic social activist, makes a similar point. Speaking of the relationship between God and the secular outlook, she says: "Some people say to me, 'The secular mind is your enemy.' I say no, no; I say the secular mind is God's huge gift to us to use for the sake of one another."[15]

Cornel West writes, "Like James, [Rheinhold] Niebuhr, and to some extent [W. E. B.] Du Bois, I hold a religious conception of pragmatism." West locates his commitment to what he calls "prophetic" pragmatism in the Christian tradition for two reasons. First, he says, "on the existential level, the self-understanding and self-identity that flow from this tradition's insights into the crises and traumas of life are indispensable *for me* to remain sane." West italicizes 'for me' to emphasize that he doesn't think it's "possible to put forward rational defenses of one's faith that verify its veracity or even persuade one's critics." Many people, however, experience a sense of "deep emptiness and pervasive meaninglessness" without some sort of religious convictions and West says he is among them. Second, West believes that his religious convictions underlie and reinforce his commitment to social justice. "[T]he culture of the wretched of the earth," he writes, "is deeply religious. To be in solidarity with them requires not only an acknowledgment of what they are up against but also an appreciation of how they cope with their situation. This appreciation does not require that one be religious; but if one is religious, one has wider access into their life-worlds."[16]

Pragmatists may, therefore, embrace certain religious beliefs without abandoning their pragmatism. The only restriction is, as James puts it, that our religious convictions "combine satisfactorily with all . . . [our] . . . other working truths." This means that pragmatism is incompatible with certain types of fundamentalism—religious convictions founded in sacred texts that are permitted to prevail over well-grounded, widely shared scientific and historical understanding.

"The fundamentalist in religion," Dewey writes, "is one whose beliefs in intellectual content have hardly been touched by scientific developments. His notions about heaven and earth and man, as far as their bearing on religion is concerned, are hardly more affected by the work of Copernicus, Newton, and Darwin than they are by that of Einstein."[17] Religious pragmatists cannot, for example, maintain the *literal* or *historical* truth of the biblical account of Genesis, the parting of the Red Sea, or the virgin birth because they cannot "combine satisfactorily with . . . [our] . . . other working truths." Religious pragmatists must construe these and similar accounts symbolically or morally rather than literally or historically.

Pragmatists, secular and religious, can, however, peacefully coexist with those who *do* believe in the literal or historical truth of these and similar occurrences. As democratic pluralists (chapters 6 and 7), pragmatists recognize the wide variety and intensely personal nature of religious beliefs and experiences and their importance in giving meaning to people's lives. Pragmatists will, insofar as possible, respect and politically accommodate individuals holding fundamentalist and other nonpragmatist beliefs, even if they think they are mistaken. The only restriction is that such beliefs must not be harmful to or forced upon those who do not willingly share them.

THE PRIORITY OF DEMOCRACY

There is therefore no "one size fits all" answer to the question of what makes a life meaningful. The convictions that give meaning to a person's life come in a wide variety of shapes and sizes. Some are religious, others not; some are widely shared, others highly personalized; some are tightly structured, others quite fluid; some are steeped in tradition, others more contemporary; some are fundamentalist, others open to revision; and so on. As with moral pluralism (chapter 6), pluralism about what gives meaning to our lives is, to use Rawls's words, "a permanent feature of the public culture of democracy." So long as people's backgrounds, temperaments, circumstances, and total experiences differ, they are likely to give differing reasonable answers to the question of what makes their lives meaningful. In some circumstances, for example, the only real (or "live") option for some people may be either religious fundamentalism or nervous breakdown. If their fundamentalism is neither harmful to nor forced upon others, it would be cruel (and unpragmatic) to criticize them for it.

More important than everyone's agreeing on a single answer to the question of what makes a life meaningful is each person's having the freedom to answer it for himself or herself. Another person's answer will not be meaningful *to you* unless (and until) you can freely and reflectively adopt it as your own. This is part of what Socrates was getting at when he said that "an unexamined life is not worth living."[18] It is also part of what Kant was getting at when he contrasted the virtues of thinking for oneself (autonomy of the will) with the pitfalls of letting others do your thinking for you (heteronomy of the will).[19] And it is echoed by Janie Woods, at the end of a long journey of self-discovery and self-creation, in Zora Neale Hurston's novel *Their Eyes Were Watching God*. "'It's uh known fact,'" Janie says to her friend Pheoby, "'you got tuh *go* there tuh *know* there. Yo' papa and yo' mama and nobody else can't tell yuh and show yuh. Two things everybody's got tuh do fuh theyselves. They got tuh go tuh God, and they got tuh find out about livin' fuh theyselves.'"[20] (I take the liberty here of interpreting Janie's "go tuh God" as "come to terms with the question of God's existence and nature.")

Democratic pluralism aims at a balance between the personal and impersonal standpoints. From a personal standpoint we each embrace a particular answer to the question of our life's meaning. From a more impersonal standpoint we realize the importance of people's answering this question for themselves and that different people, with different temperaments, backgrounds, experiences, and situations, may reasonably arrive at different answers. Again, the trick—and part of being human—is to retain both standpoints while judiciously tacking between them: *mutual respect* or at least *tolerance* in public or political contexts and *commitment* in those that are more private or personal. This will sometimes generate a good deal of discomfort or ambivalence. Not to worry. It is part of the price we pay for being human, for being and remaining true to ourselves as *both* agents and spectators.

Tolerance in the political realm, let me add, does not entail indifference, skepticism, subjectivism, or (vulgar) relativism. Personally, I'm a secular pragmatist. The answer to the question of life's meaning outlined by Dewey and embodied by Dr. Rieux is, to my mind, most nearly correct. Human lives acquire meaning that outlives the self by becoming part of one or more worthwhile plans or projects that began before we were born and won't be completed, if ever, until long after we are dead. I live my life as if this were true and, if asked, I recommend this way of looking at things to others. Things would be better, I think, if more people were to freely and reflectively accept this general conception of a meaningful life. I give reasons for my view, listen to various criticisms, and respond to them as best I can. My hunch is that it's the view that will eventually prevail. Though I think I'm right, I'm also a fallibilist. I could be wrong. I'm given pause, for example, by the many admirable people I know personally or through my reading who *do* believe in God. These are good, smart, courageous people. What do they know or experience, I sometimes ask myself, that I don't? What am I missing? Someday, perhaps, I'll have an experience or encounter an argument or situation that will persuade me to rethink and possibly revise or abandon my thoroughly secular answer to the question of my life's meaning. In the meantime, however, I'll state, defend, and act upon it while keeping my mind open, tolerating other reasonable answers, and respecting those whose lives are guided by them. Sure, I'm sometimes ambivalent. But this, as indicated above, comes with the territory. It's part of being human.

CONCLUSION

This is a fitting place to conclude the chapter and the book as a whole. Chapter 1 began with a passage from William James. "What *you* want," James said in the first of his lectures on pragmatism, "is a philosophy that will not only exercise your powers of intellectual abstraction, but that will make some positive connexion with this actual world of finite human lives" (italics added). James was responding to what he saw as a series of debilitating dichotomies in philosophy, some of which, in my terms, are: thought vs. action, reason vs. emotion, fact vs. value, and science vs. religion (here broadly construed to include Camus as well as Tolstoy, Dewey as well as James). Philosophers have generally aligned themselves with one side or the other of such series of oppositions, James thought, but at a high cost. Neither the first member of each pair nor the second speaks to the whole person for whom action is as vital as thought, emotion as vital as reason, value as vital as fact, and religion (broadly construed) as vital as science. Responding to the "entire" person "who feels all needs by turns . . . [and] . . . will take nothing as an equivalent for life but the fullness of living itself,"[21] James presented "the oddly-named thing pragmatism as a philosophy that can satisfy both kinds of demand."[22]

As a "mediating way of thinking,"[23] pragmatism refuses to choose once and for all between the two sides of this series of dichotomies. *Meaningful* survival requires tacking back and forth between the perspectives of agent and spectator. Science and intellectual abstraction may enhance our prospects for survival by increasing our powers of prediction and control. But, as Tolstoy realizes, we want not merely to survive, but to lead good and meaningful lives. What, then, makes for a good and meaningful life? We can't answer this question from the scientific or impersonal standpoint alone. For this we must turn to the personal standpoint and wide reflective equilibrium, a method of reasoning that incorporates the perspectives of both agent and spectator (chapter 5). Meaningful survival is a matter of thought *and* action, fact *and* value, reason *and* emotion, science *and* religion (broadly construed), and so on.

Most of the time most of us exhibit a pragmatic temperament, whether we know it or not. We tack back and forth between the standpoints of agent and spectator seeking meaningful survival in an all-too-hazardous world. We employ a variety of different language games to gain knowledge and understanding of the world and ourselves (chapters 2 and 3). We mediate conflicts between language games as illustrated by the pragmatic response to the mind–body and free will problems (chapter 4). We employ the method of wide reflective equilibrium in addressing new and complex questions of ethics and social and political philosophy (chapter 5). We balance personal commitment with political tolerance, as illustrated by democratic pluralism (chapter 6). And we modify our language games or devise new ones as experience or changing circumstances reveal shortcomings with those we've inherited (chapter 7). This is what we *do* and it is hard—so long as we remain embodied social agents seeking meaningful survival in a complex, rapidly changing world—to imagine doing otherwise. So if philosophy is to do more than exercise our powers of intellectual abstraction—if it is to "make some positive connexion with this actual world of finite lives"—it will have to be more responsive to the pragmatic temperament and the demands of practice in the future than it has in the past.

NOTES

1. Leo Tolstoy, *A Confession*, trans. David Patterson (New York: Norton, 1983), 30.
2. Tolstoy, *Confession*, 60.

3. Leo Tolstoy, *The Death of Ivan Ilych*, in *The Death of Ivan Ilych and Other Stories*, trans. Aylmer Maude (New York: New American Library, 1960), 117.

4. David Hume, *Dialogues Concerning Natural Religion* (Indianapolis: Bobbs-Merrill, 1947), 198.

5. Albert Camus, *The Plague*, trans. Stuart Gilbert (New York: Vintage International, 1948), 128.

6. Rachel Bespaloff, "The World of the Man Condemned to Death," in *Camus: A Collection of Critical Essays*, ed. Germaine Bree (Englewood Cliffs, N.J.: Prentice-Hall, 1962), 92.

7. John Kotre, *Outliving the Self* (Baltimore: Johns Hopkins University Press, 1984).

8. John Dewey, *A Common Faith*, in *John Dewey: The Later Works, 1925–1953*, Vol. 9: 1933–1934, ed. Jo Ann Boydston (Carbondale: Southern Illinois University Press, 1989), 57–58.

9. Annette Baier, "Secular Faith," in *Postures of the Mind* (Minneapolis: University of Minnesota Press, 1985), 293.

10. Peter Unger, *Living High and Letting Die* (New York: Oxford University Press, 1996), 4–5.

11. William James, *Pragmatism* in *William James: Writings 1902–1910*, ed. Bruce Kuklick (New York: Library of America, 1987), 606.

12. James, *Pragmatism*, 618.

13. James, *Pragmatism*, 619.

14. James, *Pragmatism*, 614.

15. Dorothy Day, as quoted in Robert Coles, *The Secular Mind* (Princeton, N.J.: Princeton University Press, 1999), 6.

16. Cornel West, *The American Evasion of Philosophy: A Genealogy of Pragmatism* (Madison: University of Wisconsin Press, 1989), 233.

17. Dewey, *A Common Faith*, 42.

18. Plato, *Apology* in *The Euthyphro, Apology, and Crito of Plato*, trans. F. J. Church, rev. and introduced by Robert D. Cumming (Indianapolis: Bobbs-Merrill, 1956), 45.

19. Immanuel Kant, *Grounding for the Metaphysics of Morals*, trans. James W. Ellington (Indianapolis: Hackett, 1993), 441–45.

20. Zora Neale Hurston, *Their Eyes Were Watching God* (New York: Harper & Row, 1937), 183.

21. William James, "The Sentiment of Rationality" (1879), in *William James: Writings 1878–1899*, ed. Gerald E. Myers (New York: Library of America, 1992), 508.

22. James, *Pragmatism*, 500.

23. James, *Pragmatism*, 504.

Bibliographical Essay

In what follows I provide selected historical and philosophical background, identify unanswered questions and scholarly controversies, and suggest additional resources for reading and research. The organization parallels that of the book as a whole. I begin with the introduction and proceed chapter by chapter, section by section. Books and articles are identified by author or by author and title. Facts of publication are listed in the bibliography. Where applicable, specific chapter or page numbers are included.

INTRODUCTION

There are a number of useful introductions to the classical pragmatism of Peirce, James, and Dewey. See, for example, Thayer, *Meaning and Action: A Critical History of Pragmatism;* Scheffler, *Four Pragmatists: A Critical Introduction to Peirce, James, Mead, and Dewey;* Rosenthal, Hausman, and Anderson, eds., *Classical American Pragmatism: Its Contemporary Vitality;* Stuhr, ed., *Pragmatism and Classical American Philosophy: Essential Readings and Interpretive Essays;* and Thayer, ed., *Pragmatism: The Classic Writings.* Menand, *The Metaphysical Club: A Story of Ideas in America* is an engaging and illuminating social history that emphasizes the influence and ideas of Oliver Wendell Holmes.

Good biographies of the classical pragmatists include Brent, *Charles Sanders Peirce: A Life;* Westbrook, *John Dewey and American Democracy;* and Simon, *Genuine Reality: A Life of William James.*

188

Though pragmatism was quite popular in colleges and universities in the first half of the century, it was eclipsed by analytic philosophy from the 1950s through the 1980s. A number of books and anthologies published in the 1990s, however, suggest a "revival" of pragmatism. This renewed interest crosses many disciplines, including law, history, literature, and cultural studies. See, for example, Dickstein, ed., *The Revival of Pragmatism: New Essays on Social Thought, Law, and Culture;* Russell Goodman, ed., *Pragmatism: A Contemporary Reader;* Hollinger and Depew, eds., *Pragmatism: From Progressivism to Postmodernism,* and Menand, ed., *Pragmatism: A Reader.* These volumes include selections by contemporary "analytic" pragmatists like Richard Rorty and Hilary Putnam and by continental philosophers attracted to pragmatism. Murphy, *Pragmatism: From Peirce to Davidson* and West, *The American Evasion of Philosophy* trace, in different ways, the path from classical to contemporary pragmatism. A number of recent books show connections between pragmatism and race, environmental ethics, bioethics, and feminism, respectively. See, for example, Koch and Lawson, eds., *Pragmatism and the Problems of Race;* Light and Katz, eds., *Environmental Pragmatism;* McGee, ed., *Pragmatic Bioethics;* and Seigfried, *Pragmatism and Feminism.*

CHAPTER 1: AGENT AND SPECTATOR

No Way Out

The classic source of radical skepticism is Descartes's *Meditations.* The brain-in-a-vat version is found in contemporary discussions, such as Putnam, "Brains in a Vat." Readers interested in learning more about standard philosophical questions of knowledge, reality, mind, will, and ethics may consult Nagel's *What Does It All Mean? A Short Introduction to Philosophy* for a brief introduction. See also Feinberg and Shafer-Landau, eds., *Reason and Responsibility: Readings in Some Basic Problems of Philosophy* and Pojman, ed., *Philosophy: The Quest for Truth.* My criticism of Divine Command theory draws on chapter 4 of Rachels's *The Elements of Moral Philosophy.*

The Cartesian Subject

The contrast between the Cartesian subject and the pragmatic subject draws heavily on Dewey, "On the Need for a Recovery of Philosophy."

Difficulties with the idea of a Cartesian subject were identified years earlier by Peirce in "Some Consequences of Four Incapacities." More recently Richard Rorty criticizes the Cartesian idea of mind as a mirror of nature in *Philosophy and the Mirror of Nature*. The connection between Darwin and pragmatism is widely acknowledged. See for example, Dewey, "The Influence of Darwinism on Philosophy"; Wiener, *Evolution and the Founders of Pragmatism*; and Richard Rorty, "Dewey between Hegel and Darwin." See, too, Menand, *The Metaphysical Club*.

To be fair to Descartes himself, we should situate his approach in the context of his times. In *Cosmopolis*, for example, Toulmin maintains that Descartes was responding to the chaotic religious and political conflicts of war-torn Europe. "The 17th-century philosophers' 'Quest for Certainty'," Toulmin writes,

Was no mere proposal to construct abstract and timeless intellectual schemas, dreamed up as objects of pure detached intellectual study. Instead, it was a timely response to a specific historical challenge—the political, social, and theological chaos embodied in the Thirty Years' War. Read in this way, the projects of Descartes and his successors are no longer arbitrary creations of lonely individuals in separate ivory towers, as the orthodox texts in the history of philosophy suggest. The standard picture of Descartes' philosophical development as the unfolding of a pure *espirit* untouched by the historical events of his time, . . . gives way to what is surely a more lifelike and flattening [sic] alternative: that of a young intellectual whose reflections opened up for people in his generation a real hope of *reasoning* their way out of political and theological chaos, at a time when no one else saw anything to do but continue fighting an interminable war. (p. 70)

On this reading, the problem is not so much with Descartes as it is with later Cartesians who decontextualize his approach to philosophy, an approach that—in the light of changing social and historical circumstances together with the legacy of Darwin—may be said to have outlived its usefulness.

The Pragmatic Subject

The idea that inquiry presupposes membership in a community of embodied, language-using agents is suggested by Peirce in "Some Consequences of Four Incapacities" and subsequently developed by Wittgenstein in *Philosophical Investigations* and *On Certainty*. Though there is no evidence that Wittgenstein had read Peirce, Amelie Rorty notes that in the 1920s he was visited in Austria by the influential British logician Frank P. Ramsey who had. "It is likely," she suggests, "that Ramsey introduced Wittgenstein to Peirce's theories on the community of inquiry and the impossibility of private languages" (Amelie Rorty, ed., *Pragmatic Philosophy*, p. 345).

The polarities of the Cartesian tradition—the sort of "all or none" choices I have identified between skepticism and certainty, realism and idealism, dualism and physicalism, freedom and determinism, and objective absolutism and subjective relativism—are criticized in different ways in James, *Pragmatism* and Dewey, "On the Need for a Recovery of Philosophy."

Agent and Spectator

James emphasizes the importance of both the personal (agent) and impersonal (spectator) points of view and the importance of mediating between them in a number of his writings, particularly "The Sentiment of Rationality" and *Pragmatism*. Too many philosophers, in the interest of simple consistency, emphasize one of these perspectives at the expense of the other. A version of the distinction may be found in Strawson, "Freedom and Resentment." Though Nagel makes much of the two perspectives in *Mortal Questions* and *The View from Nowhere*, he rejects pragmatism and the idea of mediating or tacking back and forth between them. See, in this connection, Nagel, *The View from Nowhere* (p. 11). I first used the metaphor of tacking between the personal and impersonal perspectives in *Splitting the Difference: Compromise and Integrity in Ethics and Politics*.

The Irrepressible Skeptic

The first response to the persistent radical skeptic draws on Wittgenstein, *Philosophical Investigations* and *On Certainty*. It is the power of Wittgenstein's criticism of the idea of a Cartesian subject that, in part, distinguishes contemporary from classical pragmatism. As Richard Rorty argues in "Response to Thelma Lavine" and elsewhere, pragmatism is able to make much more powerful criticisms of the Cartesian tradition once it takes "the linguistic turn" (see Richard Rorty, *The Linguistic Turn*). The second response acknowledges the limits of linguistic justification. At some points in philosophical argument and discussion, as emphasized in chapter 3, actions speak louder than words. "If I have exhausted the justifications," Wittgenstein writes in

Philosophical Investigations, "I have reached bedrock, and my spade is turned. Then I am inclined to say: 'This is simply what I do'" (§217).

CHAPTER 2: LANGUAGE, MEANING, AND TRUTH

Language

Wittgenstein's criticism of the possibility of a Cartesian subject's having a language—now called the "private language argument"—is developed in *Philosophical Investigations* (especially secs. 243–75). The argument shows that a language that would be unintelligible to others (because the words refer to the inner or private experiences of the speaker) would be unintelligible to its user as well. Given its devastating implications for the Cartesian tradition, the argument has been the subject of heated debate. For help in understanding Wittgenstein's formulation see, for example, Fogelin, *Wittgenstein;* Kenny, *Wittgenstein;* Suter, *Interpreting Wittgenstein;* and Marie McGinn, *Wittgenstein and the Philosophical Investigations.*

The idea that cognitive science, particularly that aspect focusing on the development of children's minds, can help to answer ancient philosophical questions about how we know there are minds other than our own, how we can know there is a world external to and independent of our own minds, and how we can attribute meaning to the sounds made by others is defended in Gopnik, Meltzoff, and Kuhl, *The Scientist in the Crib: Minds, Brains, and How Children Learn.* There is an interesting convergence between Wittgenstein's arguments and recent findings in this branch of cognitive science.

Meaning

Wittgenstein's anti-essentialism, his emphasis on the relationship between the meaning of a word and its use, the idea of a language game, and the notion of a family resemblance among various uses of a word are developed and interrelated in *Philosophical Investigations.* Though there is no evidence that Wittgenstein had read James's *Pragmatism,* he had read James's *The Varieties of Religious Experience* and told Bertrand Russell, "This book does me a *lot* of good" (Monk, *Ludwig Wittgenstein: The Duty of Genius,* p. 51). In *The Philosophy of Wittgenstein* (p. 218), Pitcher points out that James makes roughly the same point about the words 'religion' and 'government' that Wittgenstein later makes about his paradigm of a family resemblance term, 'game'. For example, James writes, "[T]he word 'religion' cannot stand for any single principle or essence, but is rather a collective name." And, "The man who knows governments most completely is he who troubles himself least about a definition which shall give their essence. Enjoying an intimate acquaintance with all their particularities in turn, he would naturally regard an abstract conception in which these were unified as a thing more misleading than enlightening. And why may not religion be a conception equally complex?" (*The Varieties of Religious Experience*, p. 32). It's quite possible, then, that Wittgenstein's notion of family resemblance owes something to James. In "William James's Ideas" (p. 231), Hilary Putnam and Ruth Anna Putnam suggest that James's "The Moral Philosopher and the Moral Life" also anticipates Wittgenstein's private language argument. For more on the general topic, see Russell Goodman, "What Wittgenstein Learned from William James."

Though his work shares a number of important elements with pragmatism, Wittgenstein was reluctant to identify himself as a pragmatist (*On Certainty*, §422). This may be due in part to what Monk's *Ludwig Wittgenstein: The Duty of Genius* tells us about Wittgenstein's desire to be fiercely original. Still, the connection between Wittgenstein and pragmatism is worth exploring. See, for example, Haack, "Wittgenstein's Pragmatism" and the chapter titled "Was Wittgenstein a Pragmatist?" in Putnam, *Pragmatism: An Open Question*. In "What's the Use of Calling Emerson a Pragmatist?" Cavell notes, in passing, that Wittgenstein "increasingly was called a pragmatist (or cited for his affinities with Pragmatism)" (p. 72).

Truth

For a brief introduction to traditional theories of truth—their strengths and weaknesses—see Audi, ed., *The Cambridge Dictionary of Philosophy* and Edwards, ed., *The Encyclopedia of Philosophy*. See, too, Kirkham, *Theories of Truth: A Critical Introduction*. Richard Rorty develops a (nontheoretical) Wittgensteinian approach to truth focusing on the uses of the word 'true' and its cognates and antonyms in various language games in *Consequences of Pragmatism*; *Contingency, Irony, and Solidarity*; and *Objectivity, Relativism, and Truth*. The distinction between determining truth *within* a language game and the truth *of* a language game has pragmatic/Wittgensteinian roots and is employed by Kuhn, *The Structure of Scientific Revolutions* to explain the relation between what he calls normal and revolutionary science. There is an interesting parallel between this distinction and distinguishing whether we can justify punishing a particular individual *within* a certain conception of criminal justice and the justification *of* that particular conception of criminal justice. The first is determined by constitutive rules and regulations internal to the system; the second by the overall usefulness or utility *of* the entire system of rules and regulations. See, for example, Rawls, "Two Concepts of Rules." There are, however, family quarrels among pragmatists about truth. For example, Misak in *Truth and the End of Inquiry: A Peircean Account of Truth* and *Truth, Politics, Morality: Pragmatism and Deliberation* argues for the importance of a philosophical theory of truth, while Rorty downplays its significance.

CHAPTER 3: KNOWLEDGE AND REALITY

Knowledge

This entire section is heavily indebted to Wittgenstein, *On Certainty* and Stroll, *Moore and Wittgenstein on Certainty*, though neither might approve of my situating their insights and ideas within the framework of pragmatism. In addition to Stroll, my reading of Wittgenstein has been strongly influenced by Moyal-Sharrock, "Wittgenstein's Objective Certainty: Belief as a Way of Acting."

The three ordinary conversations involving knowledge and belief are adapted from Wittgenstein, *On Certainty* (§483). Neurath's comparison of humans as knowers to "sailors who must rebuild their ship on the open sea" is, according to Scheffler, *Four Pragmatists* (pp. 42–57), anticipated by Peirce. Neurath's metaphor is closely related to the idea of wide reflective equilibrium developed in the second half of chapter 5.

Reality

The difference between the world and our ideas of it requires, as Richard Rorty puts it, that we distinguish between "the claim that the world is out there and the claim that truth is out there."

> To say that the world is out there, that it is not our creation, is to say, with common sense, that most things in space and time are the effects of causes which do not include human mental states. To say that truth is not out there is simply to say that where there are no sentences there is no

truth, that sentences are elements of human languages, and that human languages are human creations.

Truth cannot be out there—cannot exist independently of the human mind—because sentences cannot so exist, or be out there. The world is out there, but descriptions of the world are not. Only descriptions of the world can be true or false. The world on its own—unaided by the describing activities of human beings—cannot (*Contingency, Irony, and Solidarity*, pp. 4–5).

Knowledge and Reality: Pragmatic Questions

On the conflict in psychiatry between psychoanalytic and pharmacological approaches to mental illness, see Luhrmann, *Of Two Minds: The Growing Disorder in American Psychiatry*. The question is: which of the two language games or vocabularies (or what way of mediating or alternating between them) is, all things considered, more conducive to the long-run goals of psychiatry than the other(s)? For contemporary pragmatists, then, philosophical questions of knowledge and reality are those that involve concrete, practical choices between two or more language games and vocabularies that direct us to act in contrary ways. Should one prevail over the other? Is there a way of mediating between them? Or can we devise some third vocabulary or language game that serves the same purposes as the conflicting ones and in which the conflict disappears? Whatever the answer, it will be determined by the extent to which its acceptance and implementation cohere with other ways of talking and acting and fulfill our long-range purposes.

CHAPTER 4: MIND AND WILL

Mind

My account of the competing theories and arguments in this section is painted with a broad brush. For a more detailed, comprehensive introduction to these and related issues, see, for example, Block, Flanagan, and Güzeldere, eds., *The Nature of Consciousness: Philosophical Debates*; Cooney, ed., *The Place of Mind*; Guttenplan, ed., *A Companion to the Philosophy of Mind*; or Kim, *Philosophy of Mind*. Classic statements of the identity theory of mind and brain are Place, "Is Consciousness a Brain Process" and Smart, "Sensations and Brain Processes." The problem of the "explanatory gap" between brain states or function, on the one hand, and conscious experience, on the other, is emphasized by Jackson, "Epiphenomenal Qualia"; Nagel, "What Is It Like to Be a Bat?"; and Levine, "Materialism and Qualia: The Explanatory Gap." Some physicalists think the idea of such a "gap" is based on misunderstanding, while other philosophers like Jackson, Nagel, and Levine take it more seriously.

Will

See Watson, ed., *Free Will* for a good introduction to contemporary work on the free will problem. My "solution" bears a certain resemblance to that proposed in Strawson, "Freedom and Resentment." The possibility that our present concepts and theories are simply not up to providing a clear and complete intellectually and pragmatically satisfying account of the relationships between mind and brain, freedom and determinism—that we need a conceptual and theoretical revolution similar to, but larger and more radical than, those of Copernicus and Darwin—was first suggested to me by my colleague Richard J. Hall. The idea that our failure to achieve seamless solutions to the mind–body and free will problems may be due to a built-in limitation of the human mind can be found in Chomsky, *Reflections on Language* and *Language and Problems of Knowledge*; Colin McGinn, *Problems in Philosophy: The Limits of Inquiry*; and Pinker, *How the Mind Works*.

CHAPTER 5: ETHICS

Origin

The cases of Phineas Gage and "Elliott" are recounted in Damasio, *Descartes' Error: Emotion, Reason, and the Human Brain*. One reviewer of the manuscript for this book took issue with my spending so much time criticizing Descartes. "A dead horse," the reviewer wrote, "is a dead horse." Damasio, however, thinks that the ghost of Descartes has remarkable staying power and is still making mischief for us, not only in philosophy but also in medical diagnosis and treatment. Descartes's error, Damasio emphasizes, is to have radically separated the mind and the body. It keeps us from appreciating that "the comprehensive understanding of the human mind requires an organismic perspective; that not only must the mind move from a nonphysical cogitum to the realm of biological tissue, but it must also be related to a whole organism possessed of integrated body proper and brain and fully interactive with a physical and social environment" (p. 252).

My rudimentary explanation of the biological origins of ethics draws on Ridley, *The Origins of Virtue: Human Instincts and the Origins of Cooperation*; Singer, *The Expanding Circle*; and Wright, *The Moral Animal: The New Science of Evolutionary Psychology*. The behavior of vampire bats is described by Wilkinson, "Reciprocal Food Sharing in the Vampire Bat" and Denault and McFarlane, "Reciprocal Altruism Between Male Vampire Bats, *Desmodus Rotundi*." There is a family quarrel among those who accept biological accounts of the origins of ethics. Most believe the unit of selection is the reciprocally cooperative individual while a minority believe the unit of selection is the group composed of such individuals. For one account of this controversy together with an argument for group selection, see Sober and Wilson, *Unto Others: The Evolution and Psychology of Unselfish Behavior*. For an excellent comprehensive introduction to the various theses and controversies in this area, see Katz, ed., *Evolutionary Origins of Morality: Cross-Disciplinary Perspectives*.

Moral Reasoning and Reflection

The expression 'reflective equilibrium' was coined by Rawls, *A Theory of Justice* (p. 18). He notes that this way of thinking is not peculiar to ethics. Rawls identifies Nelson Goodman, *Fact, Fiction, and Forecast* (pp. 65–68) as employing basically the same method of justification to the principles of deductive and inductive inference. This method of reasoning is implicit in James, "The Moral Philosopher and the Moral Life" and in chapter 10 of Dewey, *The Quest for Certainty*. The distinction between wide and narrow reflective equilibrium is emphasized by Daniels in "Wide Reflective Equilibrium and Theory Acceptance in Ethics." Daniels notes that the distinction is implicit in Rawls, *A Theory of Justice* and later explicit in Rawls, "The Independence of Moral Theory" (pp. 288–89). For a recent overview of the notion, see Daniels, "Wide Reflective Equilibrium in Practice." My account is, for present purposes, less fully developed and nuanced than the one developed by Daniels. The "brain death" illustration is adapted from Benjamin and Curtis, *Ethics in Nursing* (pp. 41–42). For an illuminating history of this change in our understanding of death, see Pernick, "Brain Death in a Cultural Context: The Reconstruction of Death, 1967–1981." I develop the topic further in chapter 7. The characterization of ethical knowledge as practical knowledge, a kind of know-how, is indebted to Wallace, *Ethical Norms, Particular Cases*.

CHAPTER 6: DEMOCRATIC PLURALISM

Moral Pluralism

There are, in addition to Berlin, Cohen, and Rawls, a number of contemporary defenders of moral pluralism. See, for example, Hampshire, *Morality and Conflict*; Kekes, *The Morality of Pluralism*; Nagel,
Mortal Questions; Nussbaum, *The Fragility of Goodness: Luck and Ethics
in Greek Tragedy and Philosophy*; Taylor, "The Diversity of Goods"; and
Williams, *Moral Luck*. The idea and ethical significance of a worldview
are developed in chapter 7 of Luker, *Abortion and the Politics of Motherhood*, in which she compares the worldviews of political activists on
both sides of the abortion question. The notion of a way of life is
adapted from Hampshire, *Morality and Conflict*. I develop the interre-
lationship between them at greater length in Benjamin, "Conflict,
Compromise, and Moral Integrity." Rawls discusses the various factors contributing to reasonable moral pluralism under the heading of
the "burdens of judgment" in *Political Liberalism* (pp. 54–58).

Democratic Temperament

I'm indebted to Joshua Miller, *The Democratic Temperament of William
James* for both the term 'democratic temperament' and its connection
to James. Principal sources in James include "A Certain Blindness in
Human Beings" and "The Sentiment of Rationality."

Compromise

The idea of an integrity-preserving compromise is developed at
greater length in Benjamin, *Splitting the Difference: Compromise and Integrity in Ethics and Politics*. I'm indebted to Jonathan Moreno for pointing out the Jamesian undercurrents of my thinking on compromise
and integrity in ethics and politics. Moreno usefully distinguishes
consensus from compromise in *Deciding Together: Bioethics and Moral
Consensus*.

Physician-Assisted Suicide

The literature on this complex topic is vast. See Brock, "Voluntary Active Euthanasia" for a reasonable argument for legalizing physician-
assisted suicide (PAS); and Arras, "Physician-Assisted Suicide: A

Tragic View" for an equally reasonable argument against legalizing it. Each is aware of the difficulties with his position and the strengths of the opposing position. Another good source of arguments on both sides of the issue is Dworkin, Frey, and Bok, *Euthanasia and Physician-Assisted Suicide: For and Against*. Miller and Brody, "Professional Integrity and Physician-Assisted Death" develop a conception of medical practice that is compatible with PAS. For more on the importance of seeking mutually satisfactory accommodation with those with whom we reasonably disagree, see Wong, "Coping with Moral Conflict and Ambiguity." Bernat, Gert, and Mogielnicki, "Patient Refusal of Hydration and Nutrition: An Alternative to Physician-Assisted Suicide and Voluntary Euthanasia," do not propose patient refusal of hydration and nutrition (PRHN) as a possible compromise between defenders and opponents of legalizing PAS. They regard it as ethically preferable to PAS. However, I think this is mistaken. Any freestanding ethical argument for PRHN will, in similar circumstances, justify PAS; and in many cases PAS will be more justifiable insofar as it will be quicker and less likely to diminish the patient's dignity as he or she slowly withers and lapses into unconsciousness. The distinctive value of PRHN is the way it more or less splits the difference between those reasonably supporting and those reasonably opposing the legalization of PAS.

CHAPTER SEVEN: DETERMINING DEATH

Background

This chapter draws, in part, on Benjamin, "Pragmatism and the Determination of Death." For an illuminating history of twentieth-century debates over the determination of death, again see Pernick, "Brain Death in a Cultural Context: The Reconstruction of Death, 1967–1981." See, too, Youngner, Arnold, and Schapiro, *The Definition of Death: Contemporary Controversies* for a survey of recent issues.

The Main Question

Green and Wikler, "Brain Death and Personal Identity," were among the first to recognize the deep philosophical significance of "redefining" death. See also Gervais, *Redefining Death*. The distinction between a living human organism and a person may be traced at least as far back as 1690 in John Locke, *An Essay Concerning Human Understanding*. Locke distinguished a living human being (for which he used the term 'man') from a person, "a thinking intelligent being, that has reason and reflection, and can consider itself as itself, the same thinking thing, in different times and places; which it does only by that consciousness which is inseparable from thinking, and, as it seems to me, essential to it" (Vol. I, p. 280). For a moving account of one couple's efforts to donate the organs of their anencephalic infant, see Winner, *Ten Perfect Fingers*. Schectman's *The Constitution of Selves* develops a rich and original account of the nature and significance of personhood that squares with the conception underlying my thought-experiments involving anencephaly, permanent vegetative state as a possible side effect of anesthesia, and the possibility of a "permanent vegetative state drug."

Pragmatism and the Subject of Life and Death

The significance of distinguishing a living person from a living human biological organism for a wide range of bioethical issues has been noted by many. For an overview, see Michael Goodman, ed., *What Is a Person?* See also James W. Walters, *What Is a Person? An Ethical Exploration*.

Law and Public Policy

Chapters of Youngner, Arnold, and Schapiro, *The Definition of Death: Contemporary Controversies* discuss public attitudes about the determination of death in the United States and abroad. Chapters by some bioethicists in this volume argue for a return to the traditional heart-lung conception of death. Other chapters address public policy concerns.

CHAPTER EIGHT: MEANINGFUL LIVES

God, Meaning, and Mortality

The problem of life's meaning is for most people a basic philosophical question. See Klemke, ed., *The Meaning of Life* for a representative sample of answers. The philosophical problem of evil is a staple of introductory philosophy texts. See, for example, Feinberg and Shafer-Landau, eds., *Reason and Responsibility: Readings in Some Basic Problems of Philosophy* and Pojman, ed., *Philosophy: The Quest for Truth*.

Meaning without God

My reading of *The Plague* is influenced by Bespaloff, "The World of the Man Condemned to Death." The apt expression "outliving the self" is from Kotre, *Outliving the Self*, who focuses on the importance of Erik Erikson's emphasis on generativity—Erikson, *Insight and Responsibility* and *Childhood and Society*—as a source of meaning in our lives. The nature and importance of "secular faith" are illuminatingly explored by Baier, "Secular Faith."

Pragmatism and Religion

In addition to works quoted, this section draws on Richard Rorty, "Religious Faith, Intellectual Responsibility, and Romance" and "Pragmatism as Romantic Polytheism" and on Grey, "Freestanding Legal Pragmatism." I was also influenced, while writing this section, by the account of the persistence of religious belief after the rise of modern science in Wilson, *God's Funeral*.

The Priority of Democracy

The expression "The Priority of Democracy" comes from Richard Rorty, "The Priority of Democracy to Philosophy," who credits the idea to Dewey. Conceiving democracy as prior to philosophy is, as Rorty points out, central to Rawls's conceptions of social justice and political liberalism.

Conclusion

The dichotomies listed in this section follow the spirit, though not the letter, of the first chapter of James's *Pragmatism*. He distinguished the first member of each of the following pairs as characteristic of a certain general temperament (or "mental makeup") he called "tender-minded" and the second of an opposing temperament he called "tough-minded": Rationalistic vs. Empiricist; Intellectualistic vs. Sensationalistic; Idealistic vs. Materialistic; Optimistic vs. Pessimistic; Religious vs. Irreligious; Free-willist vs. Fatalistic; Monistic vs. Pluralistic; and Dogmatical vs. Skeptical. In my updated examples the first member of each pair (thought, reason, fact, and science, respectively) falls roughly under James's heading of "tough-minded" and the second (action, emotion, value, and faith, respectively) under the heading of "tender-minded." It is a mistake, James argues, to choose once and for all between the opposing sides of each pair. The "entire" person in us demands both. Thus, he says, "I offer the oddly-named thing pragmatism as a philosophy that can satisfy both kinds of demand. It can remain religious like the rationalisms, but at the same time, like the empiricisms, it can preserve the richest intimacy of the facts" (pp. 500–501). My point in this section, and in the book as a whole, is basically the same.

Bibliography

Ad Hoc Committee of the Harvard Medical School to Examine the Definition of Death. "A Definition of Irreversible Coma: A Report of the Ad Hoc Committee." *Journal of the American Medical Association* 205, no. 6 (August 5, 1968): 337–40.

Arras, John. "Physician-Assisted Suicide: A Tragic View." *Journal of Contemporary Health Law and Policy* 13, no. 2 (Spring 1997): 361–89.

Audi, Robert, ed. *The Cambridge Dictionary of Philosophy*. New York: Cambridge University Press, 1995.

Baier, Annette. "Secular Faith." Pp. 292–308 in *Postures of the Mind*. Minneapolis: University of Minnesota Press, 1985.

——. "Trust and Anti-Trust." Pp. 95–129 in *Moral Prejudices*. Cambridge, Mass.: Harvard University Press, 1994.

Benjamin, Martin. *Splitting the Difference: Compromise and Integrity in Ethics and Politics*. Lawrence: University Press of Kansas, 1990.

——. "Integrity and Policy Development in Bioethics." *Journal of Medicine and Philosophy* 15, no. 4 (June 1990): 375–89.

——. "Conflict, Compromise, and Moral Integrity." Pp. 261–87 in *Duties in Medicine*, edited by Courtney C. Campbell and B. Andrew Lustig. Dordrecht, Holland: Kluwer, 1994.

——. "Between Subway and Spaceship: Practical Ethics at the Outset of the Twenty-first Century." *Hastings Center Report* 31, no. 4 (July-August 2001): 24–31.

——. "Pragmatism and the Determination of Death." In *Pragmatic Bioethics*, 2d ed., edited by Glenn McGee. Cambridge, Mass.: MIT Press, 2003.

Benjamin, Martin, and Joy Curtis. *Ethics in Nursing*, 3d ed. New York: Oxford University Press, 1992.

Berlin, Isaiah. "On the Pursuit of the Ideal." Pp. 1–19 in *The Crooked Timber of Humanity*, edited by Henry Hardy. Princeton, N.J.: Princeton University Press, 1990.

Bernat, James, Bernard Gert, and R. Peter Mogielnicki. "Patient Refusal of Hydration and Nutrition: An Alternative to Physician-Assisted Suicide and Voluntary Euthanasia." *Archives of Internal Medicine* 153, no. 24 (December 27, 1993): 2723–28.

Bernstein, Richard. "American Pragmatism: The Conflict of Narratives." Pp. 54–67 in *Rorty and Pragmatism: The Philosopher Responds to His Critics*, edited by Herman J. Saatkamp, Jr. Nashville: Vanderbilt University Press, 1995.

Bespaloff, Rachel. "The World of the Man Condemned to Death." Pp. 92–107 in *Camus: A Collection of Critical Essays*, edited by Germaine Bree. Englewood Cliffs, N.J.: Prentice-Hall, 1962.

Block, Ned, Owen Flanagan, and Güven Güzeldere, eds. *The Nature of Consciousness: Philosophical Debates.* Cambridge, Mass.: MIT Press, 1997.

Bouwsma, O. K. *Wittgenstein: Conversations 1949–1951*, edited by J. L. Craft and Ronald E. Hustwit. Indianapolis: Hackett, 1986.

Brent, Joseph. *Charles Sanders Peirce: A Life.* Bloomington: Indiana University Press, 1998.

Brock, Dan. "Voluntary Active Euthanasia." *Hastings Center Report* 22, no. 2 (March/April 1992): 10–22.

Camus, Albert. *The Plague*, translated by Stuart Gilbert. New York: Vintage International, 1948.

Cavell, Stanley. "What's the Use of Calling Emerson a Pragmatist?" Pp. 72–80 in *The Revival of Pragmatism: New Essays on Social Thought, Law, and Culture*, edited by Morris Dickstein. Durham, N.C.: Duke University Press, 1998.

Chomsky, Noam. *Reflections on Language.* New York: Pantheon, 1975.

———. *Language and Problems of Knowledge: The Managua Lectures.* Cambridge, Mass.: MIT Press, 1988.

Churchland, Patricia. *Neurophilosophy.* Cambridge, Mass.: MIT Press, 1986.

Churchland, Paul. *Matter and Consciousness*, 2d ed. Cambridge, Mass.: MIT Press, 1988.

Cohen, Joshua. "Moral Pluralism and Political Consensus." Pp. 270–92 in *The Idea of Democracy*, edited by David Copp, Jean Hampton, and John Roemer. Cambridge: Cambridge University Press, 1993.

Coles, Robert. *The Secular Mind.* Princeton, N.J.: Princeton University Press, 1999.

Cooney, Brian, ed. *The Place of Mind.* Belmont, Calif.: Wadsworth, 2000.

Cotkin, George. *William James: Public Philosopher.* Baltimore: Johns Hopkins University Press, 1989.

Council on Ethical and Judicial Affairs, American Medical Association. "The Use of Anencephalic Neonates as Organ Donors." *Journal of the American Medical Association* 273, no. 20 (May 24–31, 1995): 1614–18.

Cranford, Ronald. "Criteria for Death." Pp. 529–34 in *Encyclopedia of Bioethics*, 2d ed., Vol. 1, edited by Warren T. Reich. New York: Macmillan, 1995.

Damasio, Antonio. *Descartes' Error: Emotion, Reason, and the Human Brain.* New York: Putnam, 1994.

Daniels, Norman. "Wide Reflective Equilibrium and Theory Acceptance in Ethics." Pp. 21–46 in *Justice and Justification: Reflective Equilibrium in Theory and Practice.* Cambridge: Cambridge University Press, 1996.

———. "Wide Reflective Equilibrium in Practice." Pp. 333–52 in *Justice and Justification: Reflective Equilibrium in Theory and Practice.* Cambridge: Cambridge University Press, 1996.

Darwin, Charles. *Origin of Species.* New York: Modern Library, 1998. First published 1859.

Denault, Lisa K., and Donald A. McFarlane. "Reciprocal Altruism Between Male Vampire Bats, *Desmodus Rotundus.*" *Animal Behavior* 49 (1995): 855–56.

Descartes, René. *Meditations.* In *Philosophical Works of Descartes.* Translated by Elizabeth S. Haldane and G. R. T. Ross. Cambridge: Cambridge University Press, 1969. First published 1641.

Dewey, John, "The Influence of Darwinism on Philosophy." Pp. 3–14 in *John Dewey: The Middle Works 1899–1924,* Vol. 4: 1907–1909, edited by Jo Ann Boydston. Carbondale: Southern Illinois University Press, 1977. First published 1909.

———. "On the Need for a Recovery of Philosophy." Pp. 3–48 in *John Dewey: The Middle Works 1899–1924,* Vol. 10: 1916–1917, edited by Jo Ann Boydston. Carbondale: Southern Illinois University Press, 1980. First published 1917.

———. *Human Nature and Conduct.* In *John Dewey: The Middle Works 1899–1924,* Vol. 14: 1922, edited by Jo Ann Boydston. Carbondale: Southern Illinois University Press, 1983. First published 1922.

———. *The Public and Its Problems.* In *John Dewey: The Later Works, 1925–1953,* Vol. 2: 1925–1927, edited by Jo Ann Boydston. Carbondale: Southern Illinois University Press, 1977. First published 1927.

———. *The Quest for Certainty.* In *John Dewey: The Later Works, 1925–1953,* Vol. 4: 1929, edited by Jo Ann Boydston. Carbondale: Southern Illinois University Press, 1988. First published 1929.

———. *A Common Faith.* In *John Dewey: The Later Works, 1925–1953,* Vol. 9: 1933–1934, edited by Jo Ann Boydston. Carbondale: Southern Illinois Press, 1989. First published 1950.

Dickstein, Morris, ed. *The Revival of Pragmatism: New Essays on Social Thought, Law, and Culture.* Durham, N.C.: Duke University Press, 1998.

Dworkin, Gerald, R. G. Frey, and Sissela Bok. *Euthanasia and Physician-Assisted Suicide: For and Against.* Cambridge: Cambridge University Press, 1998.

Eddington, Arthur. *The Nature of the Physical World.* Ann Arbor: University of Michigan Press, 1958. First published 1928.

Eddy, David M. "A Conversation with My Mother." *Journal of the American Medical Association* 272, no. 3 (July 20, 1994): 179–81.

Edwards, Paul, ed. *The Encyclopedia of Philosophy.* 8 vols. New York: Macmillan and Free Press, 1967.

Erikson, Erik H. *Childhood and Society,* 2d ed. New York: Norton, 1963.

———. *Insight and Responsibility.* New York: Norton, 1964.

Feinberg, Joel, and Russ Shafer-Landau, eds. *Reason and Responsibility: Readings in Some Basic Problems of Philosophy*, 10th ed. Belmont, Calif.: Wadsworth Publishing, 1999.

Fogelin, Robert J. *Wittgenstein*. London: Routledge & Kegan Paul, 1976.

Gervais, Karen. *Redefining Death*. New Haven, Conn.: Yale University Press, 1986.

Gibson, Eleanor J. "The Development of Perception as an Adaptive Process." *American Scientist* 58, no. 1 (January–February 1970): 98–107.

Goodman, Michael., ed. *What Is a Person?* Clifton, N.J.: The Humana Press, 1988.

Goodman, Nelson. *Fact, Fiction, and Forecast*. Cambridge, Mass.: Harvard University Press, 1955.

Goodman, Russell B. "What Wittgenstein Learned from William James." *History of Philosophy Quarterly* 11, no. 3 (July 1994): 339–54.

———, ed. *Pragmatism: A Contemporary Reader*. New York: Routledge, 1995.

Gopnik, Alison, Andrew N. Meltzoff, and Patricia K. Kuhl. *The Scientist in the Crib: Minds, Brains, and How Children Learn*. New York: Morrow, 1999.

Grandin, Temple. *Thinking in Pictures*. New York: Vintage, 1995.

Green, Michael, and Wikler, Dan. "Brain Death and Personal Identity." *Philosophy and Public Affairs* 9, no. 2 (Winter 1980): 45–53.

Gregory, Richard. *Inventing Reality: Physics as a Language*. New York: Wiley, 1988.

Grey, Thomas C. "Freestanding Legal Pragmatism." Pp. 254–75 in *The Revival of Pragmatism: New Essays on Social Thought, Law, and Culture*, edited by Morris Dickstein. Durham, N.C.: Duke University Press, 1998.

Guttenplan, Samuel, ed. *A Companion to the Philosophy of Mind*. Oxford: Blackwell, 1995.

Haack, Robin. "Wittgenstein's Pragmatism." *American Philosophical Quarterly* 19, no. 2 (April 1991): 163–71.

Hampshire, Stuart. *Morality and Conflict*. Cambridge, Mass.: Harvard University Press, 1983.

Hare, R. M. *Moral Thinking: Its Levels, Methods, and Point*. Oxford: Oxford University Press, 1981.

Hollinger, Robert, and David Depew, eds. *Pragmatism: From Progressivism to Postmodernism*. Westport, Conn.: Praeger, 1995.

Hume, David. *Dialogues Concerning Natural Religion*. Indianapolis: Bobbs-Merrill, 1947. First published 1799.

Hurston, Zora Neale. *Their Eyes Were Watching God*. New York: Harper & Row, 1937.

Jackson, Frank. "Epiphenomenal Qualia." *Philosophical Quarterly* 32, no. 127 (April 1982): 127–36.

James, William. "Remarks on Spencer's Definition of Mind as Correspondence." Pp. 893–909 in *William James: Writings 1878–1899*, edited by Gerald E. Myers. New York: Library of America, 1992. First published 1878.

———. "The Sentiment of Rationality." Pp. 504–39 in *William James: Writings 1878–1899*, edited by Gerald E. Myers. New York: Library of America, 1992. First published 1882.

———. "The Moral Philosopher and the Moral Life." Pp. 595–617 in *William James: Writings 1878–1899*, edited by Gerald E. Myers. New York: Library of America, 1992. First published 1891.

———. "The Will to Believe." Pp. 457–79 in *William James: Writings 1878–1899*, edited by Gerald E. Myers. New York: Library of America, 1992. First published 1896.

———. "On a Certain Blindness in Human Beings." Pp. 841–60 in *William James: Writings 1878–1899*, edited by Gerald E. Myers. New York: Library of America, 1992. First published 1899.

———. *The Varieties of Religious Experience.* In *William James: Writings, 1902–1919*, edited by Bruce Kuklick. New York: Library of America, 1987. First published 1902.

———. *Pragmatism: A New Name for Some Old Ways of Thinking.* In *William James: Writings, 1902–1919*, edited by Bruce Kuklick. New York: Library of America, 1987. First published 1907.

Kant, Immanuel. *Grounding for the Metaphysics of Morals*, translated by James W. Ellington. Indianapolis: Hackett, 1993. First published 1785.

Katz, Leonard D., ed. *Evolutionary Origins of Morality: Cross-Disciplinary Perspectives.* Bowling Green, Ohio: Imprint Academic Publications, 2000.

Kekes, John. *The Morality of Pluralism.* Princeton, N.J.: Princeton University Press, 1993.

Kenny, Anthony. *Wittgenstein.* Cambridge, Mass.: Harvard University Press, 1973.

Kierkegaard, Søren. *The Journals of Søren Kierkegaard*, edited and translated by Alexander Dru. London: Oxford University Press, 1938.

Kim, Jaegwon. *Philosophy of Mind.* Boulder, Colo.: Westview, 1996.

Kirkham, R. L. *Theories of Truth: A Critical Introduction.* Cambridge, Mass.: MIT Press, 1992.

Klemke, E. D., ed. *The Meaning of Life*, 2d ed. New York: Oxford University Press, 1999.

Koch, Donald F., and Bill E. Lawson, eds. *Pragmatism and the Problems of Race.* Bloomington: Indiana University Press, forthcoming.

Kotre, John. *Outliving the Self.* Baltimore: Johns Hopkins University Press, 1984.

Kuflik, Arthur. "Morality and Compromise." Pp. 38–65 in *Compromise in Ethics, Law, and Politics*, edited by J. Roland Pennock and John W. Chapman. New York: New York University Press, 1979.

Kuhn, Thomas. *The Structure of Scientific Revolutions*, 2d ed. Chicago: University of Chicago Press, 1970.

Levine, Joseph. "Materialism and Qualia: The Explanatory Gap." *Pacific Philosophical Quarterly*, 64, no. (1983): 354–61.

Light, Andrew, and Eric Katz, eds. *Environmental Pragmatism.* New York: Routledge, 1998.

Locke, John. *An Essay Concerning Human Understanding.* 2 vols. London: J. M. Dent & Sons, 1961. First published 1690.

Luhrmann, T. M. *Of Two Minds: The Growing Disorder in American Psychiatry.* New York: Knopf, 2000.

Luker, Kristin. *Abortion and the Politics of Motherhood.* Berkeley: University of California Press, 1984.

Macklin, Ruth. "Inner Workings of an Ethics Committee: Latest Battle over Jehovah's Witnesses." *Hastings Center Report* 18, no. 1 (February 1988): 15–20.

Marquis, Don. "Why Abortion Is Immoral." *Journal of Philosophy,* 86, no. 4 (April 1989): 183–202.

McEwan, Ian. *Enduring Love.* New York: Doubleday, 1997.

McGee, Glenn, ed. *Pragmatic Bioethics,* 2d ed. Cambridge, Mass.: MIT Press, 2003.

McGinn, Colin. *Problems in Philosophy: The Limits of Inquiry.* Cambridge: Blackwell, 1993.

———. *The Mysterious Flame: Conscious Minds in a Material World.* New York: Basic, 1999.

McGinn, Marie. *Wittgenstein and the Philosophical Investigations.* London: Routledge, 1997.

Menand, Louis, ed. *Pragmatism: A Reader.* New York: Vintage, 1997.

———. *The Metaphysical Club: A Story of Ideas in America.* New York: Farrar, Straus & Giroux, 2001.

Midgley, Mary. *Can't We Make Moral Judgments?* Bristol: The Bristol Press, 1991.

Mill, John Stuart, *Utilitarianism,* edited by George Sher. Indianapolis: Hackett, 1979. First published 1861.

Miller, Franklin D., and Howard Brody. "Professional Integrity and Physician-Assisted Death." *Hastings Center Report* 25, no. 3 (May-June 1995): 8–17.

Miller, Joshua I. *Democratic Temperament: The Legacy of William James.* Lawrence: University Press of Kansas, 1997.

Misak, Cheryl. *Truth and the End of Inquiry: A Peircean Account of Truth.* Oxford: Clarendon Press, 1991.

———. *Truth, Politics, Morality: Pragmatism and Deliberation.* London: Routledge, 2000.

Monk, Ray. *Ludwig Wittgenstein: The Duty of Genius.* New York: Free Press, 1990.

Moreno, Jonathan. *Deciding Together: Bioethics and Moral Consensus.* New York: Oxford University Press, 1995.

Moyal-Sharrock, Danielle. "Wittgenstein's Objective Certainty: Belief as a Way of Acting." Pp. 665–71 in *The Role of Pragmatics in Contemporary Philosophy,* edited by Paul Weingartner, Gerhard Schurz, and Georg Dorn. Kirchberg am Wechsel: The Austrian Ludwig Wittgenstein Society, 1997.

Multi-Society Task Force on PVS (American Academy of Neurology, Child Neurology Society, American Neurological Association, American Association of Neurological Surgeons, American Academy of Pediatrics). "Medical Aspects of the Persistent Vegetative State." *New England Journal of Medicine,*

Part I, 330, no. 21 (May 26, 1994): 1499–1508; Part II, 330, no. 22 (June 2, 1994): 1572–79.

Murphy, John P. *Pragmatism: From Peirce to Davidson.* Boulder, Colo.: Westview, 1990.

Nagel, Thomas. "What Is It Like to Be a Bat?" *Philosophical Review* 83, no. 4 (1974): 435–50.

———. *Mortal Questions.* Cambridge: Cambridge University Press, 1979.

———. *The View from Nowhere.* New York: Oxford University Press, 1986.

———. *What Does It All Mean? A Very Short Introduction to Philosophy.* New York: Oxford University Press, 1987.

Neurath, Otto. "Protocol Sentences," translated by George Schick. Pp. 199–208 in *Logical Positivism,* edited by A. J. Ayer. Chicago: Free Press, 1959.

Nielsen, Kai. "Relativism and Wide Reflective Equilibrium." *Monist* 76, no. 3 (July 1993): 316–32.

Nussbaum, Martha. *The Fragility of Goodness: Luck and Ethics in Greek Tragedy and Philosophy.* Cambridge: Cambridge University Press, 1986.

Peirce, Charles. "Some Consequences of Four Incapacities." Pp. 28–55 in *The Essential Peirce: Selected Philosophical Writings,* Vol. 1 (1867–1893), edited by Nathan Houser and Christian Kloesel. Bloomington: Indiana University Press, 1992. First published 1868.

———. "What Pragmatism Is." Pp. 331–45 in *The Essential Peirce: Selected Philosophical Writings,* Vol. 2 (1893–1913), edited by the Peirce Edition Project. Bloomington: Indiana University Press, 1998.

Pernick, Martin S. "Brain Death in a Cultural Context: The Reconstruction of Death, 1967–1981." Pp. 3–33 in *The Definition of Death: Contemporary Controversies,* edited by Stuart J. Youngner, Robert M. Arnold, and Renie Schapiro. Baltimore: Johns Hopkins University Press, 1999.

Pinker, Steven. *How the Mind Works.* New York: Norton, 1997.

Pitcher, George. *The Philosophy of Wittgenstein.* Englewood Cliffs, N.J.: Prentice-Hall, 1964.

Place, U. T. "Is Consciousness a Brain Process?" *British Journal of Psychology* 47 (1956): 44–50.

Plato. *Apology.* Pp. 21–49 in *The Euthyphro, Apology, and Crito of Plato,* translated by F. J. Church and revised and introduced by Robert D. Cumming. Indianapolis: Bobbs-Merrill, 1956.

———. *Euthyphro.* Pp. 1–20 in *The Euthyphro, Apology, and Crito of Plato,* translated by F. J. Church and revised and introduced by Robert D. Cumming. Indianapolis: Bobbs-Merrill, 1956.

Pojman, Louis P. *Philosophy: The Quest for Truth,* 5th ed. New York: Oxford University Press, 2002.

President's Commission for the Study of Ethical Problems in Medicine and Biomedical and Behavioral Research. *Defining Death.* Washington, D.C.: U.S. Government Printing Office, 1981.

Putnam, Hilary. "Brains in a Vat." Pp. 1–21 in *Reason, Truth, and History.* Cambridge: Cambridge University Press, 1981.

———. *The Many Faces of Realism*. Lasalle, Ill.: Open Court, 1987.
———. "Pragmatism and Moral Objectivity." Pp. 151–81 in *Words and Life*, edited by James Conant. Cambridge, Mass.: Harvard University Press, 1994.
———. *Pragmatism: An Open Question*. Oxford: Blackwell, 1995.
Putnam, Hilary, and Ruth Anna Putnam. "William James's Ideas." Pp. 217–31 in Hilary Putnam, *Realism with a Human Face*, edited by James Conant. Cambridge, Mass.: Harvard University Press, 1990.
Quill, Timothy, Bernard Lo, and Dan W. Brock. "Palliative Options of Last Resort." *Journal of the American Medical Association* 278, no. 3 (December 17, 1997): 2099–2104.
Rachels, James. *The Elements of Moral Philosophy*, 3d ed. New York: McGraw-Hill, 1999.
Rawls, John. *Political Liberalism*. New York: Columbia University Press, 1993.
———. "The Independence of Moral Theory." Pp. 286–302 in *Collected Papers*, edited by Samuel Freeman. Cambridge, Mass.: Harvard University Press, 1999.
———. *A Theory of Justice*, rev. ed. Cambridge, Mass.: Harvard University Press, 1999.
———. "Two Concepts of Rules." Pp. 20–46 in *Collected Papers*, edited by Samuel Freeman. Cambridge, Mass.: Harvard University Press, 1999.
Ridley, Matt. *The Origins of Virtue: Human Instincts and the Origins of Cooperation*. New York: Viking, 1996.
Rorty, Amelie., ed. *Pragmatic Philosophy*. Garden City, N.Y.: Anchor Books, 1966.
Rorty, Richard. *Philosophy and the Mirror of Nature*. Princeton, N.J.: Princeton University Press, 1979.
———. *Consequences of Pragmatism*. Minneapolis: University of Minnesota Press, 1982.
———. *Contingency, Irony, and Solidarity*. Cambridge: Cambridge University Press, 1989.
———. *Objectivity, Relativism, and Truth: Philosophical Papers Volume 1*. Cambridge: Cambridge University Press, 1991.
———. "The Priority of Democracy to Philosophy." Pp. 175–96 in *Objectivity, Relativism, and Truth*. Cambridge: Cambridge University Press, 1991.
———. "Dewey Between Hegel and Darwin." Pp. 1–15 in *Rorty and Pragmatism: The Philosopher Responds to His Critics*, edited by Herman J. Saatkamp, Jr. Nashville: Vanderbilt University Press, 1995.
———. "Response to Thelma Lavine." Pp. 50–53 in *Rorty and Pragmatism: The Philosopher Responds to His Critics*, edited by Herman J. Saatkamp, Jr. Nashville: Vanderbilt University Press, 1995.
———. "Religious Faith, Intellectual Responsibility, and Romance." Pp. 84–102 in *The Cambridge Companion to William James*, edited by Ruth Anna Putnam. Cambridge: Cambridge University Press, 1997.
———. "Pragmatism as Romantic Polytheism." Pp. 21–36 in *The Revival of Pragmatism: New Essays on Social Thought, Law, and Culture*, edited by Morris Dickstein. Durham, N.C.: Duke University Press, 1998.

———, ed. *The Linguistic Turn.* 2d ed. Chicago: University of Chicago Press, 1992.

Rosenthal, Sandra B., Carl R. Hausman, and Douglas R. Anderson, *Classical American Pragmatism: Its Contemporary Vitality.* Urbana: University of Illinois Press, 1999.

Russell, Bertrand. *Introduction to Mathematical Philosophy,* 2d ed. London: George Allen & Unwin, 1920.

Schectman, Marya. *The Constitution of Selves.* Ithaca, N.Y.: Cornell University Press, 1996.

Scheffler, Israel. *Four Pragmatists: A Critical Introduction to Peirce, James, Mead, and Dewey.* London: Routledge & Kegan Paul, 1974.

Seigfried, Charlene Haddock. *Pragmatism and Feminism: Reweaving the Social Fabric.* Chicago: University of Chicago Press, 1996.

Sellars, Wilfrid. "Philosophy and the Scientific Image of Man." Pp. 1–40 in *Science, Perception and Reality.* London: Routledge & Kegan Paul, 1963.

Sen, Amartya. "Rational Fools." *Philosophy and Public Affairs* 6, no. 4 (Summer 1977): 317–44.

Sereny, Gitta. *Cries Unheard: Why Children Kill; The Story of Mary Bell.* New York: Henry Holt, 1998.

Simon, Linda. *Genuine Reality: A Life of William James.* New York: Harcourt Brace, 1998.

Singer, Peter. *The Expanding Circle.* New York: Farrar, Straus & Giroux, 1981.

Smart, J. J. C. "Sensations and Brain Processes." *Philosophical Review* 68, no. 2 (April 1959): 141–56.

Sober, Elliott, and David Sloan Wilson. *Unto Others: The Evolution and Psychology of Unselfish Behavior.* Cambridge, Mass.: Harvard University Press, 1998.

Strawson, P. F. "Freedom and Resentment." Pp. 71–96 in *Studies in the Philosophy of Thought and Action,* edited by P. F. Strawson. London: Oxford University Press, 1968.

———. *Skepticism and Naturalism: Some Varieties.* New York: Columbia University Press, 1985.

Stroll, Avrum. *Moore and Wittgenstein on Certainty.* New York: Oxford University Press, 1994.

Stuhr, John J., ed. *Pragmatism and Classical American Philosophy: Essential Readings and Interpretive Essays,* 2d ed. New York: Oxford University Press, 1999.

Suter, Ronald. *Interpreting Wittgenstein.* Philadelphia: Temple University Press, 1990.

Taylor, Charles. "The Diversity of Goods." Pp. 129–44 in *Utilitarianism and Beyond,* edited by Amartya Sen and Bernard Williams. Cambridge: Cambridge University Press, 1982.

Thayer, H. S. *Meaning and Action: A Critical History of Pragmatism.* Indianapolis: Hackett, 1981.

———, ed. *Pragmatism: The Classic Writings.* Indianapolis: Hackett, 1982.

Tolstoy, Leo. *The Death of Ivan Ilych.* In *The Death of Ivan Ilych and Other Stories,* translated by Aylmer Maude. New York: New American Library, 1960.

———. *A Confession*, translated by David Patterson. New York: Norton, 1983.

Toulmin, Stephen. *Cosmopolis: The Hidden Agenda of Modernity*. New York: Free Press, 1990.

Truog, Robert D. "Is It Time to Abandon Brain Death?" *Hastings Center Report* 27, no. 1 (January/February 1997): 29–37.

Unger, Peter. *Living High and Letting Die*. New York: Oxford University Press, 1996.

Veatch, Robert M. "The Conscience Clause: How Much Individual Choice in Defining Death Can Our Society Tolerate?" Pp. 137–60 in *The Definition of Death: Contemporary Controversies*, edited by Stuart J. Youngner, Robert M. Arnold, and Renie Schapiro. Baltimore: Johns Hopkins University Press, 1999.

Voltaire. *Candide*. In *Candide, Zadig and Selected Stories*, translated by Donald M. Frame. New York: New American Library, 1961.

Wallace, James D. *Ethical Norms, Particular Cases*. Ithaca, N.Y.: Cornell University Press, 1996.

Walters, James W. *What Is a Person? An Ethical Exploration*. Urbana: University of Illinois Press, 1997.

Warnock, Mary. *A Question of Life: The Warnock Report on Fertilisation and Embryology*. Oxford: Basil Blackwell, 1985.

———. "Moral Thinking and Government Policy: The Warnock Committee on Human Embryology." *Milbank Memorial Fund Quarterly* 63, no. 3 (Summer 1985): 504–22.

Watson, Gary, ed. *Free Will*. Oxford: Oxford University Press, 1982.

West, Cornel. *The American Evasion of Philosophy: A Genealogy of Pragmatism*. Madison: University of Wisconsin Press, 1989.

Westbrook, Robert. *John Dewey and American Democracy*. Ithaca, N.Y.: Cornell University Press, 1991.

Wiener, Philip. *Evolution and the Founders of Pragmatism*. Cambridge, Mass.: Harvard University Press, 1949.

Wilkinson, Gerald S. "Reciprocal Food Sharing in the Vampire Bat." *Nature* 308, no. 5955 (March 8, 1994): 181–84.

Williams, Bernard. *Moral Luck*. Cambridge: Cambridge University Press, 1981.

Wilson, A. N. *God's Funeral*. New York: Norton, 1999.

Winner, Brenda. *Ten Perfect Fingers*. Fayetteville, N.C.: Old Mountain Press, 1999.

Wittgenstein, Ludwig. *Philosophical Investigations*, 3d ed., translated by G. E. M. Anscombe. New York: Macmillan, 1953.

———. *Zettel*, edited by G. E. M. Anscombe, translated by G. H. von Wright and G. E. M. Anscombe. Berkeley: University of California Press, 1967.

———. *On Certainty*, edited by G. E. M. Anscombe and G. H. von Wright, translated by Denis Paul and G. E. M. Anscombe. New York: Harper & Row, 1969.

Wong, David. "Coping with Moral Conflict and Ambiguity." *Ethics* 102, no. 4 (July 1992): 763–84.

Wright, Robert. *The Moral Animal: The New Science of Evolutionary Psychology.* New York: Vintage, 1994.

Youngner, Stuart J., Robert M. Arnold, and Renie Schapiro, eds. *The Definition of Death: Contemporary Controversies.* Baltimore: Johns Hopkins University Press, 1999.

Index

abortion, 122, 130, 161, 165, 198
ad hoc committee of the Harvard
    Medical School, 118, 151, 152,
    154
agency, 18, 21, 128; embodied social,
    51; practical demands of, 98;
    reflective, 24
agent: embodied, social, 7, 18, 20, 22,
    27, 28, 31, 33, 34, 36, 39, 42, 51, 54,
    55, 61, 64, 65, 70, 71, 78, 86, 88, 98,
    104, 110, 111, 182, 186; perspective
    of, 21–24, 133, 186, 191. *See also*
    pragmatic subject
agent and spectator: and democratic
    temperament, 124–25; tacking
    between perspectives of, 23–24,
    95–96, 98, 186, 191; and the whole
    person, 98, 185
agreement, reasonable, 139
Allen, Woody, 24
American Bar Association, 152
American Medical Association, 152;
    Council on Ethical and Judicial
    Affairs of, 157
anencephaly, 156–58, 160, 200
Aristophanes, 24
Arras, John, 198–99
autonomy, respect for, 142–43

Baier, Annette, 36, 180
belief. *See* certainty; knowledge
Bentham, Jeremy, 127
Bergman, Ingmar, 24
Berkeley, Bishop (George), 17
Berlin, Isaiah, 126, 128, 129, 131,
    145
Bernat, James, 145
Bernstein, Richard J., 2–3
Bespaloff, Rachel, 174, 201
Bouwsma, O. K., 51n3
Brock, Dan, 142, 198

Camus, Albert, 174–75, 177–179, 180,
    184, 185
Candide (Voltaire), 6, 26–27
Cartesian corner, 17–18, 49–51
Cartesian doubt, 29, 33, 54–55, 59
Cartesian dualism. *See* mind–body
    dualism
Cartesian subject: difficulties with,
    190; and eliminative
    materialism, 86; and ethics, 104,
    110, 111; and language use, 28,
    29, 30, 32–33, 35, 37, 43, 44,
    50–51; and philosophical inquiry,
    7, 20, 26, 35, 36; and proof, 70;
    and radical skepticism, 26;

215

216

Index

About the Author

Martin Benjamin teaches philosophy at Michigan State University, where he is also affiliated with the Center for Ethics and Humanities in the Life Sciences. He is coauthor (with Joy Curtis) of *Ethics in Nursing*, 3d ed. (Oxford University Press, 1992), coeditor (with William B. Weil, Jr.) of *Ethical Issues at the Outset of Life* (Blackwell Scientific Publications, 1987), and author of *Splitting the Difference: Compromise and Integrity in Ethics and Politics* (University Press of Kansas, 1990).